BEYOND VANITY

BEYOND VANITY

THE HISTORY AND POWER OF HAIRDRESSING

ELIZABETH L. BLOCK

THE MIT PRESS
CAMBRIDGE, MASSACHUSETTS
LONDON, ENGLAND

The MIT Press would like to thank the anonymous peer reviewers who provided comments on drafts of this book. The generous work of academic experts is essential for establishing the authority and quality of our publications. We acknowledge with gratitude the contributions of these otherwise uncredited readers.

This publication has been supported by FEKKAI and Bastide Aix-en-Provence and the MIT Press Cooper Memorial Design Fund.

This book was set in Arnhem Pro and Frank New by New Best-set Typesetters Ltd. Printed and bound in the United States of America.

Library of Congress Cataloging-in-Publication Data

Names: Block, Elizabeth L., author.
Title: Beyond vanity : the history and power of hairdressing / Elizabeth L. Block.
Description: Cambridge, Massachusetts : The MIT Press, 2024. | Includes bibliographical references and index.
Identifiers: LCCN 2023054554 (print) | LCCN 2023054555 (ebook) | ISBN 9780262049054 (hardcover) | ISBN 9780262379465 (epub) | ISBN 9780262379472 (pdf)
Subjects: LCSH: Hairdressing—History—19th century. | Hairstyles—Social aspects. | Hair—Social aspects.
Classification: LCC GT2290 .B56 2024 (print) | LCC GT2290 (ebook) | DDC 391.509/034—dc23/eng/20240104
LC record available at https://lccn.loc.gov/2023054554
LC ebook record available at https://lccn.loc.gov/2023054555

10 9 8 7 6 5 4 3 2 1

For Judith M. Block, Dr. Michael J. Block, Seth R. Friedman, Abbott Ruthson Block Friedman, Jennifer Block Martin, and Dr. Eric M. Block

CONTENTS

1

INTRODUCTION: BEYOND VANITY

The nascent field of hair studies is quickly gaining ground with a corpus of literary, visual, and material work that celebrates and interrogates women's hair. *Beyond Vanity: The History and Power of Hairdressing* advances the discourse by establishing how hairdressing and hairstyles claimed deep significance as a cultural site of meaning during one of its most industrious eras—the mid- to late nineteenth century in the United States. The considerable presence of hair becomes demonstrably evident when we study the places and spaces in which women engaged with it. Arguably, the importance of hair has been overlooked in historical studies of the period due to its ephemerality as well as a misplaced association with frivolity and triviality. This correlation may be seen as a misguided holdover in the minds of modern viewers, for whom eighteenth-century voluminous hairstyles (think miniature manicured gardens atop a powdered, towering hairdo) have had a lasting impression over the generally more contained styles of the nineteenth century. Although nonsatirical versions of big eighteenth-century styles often carried incisive, political messages in their time, to current eyes they register as preposterous. Using methods of fashion and visual and material culture studies informed by concepts of cultural geography, *Beyond Vanity* counteracts an association with triviality by identifying multiple substantive categories of place and space that hair acted within during the ever-modernizing mid- to late nineteenth century. Here are the preparatory places of the bedroom, hair salon, barbershop, and enslaved peoples' quarters. Also considered are the presentation places of parties, stages, and workplaces, including enslavers' homes. The aim is to "de-ephemeralize" hair by studying the places and spaces of hair and extracting the consequential ways it contributed to the lived experiences of women.

Although hair in the nineteenth century has been overlooked by historians, it certainly was not neglected by people in their time. Arranging hair was part of women's daily lived reality, as well as a growing profession and a mainstay of local, national, and international commerce. The years focused on here, approximately 1865 to 1900, are especially rich. Within this period, post–Civil War to the turn of the century, the hair industry grew exponentially, claiming substantial space within commercialized society. During these decades, women wore their natural hair, often augmented by hair pieces like frisettes (a curled fringe over the forehead line) or filled paddings like "rats" to achieve a seasonal style. There were not as many bells and whistles as in the late eighteenth century and early nineteenth century, perhaps, but hair claimed a permanence in daily life and business.

A cross-racial scope draws out the question of how race and racism affected who participated in the presentation and industry of hair and which standards they followed. White Eurocentric beauty norms were engrained in U.S. society, and *Beyond Vanity* investigates how visual materials like advertisements and etiquette manuals perpetuated mainstream ideals, while recentering Black women who capitalized on the opportunity to sell products directed at their communities. The quality, color, racial associations, maintenance, and presentation of hairstyles could determine a person's entry and status in U.S. culture—outcomes that were anything but frivolous.

The methodology carefully balances the performative media of paintings, photography, and advertisements with introspective journals and letters by women writers. The visual sources are not taken as veritable documents but rather are viewed as conditioned by several intermediaries. For instance, in the case of advertisements, business owners and publishers employed biases and exaggeration when selecting imagery to promote products and perpetuate dominant norms of beauty. Writings by women help to negotiate our understanding by either corroborating or contradicting how visual sources represent the ways hair actually functioned in their lives. Equally important, *Beyond Vanity* calibrates the limitations of archival sources. Archival work is inherently skewed by what white administrators in power deemed worthy of saving.[1] Here, to counter such bias, every opportunity is taken to consult images of and writings by Black women that are invaluable to understanding the narrative of hair, while acknowledging that the currently accessible records lead to a more heavily weighted conception of white hairdressing.

This aspect is admittedly problematic in a study that forefronts visual and material culture, as the majority of available images and objects related to hair care depict and were meant for white women. The book works to bring the stakes of the management of Black hair to the foreground as much as possible, benefiting from a fair amount of known documentation for entrepreneurs like Christiana Babcock Carteaux Bannister, though photographs of her or her salons are yet to be uncovered. At times when the archive is silent, some conscientious speculation is necessary, an educated imagining that Black Studies scholar Saidaya Hartman calls "critical fabulation" and that historians like Anna Arabindan-Kesson and Jennifer L. Morgan have generatively modeled in their work.[2]

HAIR STUDIES

Beyond Vanity builds on the pioneering volume *Hair: Styling, Culture and Fashion* (2008), edited by Geraldine Biddle-Perry and Sarah Cheang and interdisciplinary in its coverage of literature, performance, art, fashion, film, race, and religious studies. The six-volume series *A Cultural History of Hair* with Geraldine Biddle-Perry as the general editor and Mary Harlow, Roberta Milliken, Edith Snook, Margaret K. Powell, Joseph Roach, and Sarah Heaton as editors of the volumes that cover antiquity through the twentieth century, further provides essential analysis.[3] These books work well in conjunction with Aileen Ribeiro's discussion of hair in *Facing Beauty: Painted Women and Cosmetic Art*, Susan J. Vincent's *Hair: An Illustrated History*, Victoria Sherrow's *Encyclopedia of Hair: A Cultural History*, and Caroline Cox's *Good Hair Days: A History of British Hairstyling*.[4] A selection of articles, most notably a themed volume of *Eighteenth-Century Studies*, contributes to the rather slim corpus of critical approaches to the historical, visual importance of hair before the twentieth century.[5] For decade-by-decade chronicles of predominant styles with drawings, Richard Corson's *Fashions in Hair: The First Five Thousand Years*, first published in 1965, with several successive editions, remains indispensable.[6] Neil R. Storey and Fiona Kay's *Victorian Fashions for Women* provides descriptions of hairstyles, illustrated by photographs and fashion plates from the 1840s through 1890s.[7] Corson's and Storey and Kay's books are based in the British context. For early twentieth-century French hairstyling, the field is fortunate to draw on work by historian Steven Zdatny.[8] A selection of illustrated book compilations on single topics such as red, blond, curly, or Pre-Raphaelite hair, often in the form of personal musings, must be considered noncritical.

A few scholars of British and French literature have engaged the topic of hair, and scholars of visual, material, and social culture are served well by them. Most notable for the nineteenth century are Galia Ofek and Carol Rifelj, who have persuasively and thoroughly analyzed the role hair plays in novels of the period. Their discussions of its use as a symbol for a character's virility, magical properties, sexual power, and fetish are worth reading.[9]

Visual culture studies of Black hair in the United States are increasing. Jasmine Nichole Cobb's book *New Growth: The Art and Texture of Black Hair* is a welcome addition to the corpus and considers how textured hair of people of African descent and images of textured hair constitute an archive of feeling.[10] *Textures: The History and Art of Black Hair*, an exhibition catalogue edited by Tameka N. Ellington, Joseph L. Underwood, and Sarah Rogers-Lafferty, adeptly explores the complexities of Black hair in twentieth- and twenty-first-century art and society in the United States.[11] They build on the foundation of Shane White and Graham White's research on enslaved peoples' hair practices as well as work by Paul Dash.[12]

Sociological and anthropological analyses of Black hair prove invaluable to the present study. Most of them focus on twentieth- and twenty-first-century culture with references to earlier periods. *Black Hair in a White World*, edited by Tameka N. Ellington, comprises an anthology of essays about past and present receptions of Black hair.[13] *Trauma, Tresses, and Truth: Untangling Our Hair through Personal Narratives*, edited by Lyzette Wanzer, presents essays by twenty contributors as forms of narrative therapy for the authors.[14] Seminal publications include Noliwe M. Rooks, *Hair Raising: Beauty, Culture, and African American Women*; Julie A. Willett, *Permanent Waves: The Making of the American Beauty Shop*; Cheryl Thompson's writings on the relationship of hair and Black women's identities; Tiffany M. Gill, *Beauty Shop Politics: African American Women's Activism in the Beauty Industry*; Tabora A. Johnson and Teiahsha Bankhead, "Hair It Is: Examining the Experiences of Black Women with Natural Hair"; and Ayana D. Byrd and Lori L. Tharp, *Hair Story: Untangling the Roots of Black Hair in America*.[15] Finally, Kobena Mercer has written persuasively about the need for a historical perspective on Black hair.[16]

PLACE, SPACE, AND TIME

While considering hair studies as closely related to but separate from fashion studies, *Beyond Vanity* looks to well-established conceptions of fashion in places and spaces by several scholars. Anna-Mari Almila urges that "dress should be understood as spatial practice."[17] John Potvin's attention to the fleeting aspects of fashion and interior design in counterbalance with the intended permanence of architectural structures is especially motivating here.[18] *Beyond Vanity* resists a strict division between discussions of private and public spaces as overly reductionist. Women moved from home to workplace, from street to home, and within commercial neighborhoods and buildings in a fairly fluid manner, either alone or with a companion. In *Fashioning Spaces: Mode and Modernity in Late-Nineteenth-Century Paris*, Heidi Brevik-Zender effectively puts into practice some of Potvin's conceptions of how fashion operates in certain places and spaces and how it thus becomes more grounded.[19] As a literature scholar, she focuses on the fashion spaces as they appear and are described by French authors like Émile Zola in works such as *La Curée* (1871). In particular, she examines "in-between" spaces, like the staircases and theater foyers that claimed the interstices of the newly Hausmannized Paris. We share an interest in circulation: fashionable garments and hairstyles alike moved through and acted on social spaces.[20]

Louise Crewe rightly refers to fashion as "a set of practices that are co-negotiated between people and communities in space" and considers the interrelated element of time.[21] With regard to temporalities, hair operates differently from fashion. As Cheang and Biddle-Perry so clearly assert, the symbolic power of hair is distinct from that of clothing because it is a part of the body.[22] Or as Kim Smith puts it, hairdressing is a "craft whose work has no permanence."[23] We must therefore contend with its ephemerality. A certain style, like an updo for a ball, might last only a number of hours, but a portrait or photograph can preserve it for decades (fig. 1.1). Similarly, the curling of straight hair or vice versa survives until the next washing, but the instructions on how to attain the desired result might be passed along for years via family and community members. And as *Beyond Vanity* shows, the cumulative hours allocated to maintenance, preparation, and presentation all happened *somewhere*—namely, in built and lived-in structures. Whether or not the buildings endure, the documentation of the activities that transpired within them attests to the value invested in hair. It is that value that outlives and counteracts the ephemerality that arguably has led to its devaluing and dismissal. Karen Stevenson's chapter in Ruth Holliday and John Hassard's book *Contested Bodies* considers the hair salon as a "space of consumption," as does Kim Smith's chapter in Biddle-Perry and Cheang's *Hair: Styling, Culture and Fashion*.[24] Both inform the present study and position hair on the head as a material that matters, even if the result of its manipulation into a hairstyle is now gone.

FIGURE 1.1

Carl A. Weidner (U.S., 1865–1906) and
Fredrika Weidner (U.S., 1865–1939). *Mrs.
Walter Rathbone Bacon (Virginia Purdy
Barker)*, 1898. Watercolor on ivory, 8.6 ×
6.7 cm. New-York Historical Society. Gift
of the Estate of Peter Marié (1905.13).
Photography © New-York Historical Society.

Considerations of fashion and hair in place, in space, and through time rely on definitions by cultural geographers. The field of cultural geography is vast, formed by generations of philosophers studying how people relate to their environments and resulting in nuanced definitions of these key concepts. *Beyond Vanity* takes the work of cultural geographer Yi-Fu Tuan, particularly his book *Space and Place: The Perspective of Experience*, first published in 1977 and now in its ninth printing, as an essential touchpoint. Tuan's complex philosophies are best read in full, but distilled definitions of his main formulations prove useful here. In the Tuanian sense, the terms *place* and *time* will be used most frequently. Tuan regards *space* as an abstract, free arena that has not yet been ascribed meaning by people.[25] The result of human experiences, performed by individuals and in groups, is that "Space is transformed into place as it acquires definition and meaning."[26] We may think here of an uncultivated pasture. Tuan conceives of "places" as "centers of felt value where biological needs, such as those for food, water, rest, and procreation, are satisfied."[27] Now think of settlers choosing the uncultivated pasture, methodically building on it and converting it into a bustling village. The meaning of a place is created by repeated practices, a prolonged commitment over time.[28] Consider built structures, like a house that becomes a family home or a hair salon that after repeated visits becomes like a second home or a community center to a customer. We may productively use Tuan's formulations of time and place as we appreciate the slow work of creating and implementing a shampoo recipe; washing, combing, or styling hair; and cultivating relationships between stylist and client, employer and employee, and family members as they conduct hair practices together. Philosopher Henri Lefebvre's tenet that a place (to use Tuan's conception; Lefebvre used the term *space*) is "never empty: it always embodies a meaning" is a key principle here.[29] When considering the significance of the practices happening within the places, Tuan refers to places as "centres of felt value," a concept that guides the study of hair places in *Beyond Vanity*.[30]

In tandem with Tuan and Lefebvre, *Beyond Vanity* uses cultural geographer Nigel Thrift's theories on space and the ways it supports and inspires "material thinking" and the study of material culture.[31] His perceptions are especially helpful when comprehending the varying scales of places, from tiny to enormous and the close relationship of space and time. He also challenges the existence of boundaries.[32] Further, *Beyond Vanity* engages the field of mobilities studies, a close relative of spatial studies, particularly in how it casts light on the "travel of material things within everyday life" and the movement of bodies through space and time.[33]

Mobility as an analytical paradigm was originally aimed toward use in the social sciences but has proven constructive within humanities contexts. It is especially generative when conceptualizing the meanings of in-between movements like traveling to a destination by steamship or train, riding a bicycle, or working itinerantly, as with door-to-door sales.

Michel Foucault's theories of power and territory are central to understanding the imperialistic, patriarchal dividing and controlling of space.[34] *Beyond Vanity* considers the lives of Black and white women of varying regions, classes, and communities. The places they embodied, inhabited, and contemplated range from elite homes to enslaved, laboring, and commercial places. The language used within patriarchally distributed places directly impacted peoples' lived experiences. Anthropologist and environmental psychologist Setha Low's concept of the "discursive transformations of space" is useful when examining the language used for hair in certain places and the ways words can serve to include or exclude people.[35] She relies on a theory of embodied space that she defines as "a heuristic model for understanding the creation of space and place through trajectories, movements and actions."[36] Both premises are generative frameworks in which to conceive of hair's relation to place and are called on throughout this book.

As with clothing, the preparation and styling of hair in the United States were transnationally informed, either by cultural practices that came with women when they arrived, through immigration or force, and by a constant flow of information from Europe. Within this context, *Beyond Vanity* focuses on women's hair, while acknowledging and considering the prominent role played by men in hairdressing and barbering. The concentration on women's hairdressing and hairstyles—hair on the head—sets aside hair jewelry and commemorative hairwork, rich topics steeped in memory and mourning practices. Those subjects are thoroughly addressed in publications by Helen Sheumaker.[37] Likewise, the present volume does not engage in the topic of body hair and its removal, which is discussed to full effect by Rebecca M. Herzig in her book *Plucked: A History of Hair Removal*.[38]

EIGHTEENTH-CENTURY EXCESS

In order to destabilize the lingering association of hairdressing and hairstyles with triviality and thus an avoidance of hair as a serious topic of study in the context of the nineteenth-century United States, we must first determine where and when the linkage first took hold. Large, heavy wigs of human hair (from women) worn by aristocratic men in the seventeenth-century circles of Louis XIII and Louis XIV led to their correlation with elevated social rank, wealth, and desirability.[39] Karin Calvert, Lynne M. Festa, and others astutely write about how wigs were read as signs of a person's rank in society.[40] Marcia R. Pointon underscores the cost of high-quality wigs by stating that in many eighteenth-century portraits of men, the wig was likely more expensive than the clothes represented and the painting itself.[41] Although as Michael Kwass charts in his article on the history of wig consumption in France in the eighteenth century, certain types of men's wigs became a consumer item that, with increased production by wigmaker guilds, became attainable by moderate-income citizens in urban and country settings.[42] The finest ones were made with human hair, comprising a large international market, and the less expensive ones with horsehair or the hair of other animals like cows, goats, and sheep.[43] With this broader reach came a shift toward more contained styles that were advertised for their convenience and more natural appearance.[44] For example, by the 1780s, the shorter bagwig (with the hair gathered into a black silk or satin bag, fastened with a drawstring covered by a ribbon bow) was suitable for daily errands or even walking in the rain. One might also forego the bag, which was considered even more informal, but it was verboten to appear in public without the head covered, lest one be regarded as a deviant.[45] Wigs had been associated with masculinity in the seventeenth century and first half of the eighteenth century and rarely were worn by women, but by the second half of the eighteenth century, women began to don wigs as well. Styles and adornments proliferated.[46] Built up with pads and false pieces, the concoctions were subsequently curled, treated with pomatum (made with animal fats), powdered, and fragranced.

As with clothing fashions, these trends in wig-wearing held transnational reach and were adapted by colonial Americans.[47] Excavations at George Washington's estate in Mount Vernon, Virginia, the land of which was worked for tobacco, corn, and wheat, uncovered more than two hundred ceramic wig hair curlers and identified the wig maintenance area of the work yard.[48] The curlers were used by enslaved people and servants to maintain and style wigs for male household members, though not for George Washington, who preferred to wear his natural hair styled to look like a wig.[49] On plantations, some enslaved people wore wigs or styled their natural hair to look like one. Douglas W. Bristol Jr. writes extensively about enslaved waiting men who were responsible for styling their owner's hair and, in turn, adapted styles for themselves.[50]

How did the association of hair with frivolity and triviality become so ingrained in the collective Euro-American imaginary? The proliferation of satirical prints in the 1770s by such English artists as Philip Dawe and such artist-publishers as Matthias Darly and Mary Darly and their followers (see fig. 1.2) are largely responsible. Sets of prints by the Darlys and the artists whom they published lampooned the excessive luxury signaled by impossibly voluminous hairstyles.[51] The etchings and engravings, often vibrantly hand-colored, take aim at showy macaronis (in England) and *élégants* (in France)—men who reveled in wearing slimly cut, long-waisted coats with large buttons over high-waisted breeches, paired with shoes with oversized buckles.[52] They were reviled as being all show and no substance, as crassly valuing commodities, and as seeming effeminate.[53] As Potvin explains, concepts of decoration and excess became "coded as feminine and frivolous."[54]

Caricatures derided the hours of hairdressing artistry required to achieve women's preposterously tall or wide concoctions, either a fully artificial contrivance (with the head shaved underneath) or a delicate balance of sections of natural hair and false hair pads.[55] The space they required during their creation by hairdressers and maids and their presentation was also lampooned. A hand-colored engraving published by Matthias Darly in 1776, *The Vis-a-Vis Bisected, or the Ladies Coop*, humorously depicts two women crouching inside a carriage, the roof barely accommodating their coiffures.[56] The Darlys issued the prints in sets, with some warranting reissue due to popularity, resulting in a wide and extended circulation. They also exhibited their caricatures.[57] Susan J. Vincent's research into hairdressing manuals bears out the extent to which the Darlys' representations were exaggerated.[58] In the end, however, the satires in addition to prints of Marie Antoinette, whose voluminous, powdered, and adorned hairstyles were broadly emulated, solidified the collective image of time-consuming, impractical hairstyles as frivolous and trivial.[59]

As Amelia Rauser points out with regard to the English macaroni especially, the styles were based on concepts of artifice and performance that obscured gender divisions and became "cautionary and moralizing."[60] In the French context, which in turn influenced fashions throughout the Continent and in America, the wearing of wigs by men declined after the Revolution but did not disappear completely.[61] During the Old Regime, elaborate, artificial wigs were associated with the aristocrats who possessed the time and money to commission the most refined

FIGURE 1.2

Anonymous (French, late 18th century). *Fantastic Hairdress with Fruit and Vegetable Motif*.
Watercolor on canvas laid down on board, 55.9 × 43.8 cm. The Metropolitan Museum of Art,
New York, Alfred W. Hoyt Collection, Bequest of Rosina H. Hoppin, 1965 (65.692.8).

examples, like Louis XIV and Louis XV.[62] Although the popularity of wigs began to flag in the 1760s, by the 1780s and continuing after the Revolution, big wigs for men were decidedly out of favor.[63] More natural, restrained styles were preferred, as they were associated with Revolutionary ideals of industriousness and the disavowal of luxury.[64] They were also derided for their disingenuous use as disguise by people hiding their true selves or station in society.[65] The use of powder plummeted, and in 1795, England secured its demise by excising an annual one-guinea tax on it.[66] For men, toupees of false hair manufactured to look natural soon fit the need to cover baldness, which was associated with aging and lack of virility.[67] The wearing of full-fledged wigs was enacted only on ceremonial occasions by certain professionals like physicians and lawyers.[68] In the American colonies, too, wigs were shunned as a symbol of extravagance, and Republican ideals called for dropping them, as did Benjamin Franklin.[69]

By the last decade of the eighteenth century, women also turned away from towering wigs and headdresses, with some styles fully at the other end of the spectrum; downright short, they were modeled after styles from classical antiquity.[70] By the turn of the nineteenth century, hairstyles for middle- and upper-class white and Black women were fashioned with their natural hair, and although built up with pads or false braids in constantly changing arrangements, they were significantly more contained than those of the last decades of the previous century. Powder-free, except at historically themed costume balls, hair was now on display in a range of colors. Taken together, capricious hairstyle fashions that required skilled hairdressers and maids, the manufacturing of hair dyes, and the need to periodically clean the hair and scalp, resulted in an ecosystem that extended its reach throughout all levels of society.

BEYOND VANITY

The chapters of *Beyond Vanity* are organized thematically and address within them the chronological arc from the bound, contained hairstyles of the mid- and late nineteenth century to the looser, less constricted styles that signified the independence of the New Woman at the turn of the twentieth century. "Bedrooms, Barbershops, and Parlors" (chapter 2) looks at where women washed and dressed their hair. The focus is on the built environment, inquiring after the infrastructure and interior decoration of domestic hair places, including the fixtures within commercial places and their location, signage, and window displays. The explorations result in a broader understanding of how these places provided necessary outlets for hair practices and how they signaled the gender, class, and race of people who were welcome to enter them. The chapter further addresses the temporal dimension—how much time was spent on daily hair rituals. The next chapter, "Parties, Stages, and Studios" (chapter 3), concentrates on places of hair display—the more performative arenas of social events, theaters, and painters' and photographers' studios. The decisions and thought processes that women made before entering these places differed from regular, preparatory ones, and the intentionality of choosing a certain style or hair color is considered with renewed importance as a reflection of individual and communal values.

"Workplace and Marketplace" (chapter 4) attends to how hair figured into places of labor, including domestic, outdoor, commercial, itinerant, and enslaved work. The exploration privileges the lived experiences of women who needed to wear or cover their hair a certain way while working, either by choice or by force, the result of social norms that differed greatly for Black and white women. In turn, the chapter takes on the topic of the robust marketplace for hair products, a number of which were developed by Black entrepreneurial women who invented product lines for diverse clients. Recognizing the psychic exertion that accompanied physical and commercial labor, the chapter also discusses the vast and often racially loaded vocabulary used for hair within the embodied places of work and market.

"In Motion and Outdoors" (chapter 5) turns to the more unusual, transient places and spaces of trains, bicycles, and the seaside. These mobile spaces called for different hair-care requirements than the fixed sites of home or workplace. Ocean breezes and the wind created by the movement of a bicycle necessitated lighter hairstyles and hats that could be held down with one hand. Women's embodiment of cycling paths and open beaches eventually transformed their relationship to patriarchally organized society, leading to the New Woman aesthetic at the turn of the century, epitomized by the airy bouffant hairstyles adopted by middle- and upper-class white and Black women.

Broadening out the theme of how space and power figure into the study of women and their hair, "The International Marketplace" (chapter 6) undertakes an investigation into the human hair market. To establish the imperialist impulse that underlies the market, the chapter begins by looking at the exoticized ways that hair was displayed at the World's Columbian Exposition of 1893 in Chicago. The study then scrutinizes data from official records and points out the data's inconsistencies and shortcomings. Finally, the analysis challenges the imperially conceived archive and inserts the human dimension of the lived reality of women who participated in the market across multiple continents. Taken together, the chapters draw out the salient ways the practices, labor, maintenance, and presentation of hairstyles claimed substantial amounts of place, space, and time.

2

BEDROOMS, BARBERSHOPS, AND PARLORS

If, as cultural geographers like Yi-Fu Tuan and Nigel Thrift assert, repeated daily practices within a space over time aggregate into a wellspring of meaning, hair practices stand high on the list of individual and communal activities that ascribe meaning.[1] This chapter engages with the settings where these practices transpired, both the interiors and exteriors. While it does some useful mapping of where hair-related buildings stood in their environments, the goal is not to catalogue hair goods and services districts, for instance, but rather to view them, borrowing here from mobilities studies, as dynamic sites within a network of other places and the people that enter them.[2] As a result, our understanding of how hair-related places looked and felt and how they functioned in society greatly expands. Most hair businesses did not remain in a single location for the duration of their owners' lives, regardless of the weighty fixtures within them. Bedrooms were not only for sleeping or preparing for sleep but also for hair preparation (fig. 2.1). Barbershops were not only for men, but many were co-ed, for clients and employees alike. Hairdressing parlors or "hair rooms," the progenitors of twentieth-century hair salons, developed gradually and became communal meeting places serving women, children, and men and offering a sense of belonging. In tandem with looking at places, this chapter also focuses on the time that women devoted to the rituals of hair care and dressing. It follows Thrift's conception that space is inextricably linked to time and that space and time are "equally dynamic" in nature.[3] The time spent on hair activities cannot be fully quantified, but accounts in journals, letters, etiquette books, and advertisements attest to roughly the hours taken by washing, drying, or dressing.

FIGURE 2.1

Pierre A. Gentieu (French, 1842–1930).
*Bureau in "Miss Annie's" (Anne Ridgeley
du Pont Peyton) Room at Nemours, Eugene
du Pont's House*, ca. 1900. Photograph,
20.3 × 25.4 cm. Hagley Museum and
Library, Wilmington, Delaware (1970.001).

By foregrounding place and time, we can restore the cultural significance of daily hair practices.

––––––––––

Where did women dress their hair? As with all cultural inquiries in the United States in this period, the answer depends on the particulars of class, race, freedom, community, and surroundings. One of the common factors was the built environment. For most of the nineteenth century, women's hair was styled within the home, eventually shifting to a balance between the home and commercial salons later in the century. The gradual and nuanced nature of this change must be emphasized, as some women also patronized barbershops when they required a cut. For white women, most activity with hair pertained to its styling rather than its cutting, as long, abundant hair was considered most desirable so that it could be upswept into endless configurations.[4] Thick, lustrous, wavy, or curly hair was the ideal, achieved through frequent brushing, infrequent washing with cleansers, and the application of sundry oils and restorers. Hair cleaning and dressing were messy endeavors that involved activities like cracking eggs for yolk shampoos and collecting extra hair combings to stuff pads for voluminous styles. As is discussed in chapter 3, "Parties, Stages, and Studios," these qualities and processes were coded within white ideals of beauty and resulted in pressure on Black women to adopt the routines and styles for their own hair. The needs of and vocabulary for Black, mixed-race, and white hair differed greatly.

HOME

White women of moderate means cared for and styled their hair in their bedrooms. Numerous product advertisements depict women in these rooms either alone, in pairs, or with an adoring child observing. A series of trade cards for Barry's Tricopherous, a tonic produced by Alexander C. Barry of New York and meant to counter hair loss, proves instructive.[5] In a selection of extensively circulated cards, a partially dressed woman sits or stands in front of an ornate dressing table displaying bottles of the product (fig. 2.2). A vase of flowers might sit on the table; a small rug might cover the floor below the chair, helping to warm the room. The woman brushes her hair or gazes at her hair in a large or handheld mirror. Other advertisements demonstrate that hair preparation was often a two-person practice. A print

FIGURE 2.2

Barry's Tricopherous trade card, late
nineteenth century. Chromolithograph,
14 × 8 cm. Boston Public Library
(2012.AAP.7).

for Kendall's Amboline, a supposed growth stimulant, shows a setting similar to those in the Barry's Tricopherous cards—a dressing room interior with vanity table and mirror. Two women share the space, with one brushing the hair of the other (fig. 2.3).

Not only is it an intimate act, but it also is a practical one. Throughout the century, long, lustrous hair predominated on promotional materials for hair products. In 1888, Martha Matilda Harper opened a salon in Rochester, New York, later successfully franchising it and the "Harper method" of cutting and styling. Photographs highlighting her nearly floor-length hair were distributed widely.[6] The most ubiquitous imagery of ideal, long hair occurred on the Seven Sutherland Sisters packaging and promotional materials, especially for a hair-grower tonic and powdered shampoo (fig. 2.4).[7] Hailing from Niagara County, New York, the Sutherland family of singers toured the country and also traveled with Ringling Bros. and Barnum & Bailey Circus, stints that were recorded in novelty and publicity photographs.[8]

Brushing such long tresses was made easier by having someone to help. Talking and presumably sharing hair-care tips helped make the practice more social and time to pass more quickly. Themes of assisting, teaching, and playing with hair are evident throughout visual and written resources (fig. 2.5). The influential middle-class women's magazine *Godey's Lady's Book* (1830–1898) provided guidance, like instructions for "simple arrangements that may easily be executed at home by sisters for one another."[9] Some features in *Godey's Lady's Book*, *The Delineator*, and *Harper's Bazar* were accompanied by illustrated directions and back views of finished coiffures (fig. 2.6).

Friends wrote to one another to describe how to obtain a certain style like a French twist.[10] In December 1867, a woman named Jennie wrote to Mattie Tackitt in Buffalo, New York, with advice on how to achieve an elaborate hairstyle, augmented by a diagram with each of eleven "puffs" at the back of the head carefully numbered.[11] She explains, "on dressy occasions the hair is puffed in the back on hair puffs about a finger long (a short finger) you take the hair & comb it rather high & tie it, part it off in three parts the center bunch being the thickest puff. . . . 11 puffs are needed & takes 22 hair pins to do up just the puffs."

Assistance with hair care at home for middle- and upper-class white women might also be provided by maids, whose skills in this area were highly valued.[12] The *Evening World* wrote in 1894, "At a fashionable luncheon recently only two out of the twelve women presented professed to be able to arrange their own hair."[13] Want ads for ladies' maids abound in the papers with available workers touting their

FIGURE 2.3

L. Geissler. Kendall's Amboline for the
Hair, 1860s. Chromolithograph, 48.2 ×
38 cm. Library of Congress, Washington, DC
(2003674282).

FIGURE 2.4

Seven Sutherland Sisters Hair Grower box and bottle, 1880s. Box 14.3 × 6.4 × 3.8 cm; bottle 12.4 × 5.4 × 3.8 cm. Division of Medicine and Science, National Museum of American History, Smithsonian Institution, Washington, DC (1980.0317).

FIGURE 2.5

Photograph album, ca. 1898–1905. Winterthur Library, Joseph Downs Collection of Manuscripts and Printed Ephemera, Winterthur, Delaware.

FIGURE 2.6

Evening coiffure. *Harper's Bazar*, February 7, 1880, cover.

hairdressing skills, often claiming French training.[14] Maids cleaned their employers' hair in the home, work that was sentimentalized in numerous trade cards like those for Lyon's Kathairon and Murray & Lanman's Florida Water (figs. 2.7, 2.8). Underlying the colorful scenes meant to signal luxury are complicated labor dynamics. The status of maids is communicated not only by the work of brushing and applying tinctures but also by their posture, clothing, and headwear. They stand to work over their employer, who sits, often slumping in repose. In the Kathairon card, the worker wears a red tignon headwrap, associated with Caribbean and African heritage, and layered clothing. The wrap visually conveys her exclusion from receiving hairdressing within a white home and offers no sense of the care and management of her own hair, a topic that is further discussed in the next chapter. In the Murray & Lanman's card, the standing white woman wears a servant's outfit and white lace cap. The cap is secured around the middle of her head, leaving visible her dark brown hair at the forehead and back of the head. These sections of hair that are allowed to show convey inclusion in white hair places in a way not signaled by the woman wearing the tight-fitting, full-coverage tignon.

The heritage of such scenes derives from seventeenth-century Dutch genre paintings by artists like Caspar Netscher, copies of which were fashionable home decor in the United States.[15] Cozy domestic scenes of women tending to children's hair also featured in popular prints, like that in a steel engraving set in a bedroom with an adult woman curling the hair of a young girl who stands on a cushioned stool in front of a dressing table (fig. 2.9).[16] Warmth and caring is further indicated by the carpeted floor, canopied bed, and oval-framed portrait on the far wall.[17] As conveyed in these scenes, the bedroom was a woman's private room that was most often located on the second floor of the home, set well apart from the entertaining rooms of the first-floor parlor, dining room, library, and drawing room. Decor and color ways were more muted than in public-facing rooms.[18]

In stark contrast, two paintings by Hans Heinrich Bebie, a Swiss artist who worked in Baltimore, Maryland, depict hair practices in brothels. In *The Toilette*, a standing attendant begins to style the hair of a young woman, partially covered by a white, unstructured dressing gown, who sits, bare feet crossed.[19] In *Conversation (Group of Baltimore Girls)* (fig. 2.10) an attendant, white lace cap partially covering her hair, brushes the long blond hair of a seated prostitute, who reclines in an unnatural position, slippered feet splayed out atop two upholstered stools of different heights. The bodice of her bowed white undergarment is low-cut and

FIGURE 2.7

Lyon's Kathairon trade card, ca. 1870s,
12 × 10 cm. Division of Medicine and
Science, National Museum of American
History, Smithsonian Institution,
Washington, DC.

FIGURE 2.8

Murray & Lanman's Florida Water trade card,
ca. 1894. Chromolithograph. Boston Public
Library (10_03_002079).

FIGURE 2.9

Woman and Young Girl, 1885–1890. Steel
engraving, 17.8 × 11.7 cm. Grand Rapids
Public Museum (149641).

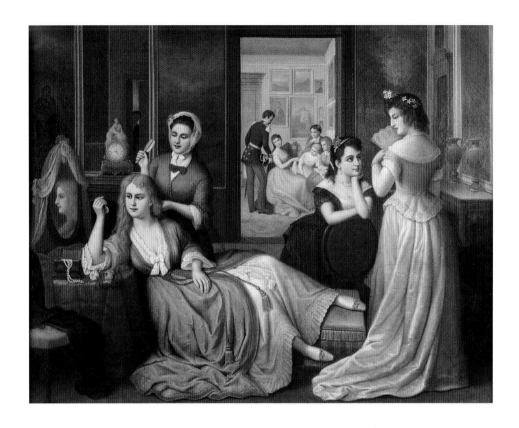

FIGURE 2.10

Hans Heinrich Bebie (Swiss, 1799–1888).
Conversation (Group of Baltimore Girls),
1870s. Oil on canvas, 71 × 76.2 cm. Courtesy
of the Maryland Center for History and
Culture (BCLM-MA.849).

revealing. In addition to loose locks, Bebie employed the blond color here and in *The Toilette* to signify a lack of morals, as did other artists and authors (see chapter 3).[20] Two darker-haired prostitutes gather to the right, while four more women are seen engaging with a uniformed male customer in the adjoining room, paintings arranged salon-style on the walls. In the wall mirror at left, we spot the reflection of another man spying on the grooming scene. The transgressive act of voyeurism led to fetishes for men watching women arrange their hair, a practice that French artist Edgar Degas engaged in at brothels and in his studio throughout his career.[21] About 1878, he asked to watch Geneviève Halévy, his friend Ludovic Halévy's cousin, comb her hair. The model told writer Edmond de Goncourt that Degas was "a strange gentleman—during an entire four-hour sitting he had done nothing but comb her hair."[22] He also repeatedly depicted maids combing their nude employer's hair in their bedrooms.[23] Henri de Toulouse-Lautrec and Pierre-Auguste Renoir also drew and painted women in various states of undress tending to their hair in private settings.[24] U.S. artist James Carroll Beckwith made a number of intimate sketches showing women braiding their hair, and in the first several decades of the twentieth century, U.S. artists George Bellows and John Sloan frequently took up the subject of women's hair.[25]

Applying feminist art historian Griselda Pollock's rubric of ways to read space and gender in paintings by male artists of women tending to their hair leads to questions of how these paintings relate to the lived spatial dynamics of women in the period. Pollock sets up three dimensions for considering space—which spaces were depicted, how space is ordered within the image, and which social space is inhabited by the producer of the image.[26] In Bebie's *Conversation (Group of Baltimore Girls)*, women's hairdressing takes place in a homelike setting. The intimate acts of finger combing and brushing the blond woman's long locks are foregrounded, for the presumed male viewer to take in. The soldier in the room beyond stands as the interlocuter for yet another male viewer—ready to receive the fully primped prostitute. Finally, the man who stands at a door cracked open and sneaks a peak of the hair preparation room is visible only in the reflection of the wall mirror at left, beyond the ornate golden clock—a true voyeur. According to Pollock's conception, the rooms are spaces of femininity invaded by the male gaze of the painter, the viewer, and the two men represented on the canvas. However, a substantial amount of looking also is being done by the women in the painting. The gazes of each of the eight women are easily traced, whether by the maid focusing on the blond woman's hair or the blond woman viewing what appears to be a gold earring in her right hand, her selection from the jewelry box on the dressing table. The power relations of looking and the patriarchal conceptions of space must be negotiated as we consider the lived experiences and representations of women in the world of hair.

There is evidence that the intimacy of engaging with women while they tended their hair was sanctioned for male barbers and hairdressers and possibly, at times, for spouses. In an advertisement for Hovey's Cocoa Glycerine, manufactured in Cambridge, Massachusetts, the matron of the home sits while an attendant applies the liquid to her shining wavy hair (fig. 2.11). She reads a sheet of paper, perhaps a dossier of information about the tonic, while her young daughter vies for her attention and a baby in a carriage raises its arms. The man at right, who brushes his hair while gazing in a mirror, is presumably the husband and father. In this picture, they share the common space of the parlor for grooming, a room that normally was used for entertaining guests. It usually was considered gauche to brush one's hair in a public-facing room. The large chandelier and the tall cabinet in the background would suit a parlor, and the man leans on a mantel-like shelf, here covered with fabric and topped by assorted hair products. The company may have contrived the scene to show that the tonic works just as well for men, a clever tactic for increasing sales.

Given that advertising materials must be viewed with an equal eye for legitimacy and persuasion, it is helpful to augment this mixed-gender scene with one in a work of serialized fiction. In *Hazard of New Fortunes* by William Dean Howells, Basil March sets out to talk with his wife, Isabel March, about relocating from Boston to New York in pursuit of a publishing venture: "When he went to her room from his library, where she left him the whole evening with the children, he found her before the glass thoughtfully removing the first dismantling pin from her back hair." The episode was illustrated by William Allen Rogers in the serial installments of the story in *Harper's Weekly*, which ran from March 23 through November 16, 1889.[27] The illustration conveys the familiarity of the married couple conversing in the modest room, enormous hair pins stuck into a large pillow atop Isabel March's bureau (fig. 2.12).

PLACES FOR HAIRDRESSERS AND BARBERS

For most of the nineteenth century in Europe, formal hairdressing was an occupation performed by men.[28] France was known for its impeccably stylish coiffeurs,

FIGURE 2.11

Hovey's Cocoa Glycerine, ca. 1860s. Color
lithograph. Library of Congress, Washington,
DC (2002718903).

FIGURE 2.12

William Allen Rogers (U.S., 1854–1931).
Illustration in William Dean Howells, *Hazard
of New Fortunes*. In *Harper's Weekly*, March
30, 1889.

extending back to Champagne (d. 1658), who opened a women's hair salon in Paris in 1635, and Léonard (Léonard Alexis Autier; probably born between 1746 and 1751), Marie Antoinette's chief coiffeur.[29] They were so revered they were called by their first names, a practice that carried into the nineteenth and twentieth centuries for high-end coiffeurs like André of West 29th Street in New York, a prolific advertiser in *Vogue*, and Léon, whose salon de coiffure was on the ground floor of the Hotel Martin at 19 Lafayette Place.[30] In the case of Marcel Grateau, who in 1882 invented the "Marcel wave" of ondulating the hair with a certain curling iron technique, a cultural fad bore his first name for years.[31] The field had been professionalized in Europe since the early seventeenth century.[32] In the United States, the process took place by the last quarter of the nineteenth century, with the establishment of the trade magazine *The American Hairdresser*, which began publishing out of Brooklyn in 1877 and was affiliated with the Hairdealers Association. In 1890, a hairdressing academy was founded by the Frenchmen Brisbois and Federmeyer in Chicago.[33] These official organizations were open only to men, but women advertised their services and wrote articles for *The American Hairdresser* on a regular basis. The journal was shipped to U.S. and international subscribers and featured fashion plates from France and New Zealand, among other countries.

As in Europe, U.S. hairdressers made house calls, and it was acceptable for them to perform their duties in women's bedrooms, as evidenced by the Currier and Ives print *An Artist in Hair* of 1871 (fig. 2.13).[34] In the modest room, the stylishly dressed hairdresser combs his client's long blond hair, preparing to trim it with the scissors set next to him on the table. Reminiscent of such a scene, in his memoir, Cecil Beaton, a fashion photographer in the 1920s, recalled that his mother, who did not employ a maid, prepared her own hair but that on occasion a male hairdresser visited, set up his tools in the bedroom, and curled her hair.[35]

On occasion, women also visited barbershops. In a famous scene in Louisa May Alcott's *Little Women* (1868), Jo, one of four daughters in the March family of Concord, Massachusetts, walks into a barbershop to sell her hair when her father becomes ill in Washington, DC, during his service in the Civil War. She details the experience of surprising the "little man who looked as if he merely lived to oil his hair": "He rather stared, at first, as if he wasn't used to having girls bounce into his shop and ask him to buy their hair." The barber's wife overhears Jo trying to sell her hair and persuades her husband to agree to the transaction. Responding to her sister Meg's incredulity, Jo explains:

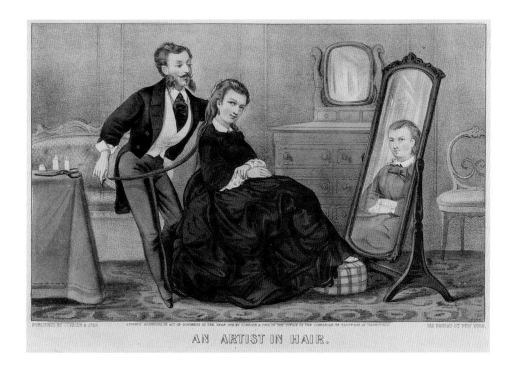

FIGURE 2.13

Currier and Ives (U.S., 1857–1907). *An Artist in Hair*, 1871. Hand-colored lithograph, 33 × 42.8 cm. Library of Congress, Washington, DC (90708792).

I took a last look at my hair while the man got his things, and that was the end of it. I never snivel over trifles like that; I will confess, though, I felt queer when I saw the dear old hair laid out on the table, and felt only the short, rough ends on my head. It almost seemed as though I'd an arm or a leg off.[36]

The scene is so vividly described that it was selected for illustration in the novel. The shift in locale in three representative editions is notable. An 1880 rendition in black-and-white shows only a barber wearing a long white coat and holding large scissors in his right hand and a swath of Jo's hair in his left.[37] A 1912 printing for children illustrated by Harold Copping depicts a colorful scene in a barbershop with the barber standing over Jo, his wife sitting nearby, and a window sign with the truncated words "Hair Cutting" (fig. 2.14).[38] Alice Barber Stephens's illustration for a 1918 edition also depicts Jo and the barber in a barbershop; the barber's wife brushes a long switch of hair that has been already cut.[39]

In another memorable scene often chosen for illustration, Jo and Meg gather in the parlor of their home to prepare for a New Year's party. Jo attempts to curl a fringe of Meg's hair using heated tongs, only to burn the pieces: "the horrified hairdresser laid a row of little scorched bundles on the bureau before her victim."[40] The scenes are instructive in describing the two most common locations for middle-class white girls' and women's hair practices—the home for most styling and a visit to the barber when in need of cutting.

In her progressive volume *The Employments of Women: A Cyclopaedia of Woman's Work* (1863), reformer Virginia Penny writes in a lengthy entry that "Both men and women are engaged in the United States in the business of dressing ladies' hair. We think women most suitable for it, and should be patronized to the exclusion of men."[41] With the aim of encouraging women to enter various occupations, she details the pricing charged by a certain Mrs. W. in New York: 50 cents for dressing only, and 75 cents for shampooing and dressing.[42] She estimates that there were

FIGURE 2.14

Harold Copping (British, 1863–1932). *Jo's Sacrifice*. Illustration in Louisa May Alcott, *Little Women: A Story for Girls* (London: Religious Tract Society, 1912). Image: National Library of Wales.

two hundred hairdressers in New York,[43] a count that is nearly impossible to verify, as city directories like *Trow's New York City Directory* did not provide complete business category listings until later years.[44] The 1867 edition of *Wilson's Business Directory of New York City* (the earliest edition available in the Library of Congress), also published by Trow, contains a section titled "Hair Dressers," but the index at the beginning of the book indicates that barbers were also listed in this section. Although the vast majority of the names in this directory are male, we must not conclude that all hairdressers were male, as the listing may reflect the nomenclature and methodology of the directory publisher.[45] In comparison, an 1875 city directory for Baltimore has a section for barbers (all men) and one for ladies' hairdressers in which the majority are women.[46] The matter may have been further complicated because some proprietors referred to their businesses as "barber and hair-dressing rooms."[47] Wig and toupee makers and dealers in human hair more consistently comprised separate sections in directories. Written accounts like educator Eliza Frances Andrews' diary from 1870 help fill in the range of vocabulary used to refer to hair services. During a visit from Georgia to New York with a companion, she writes that after spending nearly all her money shopping at Macy's, "We went to see our little hairdresser too, on the upper part of Sixth Avenue. She arranged our hair beautifully, and I left my braids with her to be made over."[48] In 1892 while visiting New York, Englishwoman Nora C. Usher "discovered a very nice shop in Fifth Avenue, with the notice in the window, 'Hair-cutting, 25 cents."[49] Much to her shock, the hairdresser (her term) charged a total of $2, stating that 25 cents covered the bang (fringe) only.

Some women successfully practiced barbering, although they remained in the minority and often the subject of novelty stories or satirical treatment by male authors.[50] However, the trade journal *The American Hairdresser* appears to have supported women's barbering, which it regarded as a profession of the progressive New Woman. In 1896, it praised them as skilled and reliable, receiving the same wages as men but not accepting gratuities.[51]

Directories do not indicate which barbers and hairdressers were Black, but historians have worked toward restoring this information where possible. For instance, Juliet E. K. Walker has found that by 1850 in Boston, out of 935 barbers, 26 (approximately 2.7 percent) were Black.[52] Whether they owned their own shops, leased space, worked on steamboats, or made house calls, they served a mostly white clientele.[53] Quincy T. Mills makes the important point that racial terminology in censuses was inconsistent, and a barber might be referred to as Black in one census and "mulatto" in the next.[54] Light-skinned barbers were more successful in the trade. Among the successful Black barbershop owners Mills has researched from the first half of the century are John Vashon, John Peck, and Lemuel Googins of Pittsburgh.[55] Douglas Walter Bristol Jr. has studied the Black barbering trade in depth, elucidating how enslaved barbers, indentured servants, and free people capitalized on their skills to elevate their status and grow their businesses.[56]

Accounts like Penny's *The Employments of Women* are essential adjuncts to city directories and other official, but inconsistent reports. She explains that many experienced practitioners were fairly itinerant and would not have registered a business address. Some of them taught students, including chambermaids at hotels, charging handsome fees for lessons.[57] Furthermore, enterprising single women with hairdressing skills would travel to upscale vacation spots like Saratoga, New York, and Newport, Rhode Island, to take advantage of increased demand during the busy summer season.[58] Clients might pay hairdressers by the week or provide boarding at their home, with the expectation of on-call service. Educator Frances E. Willard, aspired to have such an amenity. She wrote in 1870: "Would give 'those eye-teeth' of mine to be rich enough to take a hair-dresser by subscription!"[59] Eliza Potter of Cincinnati, Ohio, was a Black hairdresser who worked on wealthy white women's hair at their homes and at their vacation sites. She wrote about her experiences in *A Hairdresser's Experience in High Life*, and as literature scholar Xiomara Santamarina has pointed out, Potter astutely critiqued white women's "fortune-hunting" at events in Saratoga.[60]

Upper-class Black families that vacationed in places such as Martha's Vineyard, Massachusetts, Saratoga and Harpers Ferry, New York, and Atlantic City, New Jersey, may have used the same hair providers or brought their ladies' maids with them. Josephine Beall Willson, a teacher and philanthropist whose husband was a senator from Mississippi, is known to have employed domestic help at each of her three homes in Washington, DC, Maryland, and Mississippi and likely would have traveled with assistants (see fig. 4.3).[61]

Hairdressers and barbers were engaged by grand hotels across the country, like the United States Hotel and the Grand Union Hotel in Saratoga. An extant business card for Hawx's Hair Cutting Rooms lists its location within the Hotel St. Stephen on East 11th Street between Broadway and University Place in New York.[62] Originally built in 1876, twenty years later, the Hotel St. Stephen was connected to the neighboring Hotel Albert, resulting in an establishment that stayed in business into the 1970s.[63] Many of these U.S. hairdressing businesses mirrored those of elite coiffeurs in France, like Guillaume Louis Lenthéric and Auguste Petit.[64] They kept bustling salons in the fashionable rue du Faubourg-Saint-Honoré and the rue de la Paix, respectively, but traveled to clients' homes and vacation residences at such destinations as Nice. The offering of hair services in hotels was well established in Paris, as at the Hotel Terminus at the Gare St. Lazare, which advertised to U.S. and British visitors to the Exposition Universelle of 1889.[65]

At their main residences during the social season in New York, Chicago, and Washington, DC, hostesses might entertain guests at least once a week. For balls, at which hundreds might be in attendance, hairdressers were in high demand. At the infamously extravagant fancy (costume) ball held by Bradley Martin and Cornelia Sherman Martin at the Waldorf Hotel, New York, on February 10, 1897, the top hair-dressers began work early in the morning. The gossip paper *Town Topics* reported that many guests resorted to traveling downtown and settling for any available dresser.[66] Penny's 1863 *The Employments of Women* comments on the same issue: "The demands for a hair dresser are sometimes such, in a fashionable season, that a lady must have her hair dressed as early as noon, to wear to the opera at 8, or to a party at 10 p.m."[67] Her report is valuable in tandem with the Bradley Martin party account in that it confirms that the value and time committed to proper hairdress-ing had been in place at least thirty-four years earlier.

AT THE HAIRDRESSING PARLOR

INTERIORS

What did early hairdressing parlors, the progenitors of the modern hair salon, look like, and how did they differ in character from private bedrooms where women and their maids prepared hair? Surviving drawings and photographs of business interiors are rare, and those of places tending to personal care even more so. It is necessary, then, to consider the few that exist along with written accounts. A ste-reoview from 1882 shows the interior of the hairdressing parlor of Clough & Co. at 97 Weybosset Street in Providence, Rhode Island, run by Joseph Clough (fig. 2.15).

When seen through a stereograph, the near-identical photographs would have formed a three-dimensional view of the parlor. Another trade card, this one dedi-cated to Clough's "juvenile customers," indicates that the business served adults and children. The carpeted entrance area with elaborate chandelier above is spa-cious and accommodating to multiple clients.[68] Patrons would be escorted to the subsequent room for their appointments, taking a seat at one of the chairs lined

CLOUGH & CO. } HAIR DRESSING PARLORS, 97 Weybosset Street, Providence, R. I.

at the left, which appear to be set on a bare floor. Depending on how modernized buildings were, they might be equipped with running water, allowing for wet shampooing. Splashed or spilled water would land on the floor to be swiftly dried with towels or a mop. Bottled shampoos and other methods of cleaning the hair were amply available on the market and promoted by individual businesses (see chapter 4). Clough printed a testimonial advertisement for Lauraline on the reverses of the stereoview and trade card. Lauraline was pitched as a dressing for the hair, a cleanser, a dandruff cure, and a customer favorite for more than twelve years. The text helps clarify a question that is otherwise difficult to answer: did Clough's serve both male and female customers? In the business directories, Clough, which remained open at least until 1910, when it was located down the block at 86 Weybosset Street, is most often listed as a hairdresser but in some years as a barber. The *Providence Almanac and Rhode Island Business Directory* for 1895, for example,

FIGURE 2.15

Brownell and Company, *Clough & Co.,* 1882. Stereoview, 10 × 17.7 cm. Courtesy the Rhode Island Historical Society (2006.153.1).

lists Clough under "Hairdressers" but does not specify for men or women. The 1900 *Providence and Rhode Island Register and Business Directory* lists the shop under "Hairdressers" but directs the reader to also "see Ladies' Hairdressers."[69] Adding to the complication, the headings could change from year to year in the directories. However, the Lauraline ad specifies: "as a cleanser for long hair it is excellent, as it contains no grease and can be used quite freely." Women grew their hair long and would have purchased their own products. They also would have been responsible for bringing children to the salon, and so Clough would have directed the product to women customers. Reading the ad along with the image helps clarify that some hairdressing rooms were available for both men and women. Other examples suggest that establishments serving mixed-gender clientele may have been nearly as common as those that separated the "ladies and children's rooms" from the main salon.[70] Some husband-and-wife businesses divided the services into a hairdressing parlor run by the woman and a barbershop operated by the man.[71] Business manuals reflect the need for proprietors to know how to tend to both men's and women's hair, including sections on barbering and on ladies' hair.[72]

For the most part, buildings in the United States were newer than those in Europe and were more likely to be equipped with running water, leading some French practitioners to refer to shampooing with water as the "American style."[73] At home or at a salon, one would sit or stand over a sink, bow forward, and run the water from the tap over the back of the head. The use of egg shampoos, meant to be massaged into the roots of the hair and then rinsed out with water, was also characterized as American.[74] A staggering amount of recipes for egg shampoos and washes abound in trade and consumer publications.[75] However, not all U.S. commercial or domestic buildings had running water, even toward the turn of the century. The rather straight-shooting author of a barber's manual published in Ohio in 1898 advises:

Where you have no water connections procure a sufficient amount of water at the proper temperature (luke warm) in some convenient dish in order to pour over the head. When everything is in readiness, have your customer step from the chair to the shampoo stand, and force him to lean over far enough so that the water does not run down his neck, while washing the lather from the head.[76]

Various types of shampoo stands were available on the market. Theodore A. Kochs's catalogue of barbers' furniture and supplies from 1884 shows black walnut

FOUR-BOWL CENTER WASH-STAND.

and marble stands with a choice of one, two, three, or four hot- and cold-fauceted bowls (fig. 2.16).[77] The alternative method was "dry shampooing," which involved the repetitive brushing of the hair to remove dust, a scalp massage, and the application of powder or a tonic or other concoction, not all of which were technically dry, that might be left on overnight. Some included alcohol, glycerine, and water but were bottled and sold with the description "dry shampoo."[78] The practice of dry shampooing originated with the ancient belief that water could enter pores and shift the vapors in the body, potentially causing illness.[79] Dry shampooing might include the application of kerosene or "benzoline" (petroleum spirit), which were effective softeners and cleansers but dangerously flammable.[80] An optional final step was singeing the ends of the hair, meant to strengthen it and prevent split ends.[81] The service cost less than wet shampooing—35 cents, in comparison to 50 cents at

FIGURE 2.16

Four-bowl washstand. Theodore A. Kochs, *Price List and Barbers' Purchasing Guide of Barbers' Chairs, Furniture, and Barbers' Supplies* (Chicago: Skeen & Stuart Stationery Co., 1884).

Mrs. W. F. Fields's business in Allentown, Pennsylvania, in 1896, for example. Both women and men chose between the two methods, regardless of the length of hair. In one unfortunate incident, a male client in a Philadelphia barbershop reportedly came close to drowning when a faulty drain in the shampoo bowl led to an excess volume of water.[82] After scolding the barber and releasing himself from his brace, the client insisted on switching to a dry shampoo.

Shampoo stands were only one category within the vast offerings from trade catalogues. There were work stands, mirrored dressing cases, cabinets, looking glasses, shampoo sprinklers, and chairs galore. Patented reclining chairs with head rests, foot rests, caned seats, cushioned seats, upholstered seats, and all matter of ornamentation constituted a competitive category. None other than Joseph Clough of Providence, Rhode Island, was a player in the market, with his patented design manufactured exclusively by Theodore A. Kochs, a Chicago supplier in business since 1871.[83] Crafted of black walnut over an iron chair seat frame with a brass foot-rest, the chair was adjustable to two positions—upright for hair cutting and re-clined for shaving men's faces. The seat, back, and leg rest were covered with cane, described in the catalogue copy as a comfortable, cool option. Notably, the etching shows the chair situated on a tiled floor from which any excess water could be mopped up. At a price point of $28, Clough's chair was one of the more accessible offerings for 1884. The most luxurious one was Kochs's Barbers' Chair No. 9, which was made of black walnut or cherry wood, ornately carved and inlaid, and covered with mohair plush in color choices of olive, maroon, green, or crimson, for $70 (fig. 2.17).[84]

The heft of the furniture and accoutrements speaks to the investment in hair places as sturdy, dependable community centers. Luxurious woods, iron, and brass conveyed solidity and longevity for fixtures, but they yielded to movement when a business relocated. Depending on the square footage of the establishments, they might be purchased in multiples, as seen in Clough's salon (see fig. 2.15). Kochs's catalogue boasted that no less than fourteen of the No. 9 chairs were ensconced in the Ebbitt House hotel in Washington, DC.[85] Like many hotels, Ebbitt House went through several expansions after its founding as a boarding house in 1856. Two ma-jor renovations took place in 1872 and 1895 during which Kochs's formidable chairs would have commanded the labor of several people to move. Built to last, a number of Kochs's chairs and foot rests, produced well into the 1920s, are still in use today.

As historian Katherine C. Grier has demonstrated, genteel hotel interiors served as models for home decor.[86] The public parlor rooms were especially well

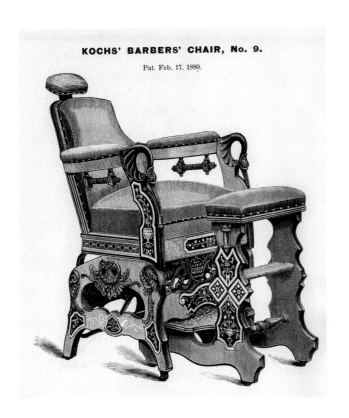

FIGURE 2.17

Kochs's Barbers' Chair No. 9. Theodore A.
Kochs, *Price List and Barbers' Purchasing
Guide of Barbers' Chairs, Furniture, and
Barbers' Supplies* (Chicago: Skeen & Stuart
Stationery Co., 1884).

INTERIOR VIEW OF PHALON'S NEW SALOON, IN THE ST. NICHOLAS HOTEL, NEW YORK.

provisioned with furniture, upholstery, and drapery from choice suppliers.[87] The service-providing areas of the hotels, including barbershops, appear to have been equally well equipped. Phalon's Saloon for men's hair cutting and dressing appears to have been an original component of the St. Nicholas Hotel in New York when it opened in January 1853 on Broadway between Spring and Broome Streets (fig. 2.18). Phalon's had been in business since at least 1837, with an establishment at 35 Bowery.[88] In February 1853, a review in the Boston magazine *Gleason's Pictorial Drawing-Room Companion* raved that "its fitting up has cost upwards of *twenty thousand dollars*."[89] The fixtures and decor of the two departments within the great hall included "polished shelves," "ornamented instruments and appliances," a chandelier, thirty mirrors, and frescoed ceilings. The hair-cutting and hairdressing room

FIGURE 2.18

William Roberts (U.S., born ca. 1829). *Interior view of Phalon's New Saloon, in the St. Nicholas Hotel, New York*. Engraving. *Ballou's Pictorial Drawing-Room Companion*, February 12, 1853. New York Public Library Digital Collections.

was outfitted with fifteen carved rosewood chairs. The cool hall lent itself to quiet conversation for clients, including travelers from France, Germany, and Italy. The lower level contained finely decorated baths. The saloon was run by longtime hairdressers Edward Phalon and son, Henry A. L. Phalon.[90] A hallmark of its stature was its "Bower of Perfume," on view in the New York Crystal Palace, which opened in July 1853 at Sixth Avenue between 40th and 42nd Streets.[91] They also sold a line of products including a complexion whitening cream and the Cocoine hair restorer, made from coconut oil, for which they were sued in 1860 for coming too close to Joseph Burnett of Boston's trademark Cocoaine product.[92] The saloon served women and was one of only seven hairdressers recommended in a ladies' shopping guide for New York in 1885.[93] The similarly ornate barbershop in the Palmer House Hotel in Chicago, run by William S. Eden, claimed that eight hundred silver dollars were inlaid into its marble floor (fig. 2.19).

Smaller shops might have modest amounts of furnishings that were less opulent but no less substantial a presence in their communities. A photograph of E. J. Dutra's Barber Shop in Oakland, California, shows three barbers tending to their clients, each in an adjustable chair. One reclines for a shave, while the other two sit upright for haircuts. Copper urns with warm water like those sold in barbers' catalogues sit at the feet of each client.[94] The floor is scuffed and the decor is simple: paintings line the upper walls above the mirrors and the familiar case of shaving mugs. The configuration is similar to that in a circa 1896 photograph of the Beehive Barber Shop in Rochester, Minnesota, suggesting a common arrangement.[95] The comfortable atmosphere bears out the aforementioned geographer Yi-Fu Tuan's definition of place, by which spaces become defined by quotidian use by people for whom the place has meaning. For the most part, all establishments had similar beginnings. The proprietors bought or leased a storefront, purchased furnishings and supplies from mail-order catalogues like Kochs's or, in big cities, from emporiums like that of Gustav Knecht's manufacturing company in Chicago.[96] Next, they customized the shop, which became familiar over time to customers who patronized the business. The welcoming, homelike setting is further borne out by the presence of resident dogs in a number of photographs.[97] Furthermore, proprietors could buy a generic electrotype of a "modern barber shop" showing barbers working on clients, mirrors, mug cases, framed landscape paintings, checkered floor, and chairs filled with patiently waiting clients who were next on the roster. Owners could then personalize the electrotype with their business name, for use as an advertisement and business card.[98] In some cases, the standard image was used

FIGURE 2.19

J. Ottmann Lithographing Company. *Palmer House Barber Shop*, 1887. Color lithograph. Library of Congress, Washington, DC (2013645268).

without any customization. In Springfield, Illinois, in 1891, the image with all-white male workers and clients was put into service for G. H. Henderson's Lady Barber Shop. The shop, advertised in the Black newspaper *The State Capital*, boasted three women on staff, available for shaving and hair cutting.[99]

EXTERIORS

Weighty and costly wood, stone, and metal fixtures anchored the interiors of hair establishments. In turn, the buildings and signs, usually bearing their owners' names, marked the streets of neighborhoods over generations. As historian Claire Zalc has shown with regard to a later period in France, which equally applies here, the names of business owners, especially those of foreigners, inscribe the places of cities and towns.[100] In the U.S. context, visual documentation is somewhat more readily available for the exteriors of hair-related businesses than for the interiors. The photographs help elucidate the substantial presence of these particular storefronts in commercial areas, and which other types of shops were in proximity. A photograph circa 1880 of a bustling street in Eastport, Maine, shows Wilkin's Hairdressing across the street from the *Eastport Sentinel* office building, a few doors down from Western Union Telegraph on its left and about five doors from a photography studio on its right.[101] The closeness of hair and photography establishments is notable, as the interrelated services benefited one another. After a hair appointment, customers might seek a photograph both as a portrait keepsake and as a visual document of their professionally created hairdos.

Some hair businesses capitalized on the demand and either offered photography in-house or shrewdly set up shop near independent photographers. Consider the business called "Mrs. R. W. Allen" in Detroit. It was begun by Richard Webber Allen (d. 1922) and Sarah Jane Allen (1845–1911), who were married circa 1867, and was continued by their son, Mark W. Allen.[102] A photograph from the early 1870s shows the compact storefront of R. W. Allen Wig Making and Hair Goods at 175 Woodward Avenue, Detroit.[103] The large glass display case contains hair pieces and dummies displaying the hair. By 1887, its storefront more than doubled, with two sizable display windows filled with hair switches and busts.[104] Taking a cue from department stores, hair professionals like Allen recognized the importance of large street-level windows.[105] Notably, a sign for an "exclusive tin type gallery" hangs next to an open door showing a stairway, presumably leading to the photograph studio, which the Allens either owned or leased space to. The Allens of Detroit were long-standing players in the hair business, consistently seizing opportunities to expand their presence and to increase their profit streams. In 1893, plans were announced for an additional building. The new four-story stone and brick-front edifice would take up a block on Michigan Avenue, with ground-floor storefront space and office or apartment space on the higher floors.[106] This is likely where the wholesale and mail-order operations were run when the company expanded into manufacturing hair and scalp products for the trade market. By 1896, the main business had moved to 251 Woodward Avenue. A rare photograph shows six saleswomen posing near display cases containing combs and tins with hair products (fig. 2.20). Several mirrors and ample seating are available for customers. Framed portraits of women, possibly advertisements, hang above the display cases on the wallpapered walls. The main business moved a few times on Woodward Avenue and then to Washington Arcade. By 1922, Mark W. Allen had purchased a 25,000-square-foot laboratory at 2109–2119 Second Avenue.[107]

Hair retailers like the Allens claimed substantial amounts of space on the main thoroughfares of U.S. cities and towns. The three-story building of Alfred Greenwood & Co. at 303 Canal Street in New York displayed hair switches in the two large windows on the ground floor and also carried hair nets, jewelry, and fancy goods.[108] Edward Rolland's Lady's Hair Store inhabited an elegant three-story brick building with cast-iron balcony on Baronne Street in New Orleans (fig. 2.21). Others leased floors in buildings that contained unrelated businesses, such as James Y. Borden Co. Ladies Hair Dressing and Shampooing Parlors on the fourth floor of a five-floor building on Chestnut Street in Philadelphia.[109] It shared the building with a hat shop, dentist, commission broker, and chiropodist (podiatrist) and manicurist. Borden's services included hairdressing and shampooing, and the shop sold human hair goods.

Finally, a trade catalogue from the 1890s for L. Shaw at 54 West 14th Street in New York states that this hair emporium and toilet bazaar filled an entire four-story building along with the basement (fig. 2.22). An illustration of the storefront depicts three window display cases on the ground floor with busts showing the latest hairstyles. The three floors above bear signs for scalp massage, manicuring, hair dyeing, hairdressing, and wigs. A photographic reproduction shows the salesroom replete with mirrors, busts, display cases, plants, and chandeliers (fig. 2.23). The rare image of the hairdressing parlor shows five clients seated and draped with protective capes in front of mirrored work stations (fig. 2.24). Three are tended by male hairdressers and one by a female hairdresser; their hair is long and loose. In the forefront is the fifth patron, her hair pinned in a low chignon, perhaps awaiting

FIGURE 2.20

*Mrs. R. W. Allen's Hair Goods Shop at
251 Woodward Avenue, Detroit*, 1896.
Mounted sepia-toned photographic print,
11.4 × 17.8 cm. Detroit Historical
Society (1953.067.027).

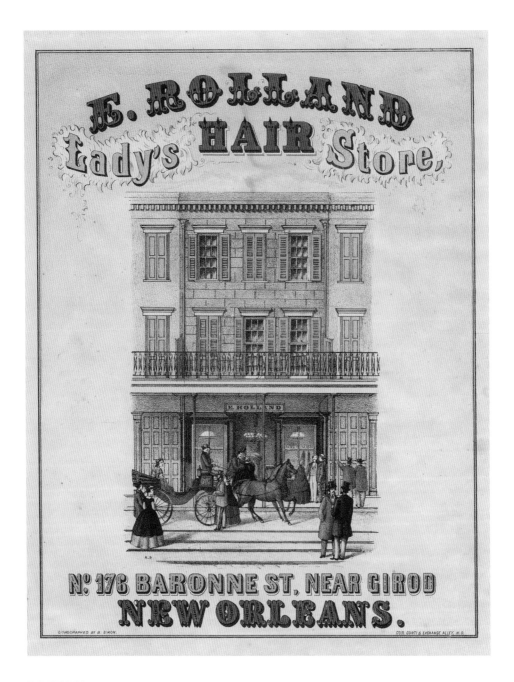

FIGURE 2.21

E. Rolland Lady's Hair Store, New Orleans,
1868–1870. Color lithograph. The Historic
New Orleans Collection, The L. Kemper and
Leila Moore Williams Founders Collection.

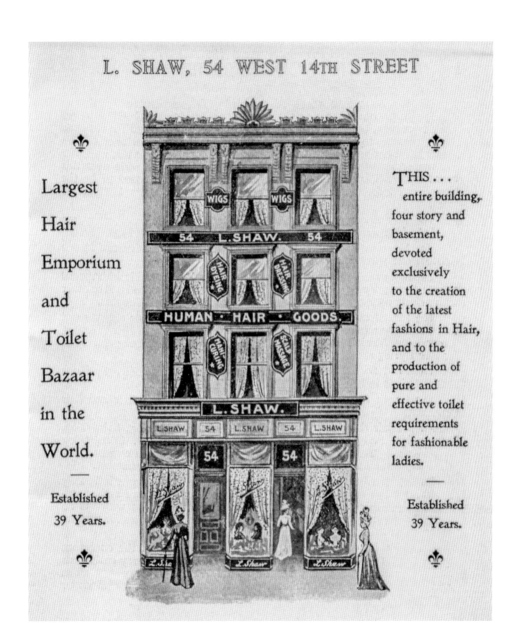

FIGURE 2.22

L. Shaw trade catalogue, 1890s. Courtesy
Winterthur Library.

her appointment. In the center, a woman manicurist attends to a client, and at back left stands another woman employee. The hall is outfitted with ornate tables and chairs, chandeliers, wallpaper, and carpets. Natural light enters the parlors through two stained-glass windows at the back.

The catalogue is an invaluable visual document that supports the textual evidence of men and women sharing spaces for hair practices. Further, L. Shaw provides an example of a woman-run business that methodically promoted itself through advertisements and circulars throughout its long history. Louise Shaw and Lawrence Shaw appear to have founded the enterprise circa 1871 at 352 Bowery.[110] Five years later, by which time Lawrence had died, it was moved to 54 West 14th Street near Sixth Avenue and retained its retail shop at that location until at least spring 1905.[111] A separate building was dedicated to the wholesale arm of the operation.[112] By 1899, Albert Edelstein served as business manager and gave a detailed interview about the firm's (referred to as "Mrs. L. Shaw") advertising strategies to *Printer's Ink* magazine.[113] The business targeted the Manhattan and Brooklyn daily newspapers, especially the morning editions that were believed to draw a larger readership of women; theater programs, emphasizing that actors and actresses used the firm's hair products; and magazines with circulations over 300,000. It sent circulars twice per year and a mail-order catalogue once per year to a list of 10,000 recipients.[114] The firm stayed in operation, taking partners at various points, until about 1920.[115]

TIME

Hair businesses marked their presence not only through the mass of their buildings and bold signage but also through the amount of time they made their services

FIGURE 2.23

L. Shaw trade catalogue, 1890s. Courtesy Winterthur Library.

FIGURE 2.24

L. Shaw trade catalogue, 1890s. Courtesy Winterthur Library.

available on a daily basis. Special events often began late in the evening: formal dinners might be served at 11:00 p.m., after musical entertainment or dancing. Hairdressers set their hours accordingly. Miss M. C. Rooney of Providence, Rhode Island, welcomed women to call at her hairdressing room from 8:00 a.m. until 10:00 p.m.[116] Depending on the services performed, the length of the appointment would vary. General practice held that shampooing women's hair should be conducted at maximum once per week, with some experts and etiquette books advising no more than on a monthly basis.[117] The infrequency led to a multistep process when it was performed, with hairdressing taking place afterward. The most skilled practitioners engaged only in the dressing of the hair, not its cleansing. As columnist Frank G. Carpenter comments: "Most ladies of fashion have their hair dressed by an artist for every evening reception, and some call for his services twice in one day."[118] Caring for the hair with cleaning, cutting, and singeing was handled by assistants or those newer to the profession.[119] With white beauty standards calling for long hair, the drying process after a shampoo was time-consuming. Empress Elisabeth of Austria, whose trademark hair extended well past her waist, reportedly spent a full day every three weeks washing (with cognac and egg) and drying her brown tresses.[120]

While tending to their hair at home, U.S. women might wear a dressing jacket, sometimes called a combing jacket.[121] There were also combing bibs or capes, simple linen vests worn to protect finer clothing from wet hair.[122] A dedicated garment was apropos for an activity that could last so long that some might read a magazine or book while doing it. Frances Ann Kemble, an English actress married to Georgia plantation owner Pierce Mease Butler, wrote in her autobiography about her habit of reading books while combing and brushing her hair at night.[123] A photograph by Albert L. Jackson of Tacoma, Washington, titled *The Last Chapter* pictures a woman perched on the side of a bed, braiding and reading (fig. 2.25).

The extraordinary diaries kept by May Bragdon of Rochester, New York, from 1893 to 1914 offer a sense of the time commitment and the places dedicated to hair care in daily life. She writes of combing her hair, pinning it up, and disliking a curling iron.[124] After a bath and dinner one evening, she visited her friend Charella, who wanted to curl her hair.[125] A wedding on a muggy June day was a "hard day on hair and tempers."[126] For washing, she alternated between visiting a professional or doing it at home. At a certain Miss Harper's place, a shampoo could last an hour.[127] Harper may have owned a salon and employed a staff, as one morning Bragdon names four people who were on site during her appointment.[128] At home, Bragdon might wash her hair after breakfast or in the evening, either alone or with a friend.[129]

FIGURE 2.25

Albert L. Jackson (U.S., active late 19th
century), *The Last Chapter*, ca. 1897.
Cabinet card (mounted albumen print),
image 16.7 × 21.5 cm. Library of Congress,
Washington, DC.

An entire morning might be devoted to washing and drying her hair by the fire.[130] Or at night, she would wash and then dry it by a window "watching a full moon going to waste."[131]

After wet shampooing, advice columns prescribed sun baths and recommended myriad ways to pass the time—snip at split ends, read a "chatty book" or an unopened letter, or mend clothes.[132] A solution that appears to have been a short-lived fad among white society women one early autumn in Bar Harbor, Maine, was morning shampoo parties.[133] Formal invitation cards were issued for the hour-long get-togethers. "Those who had maids took them and there was a professional hairdresser for those who were maidless."[134] At salons, air drying indoors took longer and led to the reputation of salons as becoming centers of neighborhood information and gossip. The first hairdryer machine was invented in 1888 by Alexandre Ferdinand Godefroy, a Frenchman who ran a hair business in St. Louis, Missouri.[135] The large, heavy contraption consisted of a metal hood connected by a pipe to a gas heater.[136] Owning one of the machines became a selling point. In 1897, Mrs. Shellabarger of Deadwood, South Dakota, advertised that she could shampoo and dry hair within fifteen to eighteen minutes.[137] All matter of time-saving and therapeutical devices appeared throughout the decades, including shampooing apparatuses, a hair-fanning machine, magnetic hair curlers and crimpers, and mechanical brushes.[138] Portable hairdryers for home use were invented in the 1920s.

The rooms, fixtures, buildings, and expenditure of time and energy devoted to hairdressing speak to the centrality and requirements of hair in the mid- to late nineteenth-century U.S. culture. Recasting hair as a matter that affected town and city streetscapes, vernacular building plans, vocational livelihoods, and daily schedules transforms our perception of its cultural weight. No longer an ephemeral or dismissible castoff material, hair stakes its claim within the cultural landscape. Using this new understanding of the places of preparation, the next chapter pursues places in which hair was on performative display.

3

PARTIES, STAGES, AND STUDIOS

Having established the places where daily hair preparation transpired—the quotidian spaces of bedrooms, barbershops, and parlors—we now turn to the places where the results were put on display. The social, celebratory purposes of these dramatic places reflect the same commitment as everyday places did to the aggregate, communal meaning ascribed to hair practices. Cultural geographer Yi-Fu Tuan's concept that emotion infuses places is a useful framework as we consider the complex decisions women made about their appearance before presenting themselves in social settings, not least of which were the color and style of their hair.[1] Social places served as venues for individual and communal performances, and, in turn, as cultural geographer Nigel Thrift says, the "urgencies and needs of performances produce and shape those places."[2] This chapter focuses on the ways that women's decisions and considerations about their hair acted within and reacted to certain performance-based places. These include a Black performer refusing to wear a wig, a brunette actress dyeing her hair blond for a play, and a family of four posing for a tintype in a photography studio, documenting their appearance for posterity.

PARTIES AND STAGES

It is noon on New Year's Day in New York, and the "artistes in hair" have been working since midnight to accommodate their clients before they begin their rounds of calling at friends' homes. As James Dabney McCabe, author of *Lights and Shadows of New York Life* (1872), observed: "Of course those whose heads are dressed at such unseasonable hours cannot think of lying down to sleep, as their 'head-gear' would be ruined by such a procedure. They are compelled to rest sitting bolt upright, or with their heads resting on a table or the back of a chair."[3] McCabe sometimes exaggerates, but for upper-class white women who attended society events, displaying a proper hairdo was as requisite as wearing a fine outfit. Hairdressers put in many hours of work to meet the demand. Christmas Day, Thanksgiving Day, and the Fourth of July were also grand events, but in some circles, a Monday night dinner party at a friend's home after the opera might require near-equal elegance. In high society, dressed hair signaled respectability, and unbound hair was a sign of disrepute because it was believed to be irresistibly alluring to men.[4] The norm was for girls to wear their hair long or pulled back into a middle braid fastened with a bow or perhaps under a hat (see figs. 3.12, 5.2). When they reached their teens and were officially available for marriage, they began to bind and dress their hair. Wealthy families marked the occasion with a coming-out party that introduced the young woman to society. In her autobiography, Frances E. Willard, educator and founder of the World Woman's Christian Temperance Union, quotes a vibrant entry from her girlhood journal describing the difficulties of the transition for her: "This is my birthday and the date of my martyrdom. Mother insists that at last I must have my hair 'done up woman-fashion'. . . . My 'back' hair is twisted up like a corkscrew; I carry eighteen hair-pins; my head aches miserably."[5]

The places in which social activities took place varied by class and race, and each had its own code of acceptable hairstyles. As guided by etiquette books, upper-class and middle-class white women adhered to the norm of having their hair fully prepared before stepping into social places, whether their own dining room with family members for breakfast, the parlor in which they entertained friends, a friend's home, a department store, a museum, or an opera house.[6] Having "smoothly-arranged hair" was one of the hallmarks of a lady, along with walking and speaking well, standing with proper posture, and acting politely.[7] Etiquette books warned women against fussing with their hair after arriving at the destination. At a friend's home, they should "avoid all such tricks as smoothing your hair with your hand, arranging your curls."[8] At a ball, they should "Be very careful, when dressing for a ball, that the hair is firmly fastened, and the *coiffure* properly adjusted. Nothing is more annoying than to have the hair loosen or the head-dress fall off in a crowded ball room."[9] Such guides make clear that social settings were performance places and that any adjustments needed to be made "off stage" in a dressing room that was stocked by the host with extra hairpins for guests.[10] A misstep could condemn a woman as slovenly and unkempt.

Women in the public eye might become known especially for their hair, setting styles to which middle-class women could aspire. First Ladies, socialites, and actresses became hair icons, with their choices chronicled in magazines and newspapers and reproduced in cabinet cards. Throughout her years in the White House (1877–1881), First Lady Lucy Hayes was admired for her modest self-presentation, exemplified by her "shining mass of satin hair," consistently worn in a tight, center-parted bun.[11] In 1886, the fashionable twenty-one-year-old Frances Folsom of Buffalo, New York, married sitting president Grover Cleveland. Her short bangs, curled at center away from her forehead, and the rest of her hair pulled into a back knot swiftly earned the moniker "à la Cleveland," and women across the country strove to copy the look, consulting the abundance of available images, many of them unauthorized (fig. 3.1).[12] Her hairdresser that year was Joannes (John) Rochon, who owned a hairdressing and wig establishment on Fourteenth and Fifteenth Streets in Washington, DC. President Cleveland reportedly curtailed Rochon's employment after learning that he apparently had abandoned his wife in Lyon, France, when he moved to the United States.[13] Rochon remained in business well into the 1890s, however, advertising frequently and often claiming the title "Professor." Frances Cleveland's later hairdressers were also successful, as her styles (always with brown hair) were still making the papers in 1894 when she sported a "Diana knot" situated at the top of the head and with the front hair in a middle part (fig. 3.2).[14]

When Frances Cleveland introduced her new styles at state events in the White House and soirées throughout Washington, DC, elite guests saw and copied her hair, but so did middle-class U.S. women who read the press coverage in their local papers. Cleveland's personal style inflected places well beyond the homes of government leaders, spreading throughout the country. Following Cleveland, socialites in major U.S. cities also experimented with novel styles, often gaining national attention. As the *Arizona Republican* reported in 1891: "There are few noted beauties among New York society women whose coiffures, no matter how seemingly natural, have not been the subject of careful study to themselves, their maids and the clientele of admiring hangers on who hover around the shrines of wealthy belles."[15] A few of the most notable were Amy Bend ("hair, of the lightest gold, as pale as wheat ears in moonlight and as fluffy as spun silk");[16] Sarah Lawrence "Susan" Endicott Roberts; and Florence Hamilton Davis, later Flora Curzon, Lady Howe.

FIGURE 3.1

Charles Milton Bell (U.S., 1848–1893).
Frances Folsom Cleveland, 1886. Albumen
silver print, 12 × 9 cm. National Portrait
Gallery, Smithsonian Institution. Gift of
Francis A. DiMauro (NPG.2007.292).

FIGURE 3.2

Anders Leonard Zorn (Swedish, 1860–1920).
Frances Folsom Cleveland, 1899. Oil on
canvas, 138.3 × 93.2 cm. National Portrait
Gallery, Smithsonian Institution. Gift of
Frances Payne (S/NPG.77.124).

In addition to its color and texture, the hair of women of high society was admired for its tasteful arrangements, most often described in the ways in which it was contained, including soft knots, tight braids, or compact coils. In nineteenth-century literature, undone hair carried associations of promiscuity or of fallen women, such as Mary Magdalene.[17] Wisps or curls of hair escaping from a chignon could be considered unruly.[18] Only on rare occasions was it acceptable for society women to wear their hair unbound and flowing in public. One of those times was when masquerading at a ball, wearing the costume of Ophelia from *Hamlet* or Juliet from *Romeo and Juliet*, for instance.[19] Then the hair could extend well past the shoulders, taking a cue from performers like the British actress Ellen Terry, who wore her hair relatively undone when she played the role of Ophelia at the Lyceum Theatre, London, in 1878. On the same stage in 1888, she played Lady Macbeth, donning enormously long red braids beneath a crown. John Singer Sargent captured the dramatic look in a celebrated portrait of 1889, now at Tate Britain.[20]

French actress Sarah Bernhardt frequently appeared on U.S. stages, and her image, like that of Ellen Terry, circulated widely in cabinet cards and in the press. Her "Titian hair"—red and curly or frizzy—delighted audiences and artists. It might be described as hanging in a "neglected manner" or "scattered," but it also represented the freedom granted by the stage setting for how women could present themselves.[21] Polish actress Helena Modjeska often arranged her hair to "float naturally over her shoulders," as when she played Ophelia in Kraków in 1867.[22] Certain parameters were maintained, though. For the role of Gismonda in the eponymous play by Victorien Sardou at the Théâtre de la Renaissance, Paris, in 1895, Bernhardt wore her hair at shoulder length, rather frizzy, with bangs (fig. 3.3). On the top of her head, depending on the scene, she alternated between wearing a faux orchid headdress, a Byzantine cap, and a large, round dark hat with white feathers. Czech artist Alphonse Mucha, who worked in Paris, captured the dreamy, classical look of the floral headdress for posterity in his Art Nouveau poster created for the opening (fig. 3.4). In the image, Mucha straightened Bernhardt's hair considerably, drawing attention to it by depicting her left forefinger touching the ends. Théobald Chartran softened and lengthened her curls in his portrait of her in 1896.[23] Mucha and Chartran were not the only ones to use artistic license with the Gismonda hairstyle. By 1900, the style was still holding the popular imagination. In February that year, Violet Lee Willing of Philadelphia, whose sister Ava Willing married John Jacob Astor IV, favored a style called "the Gismonda," supposedly inspired by Bernhardt.[24] However, images of the arrangement along with instructions of how to obtain it

show a puffed, tripartite updo. Ornamentation might include ribbons, velvet, flowers, or gauze butterflies. Other than a sense of roundness and volume, the outcome hardly resembles Bernhardt's original look, suggesting that society women deliberately tamed the style while retaining its name and association with one of the international stars of the stage.

U.S. actress Maude Adams wore her hair at different lengths while performing. The prominent Sarony photography studio captured her looks from *The Little Minister* (Empire Theatre, New York, 1897) (figs. 3.5, 3.6) and *Romeo and Juliet* (Empire Theatre, New York, 1899),[25] as did Pach Brothers and the Byron Company. Mucha

FIGURE 3.3

Studio of Nadar (French, mid- to late 19th century). *Sarah Bernhardt in "Gismonda,"* 1895. Photograph (silver gelatin print), 14.5 × 10.5 cm. Image: Bibliothèque nationale de France, Paris.

FIGURE 3.4

Alphonse Mucha (Czech, 1860–1939),
*Sarah Bernhardt as Gismonda at the Théatre
de La Renaissance, Paris*, 1895. Color
lithograph print on paper, 216 × 75.3 cm.
Image: Victoria and Albert Museum, London
(E.261-1921).

FIGURE 3.5

Sarony photography studio (New York),
*Maude Adams as Lady Babbie in "The Little
Minister,"* 1897. Cabinet card (mounted silver
gelatin print), 16.5 × 10.8 cm. Houghton
Library, Harvard University.

later painted her as Joan of Arc, altering her long hair from brown to strawberry blond.[26] Adams's hair appears natural, even in the collage photograph showing three different styles, but some performers might use quantities of false hair to achieve stage-worthy looks.[27] Actresses' countenances were so well recognized from cabinet cards and posters that one newspaper article of 1893 about dress and beauty ran line drawings without a single caption providing a woman's name.[28] Actresses with top billing could sway the season's hairstyles, despite the wishes of the premier hairdressers (*coiffeurs* in French). French actress Jane Hading was known for her

FIGURE 3.6

Otto Sarony (U.S., 1850–1903). *Maude Adams.* Cabinet card (likely mounted platinum print), 1901. Courtesy of the Ringling Theatre Collection, Belknap Collection for the Performing Arts, Special and Area Studies Collections, George A. Smathers Libraries, University of Florida.

naturally wavy and abundant red hair, so in 1886, when she opted for a simple Greek bandeau style that did not require much expertise, the *coiffeurs* were displeased.[29] Italian opera singer Adelina Patti, who wore elaborate hairstyles on stage, lent her name to hair product testimonial advertisements for the Imperial Hair Regenerator Company.[30]

In the case of Sissieretta Jones (Matilda Sissieretta Joyner Jones), a U.S. Black woman who sang soprano on stages in the 1890s, we have a statement attributed to her with regard to her intention with her hairstyle. Jones, from Portsmouth, Virginia, wore her hair pinned back with curls in a front pompadour (fig. 3.7). This was the style she wore in front of national and international audiences, from Madison Square Garden to the White House and to the World's Columbian Exposition. As reported in the *New York Times*, she refused to wear a wig, saying she "would not hide what I am even for an evening."[31] After the turn of the century, she wore a larger, rounded bouffant.[32]

The extent to which women followed the lead of stage performers varied. As mentioned above, upper-class white women might take the opportunity of a fancy ball to try an undressed look. At this type of ball, you could set your hair free for an evening. At Alva Vanderbilt and William Kissam Vanderbilt's famously extravagant ball of 1883 at their new mansion on Fifth Avenue in New York, Alva dressed as a Renaissance duchess. Underneath a period headdress, her curly brown hair extended well past her shoulders. As Joan of Arc, Lucy W. Hewitt did the same at the party, her curls spilling out from an armorial helmet. Helen Bulkeley Redmond as the water nymph Undine and Charlotte Augusta Astor Haig as Night wore their straight hair flowing to their waists.[33]

HAIR COLOR AS PERFORMANCE

Experimenting with unbound hair at fancy balls was one way that society women claimed license with their hair, perhaps emulating the freedom of actresses on stage. Another method was by altering their natural color. This manipulation, well-documented in the press, opens a lens onto how color and dye were perceived and to what degree nonactresses made their choices visible in society. Actresses' natural shade versus a dyed variant fueled the gossip pages, as did Georgie Drew Barrymore's blond locks ("so, they whisper") in 1892.[34] *Life* mused on actresses: "She is blonde, but she hasn't been blonde so very long. On the stage, blonde hair means innocence and virtue; off the stage it doesn't—at least, not always."[35] In *Lights and Shadows of New York Life*, James Dabney McCabe writes about a naturally blond

FIGURE 3.7

Napoleon Sarony (U.S., 1821–1896).
Sissieretta Jones, ca. 1895. Albumen silver
print, 14 × 9.7 cm. National Portrait Gallery,
Smithsonian Institution, Washington, DC
(NPG.2009.37).

dancer who dyed her extra hairpieces backstage: "her diamonded fingers were hard at work saturating some superb yellow tresses in a saucerful of colorless fluid, a bleaching agent for continuing the lustre of blond hair."[36]

In reality, the blond shade was never considered fully respectable or unrespectable. At any given time, some visual and written sources praise the shade on women, and others condemn it. In her book *On Blondes*, Joanna Pitman notes that Charles Dickens typecast blonds as innocents in his novels, while the Pre-Raphaelite painter Dante Gabriel Rossetti set them as *femmes fatales*.[37] Literature scholar Edith Snook notes that the ideal woman in early modern England had an abundance of blond wavy hair, which became a marker of privilege.[38] Carol Rifelj observes a spectrum of attitudes toward blonds, with some authors assigning the hue to temptresses and others to natural beauties.[39] The Northern Italian Renaissance painter Titian often portrayed blond women both as allegorical figures and as courtesans. In the mid-nineteenth century, fair-headed Empress Eugénie of France set off a craze for flaxen hair by those emulating this noblewoman who married Napoleon III.[40] Throughout the nineteenth century, Currier and Ives and other lithographers published color prints depicting their conception of types of ideally beautiful white women. Whereas "New York Beauty," "Belle of Brooklyn," and "Star of the South" were brunettes, there was also the "Beautiful Blonde" (fig. 3.8).[41] Etiquette books might not moralize about the shade but rather focus on clothing colors that complement blond: "Pure golden or yellow hair needs blue," writes one.[42] As for Currier and Ives's "Queen of the West," she was a redhead (fig. 3.9).

Red hair had a longer history of correlation with danger and betrayal, including the biblical figure Lilith, the barbarians in Greek and Roman theater traditions, and Edouard Manet's paintings with Victorine Meurent as model, often posing as a courtesan, as in *Olympia* (1863, Musée d'Orsay, Paris).[43] The aforementioned Frances E. Willard's autobiography offers a sense of the shame that could accompany red hair. As a child, she hated her "positively red" hair.[44] Children would shout "red head" as an epithet at her, and her mother would not use the word "red," preferring "bright colored."[45] Historian Ruth Mellinkoff explains that the negative associations with red hair stems from its classification as a "minority feature," occurring in about 2 percent of people.[46]

But the Pre-Raphaelite painters in England famously celebrated redheaded beauties, accentuating their appeal to male viewers by portraying them with abundant, soft, and frequently unbound hair. Rossetti's model Elizabeth Siddall popularized red hair, and two of his other models also had red hair—Fanny Cornforth, who

FIGURE 3.8

Currier and Ives (U.S., 1857–1907).
Beautiful Blonde, 1872–1874. Hand-
colored lithograph, sheet 41 × 31 cm.
American Antiquarian Society, Worcester,
Massachusetts.

FIGURE 3.9

Currier and Ives, *Queen of the West*, 1877–
1894. Hand-colored lithograph, sheet 45
× 35 cm. American Antiquarian Society,
Worcester, Massachusetts.

became his mistress, and Alexa Wilding.[47] In his paintings, they might comb, plait, or braid their thick red hair. For John Everett Millais's painting *Portia* (1886), model Kate Dolan posed in a red sixteenth-century-inspired costume that redheaded actress Ellen Terry wore when she played the role. The influence of the Pre-Raphaelite painters' penchant for Shakespearian, decorative, and allegorical scenes featuring redheaded women is seen in paintings by U.S. artists like Albert Herter. His *Woman with Red Hair* (1894) presents a profile view of a porcelain-skinned woman whose soft red hair is pulled into a low knotted bun. Curlier hair frames her face, which is topped by a black tiara, perhaps made of jet. The composition emulates Renaissance portraiture, while the abstract floral background exerts the decorative impulse of the late nineteenth century.[48] Perhaps the most salient throughline from the Pre-Raphaelite influence appears in the proliferation of redheads starring in posters, advertisements, and other printed ephemera toward the turn of the twentieth century. Louis John Rhead, who created images for Prang and Company, *Harper's Bazar*, and *Century Magazine*, among others, foregrounded redheads in his work (fig. 3.10).

In the context of the nineteenth-century United States, the Currier and Ives "Queen of the West" print (see fig. 3.9) shows that any strict connection between red hair and either villainy or unrestrained eroticism is overstated.[49] This ideal type of redhead wears her wavy hair in a classical arrangement, center-parted with a gold and gemmed floral diadem and additional hair jewels. Her skin is pale white, and her cheeks are blushed, representing the epitome of white beauty in the period.[50] Available at reasonable prices, Currier and Ives prints like this one brought ideal beauties, redheads included, into scores of middle-class homes. As one etiquette book reassured its readers: "No shade of hair is unlovely, if luxuriant and healthy in growth."[51] Writings in women's diaries echo the sentiment that abundant hair signaled health and beauty and express concern and dismay when illness affects hair growth and texture.

Eliza Frances Andrews, an educator and botanist from Georgia, wrote that before leaving for a social engagement, she arranged her sister's hair: "I fixed Metta up beautifully, though, and she was very much admired. Her hair that she lost last fall, from typhoid fever, has grown out curly, and her head is frizzled beautifully all over, without the bother of irons and curl-papers."[52] Hair figures prominently throughout Andrews's journal. She frequently becomes wary of curling her hair only to have damp air flatten the spirals: "I am tired of frizzing, anyway, though it does become me greatly."[53] She had "false frizzettes" made up of her and Metta's

FIGURE 3.10

Louis John Rhead (U.S., 1857–1926). *Jane*,
1897. Color lithograph, 40 × 31 cm. Boston
Public Library (2012.AAP.310).

hair, but those would not stay curled either.[54] At times she wished her hair was longer, and she freely commented on the hair of other women: one had "dull, coarse hair of an undecided color," and another had "hair of a rich old mahogany color that I suppose an artist would call Titian red."[55] Advertisements for hair treatments split the difference between blonds, brunettes, and redheads but always emphasize healthy, lustrous locks.[56]

Many hair products promised to restore gray hair to its original color, like Ayer's hair vigor, or even prevent gray hair, like Hall's vegetable Sicilian hair renewer. Despite the proliferation of these products, however, gray hair was not shunned on women who chose to wear their hair naturally, and hairstyles specifically for older women appeared on the pages and covers of *Harper's Bazar*.[57] A watercolor on ivory miniature by Laura C. Prather of an unidentified woman appears to celebrate the white hair of the sitter, the light source from the upper left shining on the right and center upsweeps of smooth hair and on her forehead (fig. 3.11).

Society women's natural hair color was publicly known, so when it changed, gossip columnists took note. Alice Claypoole Vanderbilt had soft brown hair, Alva Vanderbilt's was "ruddy bronze brown," and Louise Vanderbilt's was golden and gleaming.[58] When in 1897, at the age of forty-four, Alva Vanderbilt (at this point named Alva Vanderbilt Belmont, having recently married Oliver Hazard Perry Belmont) dyed her hair to hide its silvers, the change warranted a three-paragraph item in the papers.[59] In overstated terms, she was said to have changed her "almost raven black" hair to the costly "No. 4 chestnut," now looking ten years younger and resembling more closely her daughter, the well-known beauty Consuelo, duchess of Marlborough. The cheekiness with which changes in hair color were parlayed reflects the continuing stigma against hair dyeing, which, as historian Steven Zdatny points out, lasted well into the twentieth century.[60] Accordingly, the places where this process could happen were private rooms, their candor advertised by hairdressers like the aforementioned Christiana Carteaux, who advertised that one of her establishments in Providence, Rhode Island, had a separate room for hair dyeing.[61] Likewise, Mrs. M. L. Baker of Philadelphia offered private rooms for hair dyeing and emphasized the safety of the black and brown dyes she used.[62] In the 1860s, synthetic dyes began to be used as hair colorants, although the process of "blondining" to achieve blond hair seems to have retained the formula of applying ammonia, followed by hydrogen peroxide.[63] Before then, plant- and animal-based dyes were used but might be supplemented by dangerous additions of lead or sulphuric acid. Books like Dr. Charles Henri Leonard's *The Hair: Its Growth, Care, Diseases*

FIGURE 3.11

Laura C. Prather (U.S., 1862–1932). *Seated Woman with White Hair*, 1900. Watercolor on ivory, 10.1 × 7.6 cm. Worcester Art Museum. Gift of Lewis Hoyer Rabbage (1995.68.9). Image: © Worcester Art Museum, Massachusetts, USA/Bridgeman Images.

and *Treatment* (1881), however, indicate that well after synthetic dyes were available, packaged and homemade concoctions often contained dangerous combinations of ingredients that could be poisonous if ingested or absorbed by the skin. They might include silver nitrate, lead oxide, lead acetate, copper sulphate, or iron rust.[64] Leonard warns about keeping children away from the dyes.[65] Another hair care book warned that packaged dyes did not always disclose their ingredients and should be checked carefully by the customer.[66] In 1899, physical fitness proponent Bernarr Macfadden advised against any hair dyes, stating that most of them included lead, a point supported by medical publications.[67] A safer, more durable dye would be invented by French chemist Eugène Schueller, founder of L'Oréal, in 1909.[68]

PORTRAIT STUDIOS

The portrait studio was a place where society leaders and actresses deliberated over just the right look and made their hair color and style choices eminently visible. Helen Ward, a hairdresser in Washington, DC, wrote about preparing the naturally blond hair of writer Amélie Rives Troubetzkoy for a portrait for her husband's family. Rives's second husband was Russian prince and painter Pierre Troubetzkoy. According to Ward,

That woman has driven me crazy three distinct times. She came to me three days in succession to get her hair dressed in the style of a Russian litterateur. She wanted it in a Psyche, and she was determined to have it wild. I lay awake till morning and dreamed it out in one minute after she arrived at daylight to get it done.[69]

An oil-on-canvas portrait by a leading painter could cost thousands of dollars and was meant to capture a person's appearance for posterity. Even the wealthiest patrons commissioned only a few portraits over their lifetimes, so for women, the choice of hair and dress carried magnitudes of importance. John Singer Sargent could spend weeks planning and painting a portrait, as he notoriously did for *Madame X*, a portrait of Virginie Amélie Avegno Gautreau, in 1883 to 1884 (Metropolitan Museum of Art, New York).

For *Mrs. Fiske Warren (Gretchen Osgood) and Her Daughter Rachel*, the sitters visited Sargent's temporary studio at Fenway Court, the palazzo that housed Isabella Stewart Gardner's magnificent art collection (figs. 3.12, 3.13).[70] Mother and daughter

FIGURE 3.12

John Singer Sargent (U.S., 1856–1925).
*Mrs. Fiske Warren (Gretchen Osgood) and
Her Daughter Rachel*, 1903. Oil on canvas,
152.4 × 102.5 cm. Museum of Fine Arts,
Boston. Gift of Mrs. Rachel Warren Barton
and Emily L. Ainsley Fund (64.693). Photograph
© 2024 Museum of Fine Arts, Boston.

FIGURE 3.13

John Templeman Coolidge (U.S., 1856–
1945). *John Singer Sargent Painting
Mrs. Fiske Warren and Rachel Warren*,
1903. Photograph. Isabella Stewart
Gardner Museum, Boston.

sit on ornate chairs and wear satin dresses in varying shades of pink. Sargent highlights their auburn hair from the upper right, their locks merging into one another's. Fiske was thirty-two years old at the time, and her loose hairstyle is appropriate for her, an intellectual poet. She avoids an overly exaggerated pompadour bouffant so often seen at the turn of the century (see fig. 5.22). Eleven-year-old Rachel's hair is pinned up only in the front, and the rest tumbles past her shoulders.

It was prudent to select a subdued or even outright traditional hairstyle rather than a seasonal fad so that the sitter would not regret the decision and attempt to call back the artist to adjust it. One New York writer warns of the expense incurred by a woman who wore a Langtry knot (after English actress Lillie Langtry): "fashions change, and when she took to bangs her portrait did the same."[71] Miniature watercolor-on-ivory portraits by reputable painters, although significantly smaller in size also required strategic hair choices (fig. 3.14; see also fig. 3.11).

Posing for a portrait in a photographer's studio allowed for more variations in hairstyle. It could be a formal affair, and, as noted in chapter 2, hairdressers and photography studios made happy, profitable neighbors. In the early decades of daguerreotypes (images made on a silvered copper plate; introduced in the United States in 1839) and ambrotypes (images made on coated glass; invented circa 1854), which were unique creations that could not be reproduced, we see careful self-presentations with contained hairstyles (fig. 3.15). Although by the 1850s exposure times had been reduced from several minutes to under one minute and the risk of blurring the final image was no longer as dire, sitters often appear to be holding a preconceived pose. They were also seated in straight-backed chairs, possibly leaning into a metal head brace. They rarely smiled and wore dark clothing to increase the success of the final result, and it is difficult to detect emotion, though there must have been a great sense of anticipation. In the heyday of daguerreotypes, prices varied depending on the provider. Itinerant practitioners might charge less than a dollar for an image, whereas the renowned firm Southworth and Hawes in Boston (ca. 1843–1860) charged about $15.[72] Robert Douglass Jr., a Black daguerreotypist in Philadelphia, charged about $5.[73] The advent of the durable, less costly tintype in 1856 (about $1 per image) led to a relaxing of formality. Sitters could keep the dog in the shot, if they wished.[74]

Later in the century, commercial photography studios proliferated throughout the country, producing affordable paper photographs and cabinet cards that could be made in multiples. Stamped names and addresses on the front or back of the cards became an effective way to market a business's services and show historians

FIGURE 3.14

Carl A. Weidner (U.S., 1865–1906) and
Fredrika Weidner (U.S., 1865–1939). *The
Daughters of Heber Reginald Bishop
(Elizabeth, Harriet, Mary, and Edith)*, ca.
1895. Watercolor on ivory, 9.5 × 7.6 cm.
New-York Historical Society. Gift of the
Estate of Peter Marié (1905.22). Image:
© New-York Historical Society.

how pervasive the establishments were throughout the country, from small town to bustling metropolis. The tintype's lower cost allowed people to make repeat visits to the photographer and document the growth of a family (and generational resemblances) over the years. Standard studio backdrops were painted on fabric and could be purchased from photography supply companies.[75] They might show a distant landscape through a window, classical sculptures or ruins, or an architectural scene. Photographers took great care to match the sitters with an appropriate, albeit generic, background. For instance, a family wearing winter clothing would not be set against a summer meadow backdrop.[76]

Likewise, professional retouchers of photographs were instructed to be attentive to areas around the hair and to avoid creating an unnatural division between

FIGURE 3.15

Glenalvin J. Goodridge (U.S., 1829–1867).
Mrs. Glenalvin Goodridge (Rhoda), 1859.
Ambrotype, 8.3 × 7 cm. Smithsonian
American Art Museum, the L. J. West
Collection of Early African American
Photography.

FIGURE 3.16

Aultman Studio (Colorado). [Portrait of a
family], 1897. Glass negative, 13 × 18 cm.
History Colorado (93.322.318).

the scalp and where the hair falls on the neck or clothing, which could indicate a wig.[77] Painting hair colors onto a black-and-white photograph entailed another set of detailed instructions, rivaling the recipes for homemade hair dyes, though with paint colors (burnt sienna, raw umber, a dash of sepia).[78] The well-to-do Black family photographed by the Aultman Studio in Colorado in 1897 is set against a backdrop showing a contemporary building, perhaps meant to evoke a civic building or university (fig. 3.16). The three women of the family wear their hair pinned up, and their fine dresses suit the occasion.

This chapter has examined how women strategized the presentation of their hair at parties, on stages, and in portraits taken in painters' and photographers' studios. Women contemplated how to present the style and color of their hair, knowing that their choices would be made visible to their peers either for an evening, in the case of a celebration, or for posterity, in the case of a portrait. The process of decision making before entering certain places speaks to how women's thoughtfulness, deliberation, and, for Sissieretta Jones, refusal to wear her hair a certain way, held the potential to change how entire places looked and felt. Jones's choice to wear her natural hair in a pompadour instead of under a wig meant that she brought more of her whole self to the stage in front of what was likely a mostly white audience. The viewers watched, while her natural voice and hair communicated back. Women used the medium of hair to express personality and infuse emotion into places, albeit within the communally constructed boundaries of decorum. There was a degree of self-determination in how women presented themselves that may be discerned by paying attention to their choices of hairstyle and hair color. The next chapter contends with places of labor, further emphasizing how a consideration of hair functioned not only in the workplace but also in the marketplace once the manufacturing and merchandising of hair products began to proliferate. Depending on class and race, the level of control over one's hair and head coverings differed greatly in the two arenas.

4

WORKPLACE AND MARKETPLACE

The paradigms of cultural geography and mobilities studies help us regard places of labor not only as places of exertion, oppression, or capitalism but also as places of social experience inscribed with personal and communal performances, symbols, and expressions. Hair figured into this construction across various strata of mid- to late nineteenth-century society, whether women were working in a home, agricultural field, department store, social club office, or on the road selling products door-to-door. This chapter investigates how the lived experiences of women in the workplace affected their hairdressing practices and how the demands of the marketplace led to the creation of new hair products. Women's identities were socially constructed, and they adapted their hairstyles and head coverings according to social and spatial norms. These arenas of labor range from built structures like stores and houses to the open spaces of agricultural fields and to the liminal, fluid spaces of traveling salespeople's call itineraries.[1]

Because places of labor demand physical and psychic exertion, the chapter devotes in-depth discussion to the vocabulary used around hair. Since many of the terms used for Black hair were first recorded during slavery, like missing-person advertisements (so-called runaway ads), sources from earlier in the century are drawn on, although the chapter's focus remains the period after the Civil War. The more conceptual standpoint employed here is put forth by anthropologist and environmental psychologist Setha Low. Low forefronts the "role of language and discursive transformations of space" in her studies of embodied spaces.[2] The varied terms and phrases used to describe, celebrate, and denigrate hair were loaded with meaning, value, and bias. The emphasis here is how places of work, many of them mixed-race settings, and the time spent in them fostered different meanings about hair, resulting in a diffusion and circulation of a complex hair-related vocabulary.

Finally, the chapter demonstrates how the lived reality of women in the workplace led women entrepreneurs late in the century to create and market new products on a regional and eventually national scale. Given the ample evidence of Black women entering and succeeding in this market, the chapter centers Black hair care and styling.

WORKPLACES

OUTSIDE THE HOME

Uniformity in hairstyles and dress was paramount for women in various areas of service, including in behind-the-scenes workrooms and on the sales floor. It is amply visible in an illustration of the sewing room at A. T. Stewart's dry goods store in New York (fig. 4.1). In the woodcut shown in figure 4.1, hair was pulled into a low bun to keep it off the face and from falling over the eyes. At James McCreery and Company's store in New York at the turn of the century, clerks were instructed to wear black and white clothes; shirtwaists were allowed in the summer. The overall emphasis was on neatness and good hygiene.[3] In the lunchroom at the store's second location on Sixth Avenue at 23rd Street, the New Woman style is in full effect (fig. 4.2). From

FIGURE 4.1

The Sewing-Room at A. T. Stewart's. In *Frank Leslie's Illustrated Newspaper*, April 24, 1875, 109. Wood engraving. Library of Congress, Washington, DC.

FIGURE 4.2

Lunchroom scene at James McCreery and Company, in Anne O'Hagan, "Behind the Scenes in the Big Stores," *Munsey's Magazine*, January 1900, 529. Image: Library of Congress, Washington, DC.

NEW YORK CITY.—THE SEWING-ROOM AT A. T. STEWART'S, BETWEEN NINTH AND TENTH STREETS, BROADWAY AND FOURTH AVENUE.—See Page 107.

one table to the next, the women's hair is loosely swept into a top knot, creating a bouffant, with some pieces allowed to escape (see chapter 5).

Notably, since the New Woman hairstyle blurred class lines and was widely worn by middle-class women, including shop women working in stores, employee handbooks call for saleswomen to differentiate themselves from customers by keeping their hair and dress modest.[4] The issue continued to vex managers into the first decade of the twentieth century. An editorial in *Dry Goods Economist* in 1909 lamented, "In certain departments of some stores the saleswomen are attired, hairdressed, and manicured to a point which seems to put them out of the class of business women, and thus tends to complicate their relations with the customer, or possible customer."[5]

Middle- and upper-class Black women in the workplace, either paid or philanthropic, wore their hair in a variety of styles. In 1878, Josephine Beall Willson, a teacher from a wealthy Philadelphia family, married Senator Blanche Kelso Bruce of Mississippi, a formerly enslaved man. She contributed years of service to the National Association of Colored Women, helped found the Colored Women's League, and became "dean of women" at Tuskegee Institute at Booker T. Washington's invitation.[6] A cabinet card from 1875 shows her with a fashionable updo, hair piled high, most likely with false pieces added, and with a loose tress in back and short bangs in front (fig. 4.3).[7] Line drawings in newspapers in subsequent years show that she retained a stylish updo worn close to the head throughout her career.[8]

DOMESTIC WORKPLACES

Housemaids were expected to wear a simple hairstyle and a white lace cap (often brimless or topless), a symbol of cleanliness and a demarcation of rank (see fig. 2.8).[9] Women of the family would wear a hat when in public but no head covering at home during the day, although they might wear a sleeping cap at night. In the antebellum South, enslaved Black women working in a white person's house were likely required to cover their heads, though there were possibly exceptions. A number of images and written descriptions suggest the prevalence of tignons, a type of head wrap. The practice may have stemmed from a law put in place by the governor of Louisiana, Esteban Rodriguez Miró, in 1786 that required women of African descent, regardless of whether they were free or enslaved, to cover their hair. According to dress historian Dominique Cocuzza, the intent of the law was to mark people as nonwhite, but she also points out the pragmatic benefits of the tignon, which could keep the hair and head clean and absorb sweat.[10] Wearing a wrap around the head

FIGURE 4.3

Edgar Decker (U.S., 1832–1905). *Josephine B. Willson*, 1875. Carte-de-visite (albumen), 10.2 × 6.4 cm. Meserve-Kunhardt Collection at the Beinecke Rare Book and Manuscript Library, Yale University.

was a common practice in West Africa, and either as a continuation or as a form of resistance, many Black women used bright, colorful fabrics for their tignons.[11] Some traders of enslaved people attempted to reclaim the value of the bright turbans for their own financial benefit and had women wear them as a symbol of cleanliness and as an attention-getter at the market where enslaved people were bought and sold.[12] Furthermore, as historian Jonathan Square has shown, white women appropriated madras headwraps, wearing them as a fashionable accessory in formal portraits.[13]

Looking with a critical eye at and reading beyond photographs of Black women who worked in white homes can help us visualize hair and wrapping practices. Photographs of enslaved people are not to be used indiscriminately as unimpeachable documents. They were paid for by enslavers, often with the aim of boasting ownership of enslaved people and signaling certain meanings onto them. As historian Matthew Fox-Amato points out, the composition of the photographs and the positioning of the subjects made deliberate claims about the commissioner of the image.[14] For instance, women's hands might be positioned in their laps or holding a handkerchief, conveying an air of gentility that in turn was meant to reflect on the humanity of the enslaver.[15] It follows that the representations of the hairstyle and clothing of the subjects were also mediated through the decisions of the commissioner and maker of the photographs. In the multitude of extant photographs of Black nannies with white children, both turbaned and uncovered, styled hair appears with frequency. The latter may represent either a regular practice or a special occasion when a head covering was eschewed for a formal portrait with the family's children, both in photographic and painted portraits (figs. 4.4, 4.5).

The consensus of historians is that when housemaids and nannies of African descent were working in a white family's home, they most likely wore solid or plain-patterned cloth wraps and perhaps occasionally wore their hair uncovered.[16] At night and during any work-free hours on Sundays, women fashioned their hair, as they did with their clothing, according to their own desires and comfort, as much as was possible given available supplies.[17] As Esther C. White explains in her study of enslaved life at Mount Vernon, Virginia, owned by George Washington, plantation owners allocated parts of their land for dwellings where those they enslaved lived. In other words, they prescribed the space, but enslaved people converted them into meaningful places with homes, yards, and gardens.[18] Although enslaved people created places out of spaces assigned to them, their power to enforce boundaries over who could enter the zone and thus observe their personal practices was limited.

FIGURE 4.4

[Young Black female nanny, seated, with a
baby on her lap and young boy standing],
undated. Albumen on card mount,
17 × 11 cm. The Library Company of
Philadelphia (P.2016.17.2).

FIGURE 4.5

George Fuller (U.S., 1822–1884). *Woman Dressing the Hair of a Girl*, 1861. Oil on canvas, 18.5 × 16.5 cm. Memorial Hall, Deerfield, Massachusetts, Mr. and Mrs. Harry and Lucia (Taylor) Miller (1995.14.02). Image: Courtesy Pocumtuck Valley Memorial Association's Memorial Hall Museum, Deerfield, Massachusetts.

In this vein, historian Stephanie M. H. Camp refers to "plantation boundaries of space and time."[19] Cultural geographer Nigel Thrift takes a more extreme position, stating "there is no such thing as a boundary" and regarding spaces as porous.[20] Further, he writes about power dynamics and space within the context of empire—the "organization of many interlocking and overlapping spaces."[21] These concepts frame an understanding of unwanted visits by white people as invasions of enslaved peoples' places—the generic spaces that were distributed to them but that they imbued with their own meaning by converting them into homes. Historian Whitney Nell Stewart emphasizes how objects like a hickory walking stick found in an enslaved person's dwelling speaks to the efforts made to create homes and exert a level of control.[22] As outsiders, white people could never know the full significance of the homes and the communal caring that they held. Frances Ann Kemble, a white English actress married to a Georgian plantation owner, wrote frequently about entering enslaved people's areas and commented in racist terms about their hair. After one visit, she stated her inability to understand why children's heads would be covered when their cap of "woolly hair" should be sufficient.[23] Eliza Ripley writes about an enslaved couple's wedding on the Louisiana plantation owned by her husband: "As was the custom, the whole household went to the quarters to witness the wedding."[24]

Some voyeuristic white visitors, often passing through while traveling, wrote in journals or made sketches. White portrait painter George Fuller of Deerfield, Massachusetts (see fig. 4.5), kept a sketchbook during his travels to Alabama, South Carolina, and Georgia in the 1850s. He made three sketches of the interior of an enslaved family's home on a plantation. In one, a woman sits in a rocking chair by a fireplace, creating or mending a garment. Light from the upper left falls on her head, highlighting her full, uncovered hair (fig. 4.6). This rare drawing of the inside of a Black family's home, created by a white artist, underscores the complexities of reading images by unreliable authors. We cannot access the interiority of the sitter, but we may endeavor to extract meaning from the activity and posture of the subject and the implied warmth of the room. There is no visible fire in the hearth, but the sitter wears layers of clothing and sits barebeaded in a rocking chair. Could she be mending clothing for a family or community member, not an employer? Black Studies scholar Saidiya Hartman encourages this type of speculation, which she terms "critical fabulation," the rewards of which grant us the reading of this image as a moment to consider the conditions of Black peoples' lives and not only the voyeurism of the white artist and invasion of space.[25]

Many enslaved women sewed for their mistresses and were experts in growing linen and cotton and in dyeing and weaving cloth.[26] Sewing skills appear in advertisements taken out by slave traders as one of the selling points for enslaved women.[27] Sewing and weaving appear frequently in missing-person advertisements.[28] Many free Black women earned income in the garment businesses, taking clients for sewing and dressmaking and performing work out of their own homes.[29] Elizabeth Keckley, who became a dressmaker for First Lady Mary Todd Lincoln, is perhaps the best known, in large part to the publication of her memoir in 1868—*Behind the Scenes: or, Thirty Years a Slave, and Four Years in the White House*. She writes of dressing First Lady Mary Todd Lincoln's hair and, on at least one occasion, brushing President Lincoln's hair.[30] Proficiency in hair care, dressing, and sewing were

FIGURE 4.6

George Fuller (U.S., 1822–1884). *Woman Sewing*, 1856–1858. Graphite and ink on paper, 14 × 27.3 cm. Memorial Hall, Deerfield, Massachusetts (1994.20.03.54). Image: Courtesy Pocumtuck Valley Memorial Association's Memorial Hall Museum, Deerfield, Massachusetts.

intimately related, and all contributed to Black women's creation of hairstyles and expressive headwraps that they created for their own use.

AGRICULTURAL FIELDS

Information about how women wore their hair while working in agricultural fields may be found in the Federal Writers' Project Slave Narrative Project testimonies of 1936 to 1938, which were sponsored by the Works Progress Administration (WPA).[31] Although the testimonies are primary documents, they reflect the complexities of a project in which mostly white interviewers posed selective questions to Black people who had been enslaved many decades earlier. The oral answers were then transcribed and sometimes retyped or reshaped by clerical workers, resulting in biases or errors in the final versions, which are now accessible in the Library of Congress.[32] The transcriptions must be read with care, balancing the circumstances of the interviews with the valuable information that can be extricated in the aggregate. Rather than dismiss them for their imperfections, choosing to read them as a collective of memories, flawed as they might be, provides us with a sense of the motions and conditions of Black hairdressing—the actual moving of hands, scissors, and combs.

In the testimonies, formerly enslaved people relate that when working outside in fields, women wore either a straw sunbonnet, turban, or bandana to protect their hair from sun, wind, and dust.[33] Young girls' hair might be pulled through an opening at the top of the bonnet, which was then buttoned to ensure the girl could not remove it.[34] Formerly enslaved women recalled combing and rolling one another's hair on Sundays to last a week; men would cut each other's hair.[35] They also refer to wrapping the hair, meaning that they wrapped pieces of hair from the root with cotton string, with the aim of growing the hair longer and straighter.[36] Handmade combs, brushes, and cards were used for combing, and formerly enslaved woman Jane Mickens Toombs years later opined that the cards would straighten hair just as well as the straightening combs and pomades of the 1930s.[37] Cards, sometimes referred to as "Jim Crow cards," were metal-toothed combs used to separated animal fibers before they were spun into wool.[38] William H. Robinson recalled being made to use them at the market where enslaved people were sold: "We sat around on the floor and ate our breakfast, after which we were ordered into a long hall, where we found wire cards, such as are used for wool, flax or hemp. We were ordered to comb our hair with them. . . . The women, and sometimes the men, wore red cotton bandanas on their heads."[39] Minerva Davis of Biscoe, Arkansas, stated that her father was responsible for combing, fixing, and braiding the hair of other enslaved

people at auction in Tennessee.[40] Her recollection allows us to imagine her father implementing his hairdressing skills, moving from one person to the next. We can hold the meaning of this image apart from the forced directive that set it in motion.

It is also generative to apply a speculative reading to an actual image. An etching of 1866 in *Harper's Weekly* depicts the marriage ceremony of a Black Union army soldier and bride and shows a variety of ways that the freepeople in attendance styled their hair (fig. 4.7). The bride wears a veil, the bridesmaids' hair is pinned back, and the guests wear their hair either fastened or covered by a cap. Like all reproductions in national magazines, this one would have been put through the numerous gears of the publishing house, run by white men, before publication. They may not be considered pieces of reportage. However, if we deprivilege the stance of the publisher, what meanings about Black hair at celebratory events can we access? Perhaps we can imagine the communal caring and sharing of hair techniques that took place before the wedding. We can envision bowls filled with oils and herbs, ready to be mixed into pomades and applied to freshly washed hair. Further, the joy, celebration, and kinship shown in the scene exemplify the connection of emotion to space, a relationship that Yi-Fu Tuan and Nigel Thrift have generatively put forward.[41] A simply decorated room with a wooden floor and a brick wall is transformed into a

FIGURE 4.7

Marriage of a Colored Soldier at Vicksburg by Chaplain Warren of the Freedmen's Bureau, Harper's Weekly, June 30, 1866. Image: www.slaveryimages.org.

wedding venue. Hair and head coverings along with dress and posture contribute to the depth of feeling.

Later in the century, photographs of free women of color taken at their homes or in studios show an expanded range of hair choices. In a formal photographic portrait from the 1870s taken in front of a painted backdrop, a woman wears a fashionable, dark straw hat with floral decoration that complements her horizontally striped afternoon dress.[42] Other portrait sitters chose a smooth, center-parted of-the-moment style, bun or updo, bonnet covered by a headscarf, fashionable bonnet or hat.[43] A photograph labeled "Thanksgiving Morning" was taken on the grounds of the Biltmore House in Asheville, North Carolina. Dated 1897, it shows eighteen people outside a log cabin. Of the four adult women, three wear their hair pinned up or in a low bun; one wears a white cloth wrap.[44] We may apply here Jasmine Nichole Cobb's concept of "picturing freedom." By looking at the visual culture of freeborn and free Black people, she interprets the ways they took control of their own depictions.[45] Exerting choice in clothing and, as argued here, in hair and head coverings, specifically the places in which they chose to prepare and wear those coverings, was a central strategy in defining their image.[46] Taking ownership of how they were publicly presented separated the resulting photographs and prints from the racist depictions made by white people of enslaved, freeborn, and free Black people that had proliferated in print culture, especially in the antebellum period. Cobb's telling example of the latter is exemplified by *The Lady Patroness of Alblacks*, a hand-colored aquatint that appeared in *Tregear's Black Jokes: Being a Series of Laughable Caricatures on the March of Manners of Blacks* (1834). The print is related to Edward W. Clay's lithograph series "Life in Philadelphia" of the late 1820s.[47] A Black woman is shown wearing a white underdress with sleeves capped in an exaggeration of the fashionable style, and the low-cut bodice reveals most of her breasts. Her hair is arranged in three puffs, and she holds a comb in her right hand as she looks into a full-length mirror. Her bedroom is gaudy, with pink strewn drapery and an oversized straw hat with exaggerated white ribbons streaming from it. The implication is that her sense of decorum, like her hair, is untamable.

TERMINOLOGY

The so-called taming or straightening of hair of women of African descent has a charged history that figured directly into women's workplaces and, as we will see, the marketplace. Scholar and activist Kimberlé Crenshaw sees the history and continuation of hair discrimination as rooted in white patriarchal institutional efforts to tame Black peoples' lives.[48] One of the most operative forms of expressing and spreading racial discrimination is through language. The use of racist terms to comment on the texture and appearance of the hair of Black people was pervasive. Some of the most frequent words that appear in missing-person ads, pseudoscientific journals, legal documents, novels, memoirs and diaries of white people, and the commentary by white interviewers in the transcriptions of the Federal Writers' Project (1936–1938) include *wool, woolly, kinky, nappy*, and *frizzly*.[49] In their recollections, formerly enslaved people use some of the same words when recalling how white people found it entertaining to watch Black people trying to comb their hair with inadequate implements.[50] The use of the terms *wool* and *woolly* to describe hair of people of African descent has been associated with derogatory intent, with a connection to livestock terminology. However, the use of the words by people of African descent themselves complicates the semiotics and raises questions about whether they were actively reclaiming the words for their own purposes, using their own voices.

Historians have traced the roots of certain hair terms to classical Western literature, including Aristotle's writings, which describe Moors having "curled or crisped hair,"[51] and works by Herodotus that refer to "woolly hair."[52] Literature scholar Edith Snook observes the use of the word *woolly* in relation to hair in early modern texts, denoting deviance and incivility.[53] Historian Sharon Block cites French Enlightenment author Voltaire's segregation of "the Negro race" from Europeans as based in part on the "black wool on their heads" differing from so-called European hair.[54] Literature scholar Mathelinda Nabugodi traces the usage of the terms in texts such as attorney Peter Arrell Browne's *The Classification of Mankind, by the Hair and Wool of Their Heads: With the Nomenclature of Human Hybrids* (1852) as a way of justifying the association and treatment of people of African descent with chattel.[55] Browne's tome of 1853, *Trichologia Mammalium*, further solidified his thesis of the racial and genetic differences between people of African descent and people of European descent, using hair as his version of proof.[56] The list of sources continues throughout the nineteenth century, especially in phrenological and other pseudoscientific texts.[57]

As mentioned above, enslaved women who worked in the homes of their mistresses might be tasked with combing white people's hair and helping them dress.[58] They might also be granted more time to prepare their own hair and allowed to wear higher-quality clothing than enslaved people who worked outdoors.[59] Interdisciplinary scholar Noliwe M. Rooks points out that enslaved women who worked in houses would have been exposed on a daily basis to white women's beauty standards.[60] As seen in the advertisements for hair products directed at white women (see chapter 2) long, straight, or wavy hair was considered the Western beauty norm and led to racist views of the predominantly curly hair of women of African descent.

From the viewpoint of white people, straight hair and blue eyes in enslaved people could signify mixed heritage and a higher status. Black women working in white homes would have been exposed to this so-called ideal on a daily basis. Furthermore, some enslaved women gave birth to mixed-heritage children, the result of enforced pregnancies from white men.[61] Historians Shane White and Graham White make the important point that some owners insisted on using the term *wool*, "even where the appearance of their slaves' hair differed little from their own."[62] Setha Low's position on the transformative power of language on space is useful here.[63] When we add the conceptual layers of place and space to the consideration of how different communities conceived of and spoke about beauty, however, we begin to detect the level of awareness women held about the power of their hair. They used hair language with intention in their own houses, inside white peoples' homes, and at slave auctions.

Freewoman Louisa Picquet (1828–1896) of South Carolina was considered an "octaroon" (she had one black grandparent and seven white grandparents). In 1861, she recalled to interviewer Reverend Hiram Mattison that her long hair had been a liability when she was enslaved by the Cook family. It was more beautiful than that of Mr. Cook's daughter, so Picquet's hair was cut short to curtail the rivalry. When she was put up for auction, she recalled that the auctioneer asked about her hair and was reassured that it was "good quality, and give it a little time, it will grow out again."[64] Her recollections are valuable in that they show how hair functioned in the marketplace of the slave auction and express her awareness of the value of her hair, regardless of her lack of agency over it in that space. Historian Stephanie E. Jones-Rogers writes about how enslaved women's keen understanding of the market would allow them to set prices for their freedom. She states, "They took an active interest in the market processes to which they were subjected and acquired extensive financial knowledge as a consequence."[65] Harriet Jacobs's *Incidents in the Life of a Slave Girl* (1861) further exemplifies this point when the character Linda, an enslaved girl, describes her understanding of the resentment felt by the owner, Dr. Flint, toward her desirable hair, especially after she escapes his sexual predations and becomes pregnant with a child that is not his: "When Dr. Flint learned that I was again to be a mother, he was exasperated beyond measure. He rushed from the house, and returned with a pair of shears. I had a fine head of hair; and he often railed about my pride of arranging it nicely. He cut every hair close to my head, storming and swearing all the time."[66] Like many other real victims of enslavers' violence, the fictional character Linda's head was shaved against her will, temporarily erasing a defining physical attribute and the descriptive, laudatory words associated with it.

The Last Seen: Finding Family After Slavery project, which aggregates "last seen" and "information wanted" missing-person advertisements in U.S. newspapers, is another valuable source for restoring agency to speakers about their own hair and for gauging how Black families spoke about their children and kin.[67] The advertisements were paid for by formerly enslaved people who were attempting to locate family members from whom they had been separated. When included, descriptions of hair usually follow those of skin tone and variably include length, style ("cut short"), colors and colorations ("brown," "black," "red," "reddish," "sandy colored," "blonde," "gray," "silvered," "white," "auburn,"), and texture ("curly," "bushy," "straight," "soft woolly"). The advertisements provide useful points of comparison to slave-trading for-sale advertisements and missing person advertisements taken out by white people,[68] which use some of the same descriptors, including "full suit of hair," "bushy," and "curly." The intent here is to provide a brief overview of commonly appearing hair terms. Historian and digital humanities scholar Sharon Block has done a comprehensive analysis of colonial eighteenth-century ads as "internalized belief systems put on paper." For that early period, she evaluates the data for the frequency of certain terms.[69] Block looks at descriptions of people of African descent and those of European descent, analyzing the degree to which whiteness was used as a control against which complexions were described.[70]

For the present study, given the low survival rate of written documents by enslaved and formerly enslaved people, the "last seen" and "information wanted" advertisements begin to fill in a more robust picture of how Black people described their own hair. They are a welcome, growing addition in the scholarship to the invaluable memoirs and autobiographies by such authors as Harriet Jacobs, Eliza Potter, and Harriet E. Wilson, which are discussed below. They help conjure the lived experience of Black women who moved through places, heard newly created words used by white people to describe their hair, and, by co-opting some of the same words, stripped them of derogatoriness. The power of words is especially evident in hair product packaging and advertisements. We now turn to how Black entrepreneurs entered the marketplace to sell their own products. By selling to Black and white women, they used adaptive, persuasive vocabulary to elicit sales. Naming and describing their products were powerful acts, and descriptions often referred to nourishing, restoring, or medicating the hair. This confident entrance into the hair marketplace provides yet another fruitful angle on Black women's experiences with hair.

MARKETPLACES

Circa 1860, products aimed for Black women continuously appeared on the market, dominated by pomades and tinctures promising smooth, manageable, or straight hair. On occasion, Black newspapers reported on a backlash against relaxing and straightening products and in favor of natural hairstyles that did not emulate European ideals. Thomas Hodgson, who was white, gave a lively lecture and demonstration of his "Great African Hair Unkinker" in February 1859 at Spring Street Hall in New York. According to the *New York Times*, the concoction claimed to "change [the] hair of the most indignant and persevering kink, to a perfectly straight, smooth and glossy appearance," and it was expected to "create a profound sensation among our colored brethren, and particularly among the sisters."[71] Hodgson's presentation met with mixed responses: there were counterreactions from Black audience members who did not want to "deny their race." The same year, Martin Henry Freeman, a Black professor at Allegheny Institute in Pittsburgh, Pennsylvania, spoke out in the first volume of the *Anglo-African Magazine* against the desire to strive toward white notions of beauty, including hair texture:

In many cases the child is taught directly or indirectly by its parents that he or she is pretty, just in proportion as the features approximate to the Anglo-Saxon standard. . . . Hence flat noses must be pinched up. Kinky hair must be subjected to a straightening process—oiled, and pulled, twisted up, tied down, sleeked over and pressed under, or cut off so short that it can't curl. . . . I mention these practices not so much as a matter of blame to us but as illustrations of the power of public sentiment to thwart nature in us.[72]

Abolitionist Sojourner Truth famously denounced a democracy that determined "the rights of men by the texture of their hair and the color of their skin."[73] Occasional articles in newspapers for Black readers like *The Washington Bee* (Washington, DC) urged people to value their natural hair.[74] "Kink in the hair should be no disgrace," wrote one columnist.[75] In 1891, a front-page article in *The State Capital* (Springfield, Illinois) exhorted readers to "prove that the color of the skin or texture of the hair, are not evidences of race superiority."[76] However, the years-long advertising campaigns in those same newspapers and magazines speak to the longevity of the product lines (including Angeline, Hairoline, Kinkara, Lee's Take-Out Kink, Osiline, and Straightine) and customers' interest in them.[77] As Tiffany M. Gill points out, the advertising income was likely a prime incentive for the newspapers.[78]

Newspapers for Black readers also reprinted hairstyle descriptions and hair-care recommendations from national publications that originally were intended for white women.[79] The tone of the pieces was more reportage than instructive and might be placed under line drawings of white people.[80] For years, *The Washington Bee* ran advertisements for Imperial Hair Coloring, a product meant to restore gray hair to seven colors ranging from black to ash blond, appealing to the widest possible pool of customers.[81]

Eventually, Black women, many of them hairdressers, founded commercial product lines, claimed considerable space in the existing hair marketplace, and created new markets. In the early 1890s, Rebecca E. Elliott, a Black woman based in Indianapolis, Indiana, advertised her "nutritive pomade" to readers of newspapers for people of color, including *The Freeman*, an illustrated paper published in Indianapolis from 1884 to 1927.[82] Promising to soften, gloss, and grow the hair long, the advertisement includes a three-quarter back view of a woman with hair past her waist, reminiscent of the trope of long-haired women posing for photographs (see fig. 2.5). The pomade ad includes images of a Black woman showing her hair before treatment with the product (two asymmetrical puffs) and after treatment (a middle back bun with banged curls). The images do the work of marketing to persons of color. Although the written copy refers to "ladies throughout the country" and does not mention Black women specifically, Elliott seems to have advertised only in newspapers with a Black readership. Notably, agents selling Elliott's products also advertised in Black newspapers.[83] Beneath the pomade ad is one for Elliott's "antiseptic toilet cream" meant to soothe hands chapped and red from work and to clarify the complexion, although the color of complexions is not specified. Although these products focus on European beauty ideals, the language in the promotional copy emphasizes self-care, growth, nutrition, and soothing. The words convey recognition of the humanity of the people to whom they were marketing and also their

Cultivate Your Hair and Complexion by the Great French System!

BEFORE   AFTER

These cuts were taken from one of my customers, whose hair was changed, as you see, by our treatment.

Soft, Straight and Glossy Hair Produced by the Use of

CHEVELINE!

power as consumers. In the absence of a high-resolution image of one of Elliott's advertisements, a similar one by M. C. Turner of New Orleans for her "Great French System" of straightening and growth products, which was printed regularly in *The Freeman*, is a helpful surrogate (fig. 4.8). It follows the same scheme as Elliott's pomade ad, showing the undesirable state as short, tightly curled, and puffed hair and the desirable state as longer, more loosely waved hair.

At the turn of the century, frequent advertisers in newspapers for people of color included the Boston Chemical Company of Richmond, Virginia, which marketed its Ozono hair tonic, meant to straighten "knotty, nappy, kinky, troublesome, refractory hair" and grow it long (fig. 4.9).[84] Before-and-after illustrations demonstrated

FIGURE 4.8

Advertisement, M. C. Turner, *The Freeman*
(Indianapolis, Indiana), November 16, 1895,
6. Image: Indiana State Library.

OZONO
KING OF ALL HAIR TONICS

The peer of all mediums for straightening kinky, curly, refractory, troublesome hair. Not a worthless mass of ill-smelling nostrums, but a delicate perfumed ungent, made to beautify the lady, polish the gentleman, benefit youth and gladden old age. *Used by people of taste and refinement as a certain medium to produce a long and luxuriant growth of soft fine hair.* Cures dandruff, tetter, eczema, scurf and all itching, humiliating scalp diseases. It restores gray hair to its natural color; causes the hair to grow out on all bald places, especially so about the temples. It never fails to improve all grades and conditions of hair. Ozono is guaranteed as represented, or money refunded.

BEFORE.   AFTER.

FIGURE 4.9

Advertisement, Ozono hair tonic, *The Colored American Magazine*, February 1902. Image: coloredamerican.org.

the wavy, soft locks of the "guaranteed remedy." Hartona, put out by the Hartona Remedy Company of Richmond, Virginia, appears to be a related product. It promises to straighten "kinky, knotty, stubborn, harsh, curly hair" and is illustrated by a similar before-and-after line drawing.[85] By 1902, the company sought salespeople across the country: men, women, boys, and girls could be their own "master or mistress" selling the products.[86] Madame Delmore's Hair Vigor, produced in Boston, Massachusetts, promised that customers could have "long, wavy and silky growth" and could throw away their curling tongs and irons. Its frequent placement on the first page of *The Colored American* suggests the confidence of an established business.[87] The companies, presumably white-owned, were clear that they offered a remedy to the problem of Black natural hair.

Fortunately, there are women in the hair industry for whom we have near-complete biographies. They greatly expand the historical record for hair and inspire new questions that we can ask of the existing archive. One of the most successful was Christiana Babcock Carteaux Bannister, a woman of Black and Narragansett heritage. In her business dealings, she retained her last name from her first marriage to Dessilin Carteaux, a man of Black or mixed heritage who is listed variously in Boston city directories as having been engaged in hairdressing, millinery, and cigar making.[88] In 1857, she married landscape artist Edward Mitchell Bannister, a Black man whose family came from Canada. Christiana Carteaux offered haircutting and dressing, dyeing, shampooing, and wigmaking services in Boston and Providence, Rhode Island, apparently for Black and white customers. She also sold her own products and advertised them regularly from the mid-1850s to the mid-1860s in *The Liberator*, an antislavery newspaper published in Boston from 1831 to 1865 for which the majority of readers were Black. Her ads later ran continuously in the mass-audience *Boston Evening Transcript* and *Providence Journal*. She promoted the natural aspects of her hair restorative (it was made from the "roots and herbs of the forest"), and her shampoo made from tree bark was said to ward off gray hair.[89] In her early years, she offered a complexion product that promised to remove freckles. She offered packing of the products so that customers could take them on trips to Europe, and in the 1880s, she filled special orders and mailed them from her office in Providence.[90]

Carteaux provided financial and moral support for her husband's artistic goals, and Bannister publicly recognized his wife's pivotal role in his professional development.[91] Bannister began his career as a hairdresser in Boston about 1850 and by 1853 was working with Carteaux.[92] Her success allowed Bannister to set aside his own hairdressing business and photographic work (in the 1850s and 1860s) to focus on painting.[93] Journalist and civil rights activist George W. Forbes was one of the earliest writers to recognize Carteaux's integral patronage of Bannister:

But Madam Bannister had worth apart from her establishment, and art of hairdressing; for she probably more than any other woman in the race had a right to a share in the credit of her husband's achievements. It was through her skilful (*sic*) management in business that he obtained the leisure and time necessary for laying his foundation in painting.[94]

Bannister's oil-on-panel portrait of Carteaux dating circa 1860 to 1870, a rare domestic portrait by him, is held in the RISD Museum, Providence, Rhode Island.[95] Presented in three-quarter length, the sitter's solid form dominates the picture plane. Bannister captures the formidable qualities of his high-achieving wife; however, there are no hints of her profession—no scissors, mirror, or tonics—and no indication of her civic involvement.

Carteaux relocated within Boston a number of times between 1851 and 1891, mostly on Washington and Winter Streets. The spaces she occupied are variously described as "a room," "rooms," "a saloon," or "office." Typical hours were 8:00 a.m. to 6:00 or 7:00 p.m., and early in her career she also offered house calls.[96] At times, Carteaux maintained places in Boston and Providence simultaneously. In fall 1855, she announced the opening of "a Branch of her Saloon at No. 2, Lonsdale Block" in Providence.[97] The couple traveled frequently between the cities—Carteaux to meet with hairdressing clients and Bannister to meet with patrons of his paintings.[98] In the 1870s and 1880s, when splitting her time between the cities, she took out ads to inform clients of her whereabouts. When leaving Boston, she placed a stock of her hair products with neighboring hairdressers (Mrs. Trafton, Mr. Martin, Mrs. Smith) in the same building at 43 Winter Street, Boston, ensuring that clients knew where they could purchase them.[99] She might also have an associate available for shampooing while she was away.[100] In turn, she advertised in the *Providence Journal* informing local clients when she would be decamping to Boston, and in her absence they could buy her restoratives at Miss Watt's place on Benefit Street.[101] These arrangements with fellow hair professionals and her communication with clients speak to Carteaux's allegiance to the Black community, a commitment she affirmed earlier in the century during slavery.

Carteaux and Bannister were active members of their community and were avid abolitionists. Bannister sang in the Crispus Attucks Glee Club, which played at political rallies, and acted in the Histrionic Club, comprised of Black performers.[102] In 1859, he served on a committee of the New England Colored Citizens' Convention.[103] Later, he worked on the arrangements for a celebration of the forthcoming Emancipation Proclamation on January 1, 1863, at Tremont Temple in Boston, at which a collection of funds was taken for the aid of the "National Freedmen."[104] Carteaux served during the Civil War in the Colored Women's Auxiliary, was president of the Colored Ladies of Massachusetts, and participated in numerous fundraising events. Sarah Josepha Buell Hale, longtime editor of *Godey's Lady's Book*, wrote to Carteaux in 1852, asking for "advice and aid" in support of a Christian missionary effort to send female physicians to "heathen lands."[105] In January 1860, Carteaux helped organize an event at the Meionaon, a hall within the larger Tremont Theatre in Boston, "to aid the widows of the colored American heroes of Harper's Ferry, and to promote the erection of a Monument to their memory."[106] In 1864, she was the chair of the Boston Colored Ladies' Sanitary Commission, which held a fair in October 1864 to benefit members of the Fifty-Fourth Infantry, Fifty-Fifth Infantry, and Fifth Cavalry, which were Black Massachusetts volunteer regiments.[107]

Carteaux hosted community events and abolitionist work at her hairdressing establishments.[108] Forbes wrote that Carteaux conducted "a prosperous business at 365 Washington Street where with her ne plus ultra-fair vigor she was patronized by the most fashionable of the city, and where the members of the Histrionic Club itself went to rehearse their parts." He notes that Carteaux "filled a leading role on the programmes for several successive years."[109] As a lively center of social and civic activity, Carteaux's hairdressing establishments were in keeping with the long history of barbershops serving as such places and an early progenitor of woman-owned salons that would do so.[110] Her contributions to community welfare culminated in 1890 when she founded the Home for Aged Colored Women in Providence, the heritage of which continues today in the Bannister Center for Rehabilitation and Health Care.

Carteaux's leadership in social, wellness, and placemaking efforts for her friends and neighbors was tied to her work in the world of hair. Her ownership of and movement between multiple salons and in business and social gatherings within those places are practical examples of the dynamic interactions between people, places, and material items and services like those pertaining to hair. Paying attention to the mobility and reach of her labor provides a clear sense of the extent of her management within the marketplace. In addition, Carteaux would have been responsible for running the homes that she and Bannister lived in. One of them, a two-and-a-half story midcentury house that they occupied from 1884 to 1899, stands at 93 Benevolent Street, Providence.[111] Less than a mile from her hairdressing rooms on Westminster Street, Carteaux would have been able to walk to and from work.

Finally, Carteaux also leveraged family relations for the success of her business. Carteaux's brother Charles Babcock was married to Cecilia Remond Babcock, member of the Remond family of hair professionals in Boston. Sarah Parker Remond, Charles Lenox Remond, and his sisters, Cecilia Remond Babcock, Maritcha Remond, and Caroline Remond Putnam, owned a large wig factory in Salem, Massachusetts, named "Ladies Hair Work Salon," which served white women.[112] They also marketed Mrs. Putnam's Medicated Hair Tonic to combat hair loss for Black women.[113] The family was well known for leadership in antislavery, suffrage, and women's education movements.[114] The Babcock-Remond joint involvement in the hair industry is further documented by the 1851 Salem Directory advertisement page, which indicates that the "hair manufactory" of "Miss M. J. Remond and Christina Carteaux Babcock" at 18 Washington Street was located next door to James Babcock's shaving and hair dressing room at 16 Washington Street.[115] Decades later, in 1885, Carteaux and her nieces, the "Misses Babcock," who operated shampooing parlors, ran ads in the same column of the *Boston Evening Transcript*.[116]

Edward Bannister died in January 1901, and a memorial exhibition of his work was held soon after by the Providence Art Club, with which he was closely associated. The archive for Carteaux becomes quiet after Bannister's death. By June 1901, Carteaux's root and herb hair preparation was available for sale at the Rhode Island Exchange for Woman's Work, a consignment store on Dorrance Street, suggesting that she no longer operated hairdressing rooms.[117] Her health and finances seem to have declined, and she briefly moved into the Home for Aged Colored Women in Providence, followed by the State Asylum for the Insane and Poor. She died on December 29, 1902. Her nieces apparently inherited her formula for the hair restorative and began advertising it a few months after her death.[118]

Another influential woman in the New England hair-care world was Harriet E. (Hattie) Wilson of Boston and New Hampshire. Her autobiographical novel, *Our Nig: or, Sketches from the Life of a Free Black* (1859), tells the story of Frado, a mixed-heritage girl who is indentured at the age of six to a white family in New Hampshire and endeavors to improve her standing in life as she comes of age. The story parallels that of Wilson, the daughter of a Black barrel maker and a white washerwoman who was placed into indentured servitude after her parents died. When she became free in her late teens, she used her sewing skills and hair-care knowledge to build a career. Circa 1857, she began to market a line of hair products and set up a partnership with druggist Henry P. Wilson (no relation).[119] The main products, manufactured in Manchester, New Hampshire, were "Mrs. H. E. Wilson's Hair Dressing" and a regenerator promising to restore health to the hair and remove gray. The partners advertised relentlessly in New England and mid-Atlantic newspapers to a wide and diverse readership, including the *New York Times*.[120] In Wilson's novel, Frado also enters the hair-care industry:

Providence favored her with a friend who, pitying her cheerless lot, kindly provided her with a valuable recipe, from which she might herself manufacture a useful article for her maintenance. This proved a more agreeable, and an easier way of sustenance. And thus, to the present time, may you see her busily employed in preparing her merchandise; then sallying forth to encounter many frowns, but some kind friends and purchasers.[121]

Wilson refers here to the door-to-door peddling that she practiced in order to sell hair products. It is crucial to consider the power of her salespeople, not only as they claimed space in the market but also as they determined the communities they would make their markets and then fanned out through multiple cities. She thus has been referred to as a predecessor of early twentieth-century Black hair-care entrepreneur Madame C. J. Walker (Sarah Breedlove McWilliams Walker) of Indianapolis and New York.[122] However, as P. Gabrielle Foreman and Katherine Flynn have pointed out, it is difficult to determine whether Wilson marketed her products specifically to Black patrons.[123] The advertisements disappear from the papers circa 1862, suggesting that was the year the business ended. Wilson went on to become a Spiritualist, delivering religious lectures and serving as a spiritual medium, as well as a nurse and housekeeper.[124]

The steady flow of products meant to alter the natural appearance of Black hair was slowed a bit just after 1900, when activists in the New Negro movement spoke out against racial bias. Fannie Barrier Williams and Nannie Helen Burroughs wrote essays in *Voice of the Negro* in 1904, urging Black pride in their natural beauty.[125] Noliwe M. Rooks finds an increase in advertisements for products made by and for Black women between 1906 and 1919.[126] Journalist and author A'Lelia Bundles writes about Black newspaper editors in the early twentieth century who refused to include advertisements for anti-Black hair and skin products.[127] Among the new generation was Annie Turnbo Malone, who began her business with "The Wonderful Hair Grower" and eventually expanded the line to include hair creams, pressing oils, and more. In 1917, she founded Poro College in St. Louis, which included a factory, a beauty school, and community spaces and services for Black people.[128] Franchises of the school were opened in countries across the world, and Malone became wealthy. One of her students was Sarah Breedlove, later known as Madame C. J. Walker. Walker eventually transformed and dominated the market for products made by and for Black women. As historian Davarian L. Baldwin points out, Walker advocated for healthy, natural hair that did not require straightening to be beautiful.[129] Walker's concept of Black hair beauty swiftly disseminated, and by 1916, twenty thousand agents were selling her products.[130] In 1918, against the protests of the sales agents, she distributed her products to retail establishments, prioritizing the space of store shelves over the itinerant salesperson model.[131] In both iterations of the sales model, a dynamic network of products, employees, customers, homes, and stores at a large scale had been placed in motion.

The ways in which people wore and cared for their hair while working was often the hybrid result of decisions made by employers as to what was considered acceptable and hygienic and, to a lesser degree, personal choice. The amount of agency differed significantly, depending on race, class, and setting. The range of descriptive words for hair types and styles used by and around people in places of work as opposed to in their own homes reinforces the impact of power dynamics on the presentation and description of hair. The ingenuity of Black professionals, many of them women who at first worked on other people's hair, led to remarkable entrepreneurship and influence over a segment of the market. This broadening of who could enter and expand the marketplace reinforces the extensive role women took later in the century in shaping the activities they participated in. Following on the theme of increased visibility, the next chapter demonstrates how the freer movement of women—on forms of transportation like trains and bicycles and in open areas like seaside boardwalks and on the beach—led to new ways of presenting themselves, especially through their hairstyles.

5

IN MOTION AND OUTDOORS

Yi-Fu Tuan's conception of how a place acquires meaning prudently accounts for the "fleeting and undramatic."[1] For hair studies, this supposition pairs well with mobilities theory, which allows us to expand our analysis of movements like riding a bicycle as an "unfixed site" of meaningful activity.[2] The two premises are useful when considering several aspects of women's lived experiences in the mid-to late nineteenth century—when they were traveling from one place to another and when they were claiming new freedoms outside of home or work, whether on the beach, in the ocean, or on a bicycle. Reconfiguring their relationship to environments with fewer restrictions transformed women's place in a patriarchally conceived society, leading to greater visibility and power. The epitome of the independent woman who took advantage of more accessible spaces and the ability to freely move through them was the so-called New Woman. These independent women adopted hairstyles like the pompadour and the Gibson Girl bouffant that incorporated air and circular patterns to express lightness. The hair stories of journalist and civil rights activist Ida B. Wells and actress Minnie Maddern Fiske encapsulate the cultural work that New Woman hairstyles embodied and symbolized.

IN TRANSIT

Visual evidence shows that informal settings provided opportunities for middle- and upper-class women to let down their hair and stray from refined, contained hairstyles. These settings include the beach, bicycles when touring and exercising, and the in-between "dwellings-in-motion" of railroad cars while in transit.[3] While on a long-distance railroad trip, middle-class and wealthy white women might fix their own hair, have their maid do it, or engage the hairdresser on board. A bathroom in the ladies' car was available for the task. The close quarters are attested to by a rare photograph of a woman in a dressing gown standing in front of a narrow sink to view herself in the mirror while combing her hair (fig. 5.1). Sleeper compartments might be furnished with sinks and mirrors, as in a circa 1905 photograph showing a woman sitting on a narrow bed braiding a young girl's hair.[4] Some trains were outfitted with full barbershops that would have catered to white men.[5] As historian Mia Bay has shown, train travel at the end of the century was fraught with racial and gender segregation. On trains, Black women were often required to sit in men's cars that were filled with tobacco smoke and lacked access to the washroom in the ladies' car.[6] In resistance, they initiated numerous lawsuits, most famously the one in 1884 by Ida B. Wells versus the Chesapeake, Ohio and Southwestern Railroad when she was denied seating in a first-class car despite having purchased a ticket. She won the case with a monetary settlement, but the Tennessee Supreme Court overturned the decision in 1887.[7]

Hairdressing spaces on oceangoing steamships are rarely visually documented, although it is known that some ships—like those of the Collins Line, which was founded in the late 1840s—were equipped with barbershops for men. These included the *Arctic*, *Atlantic*, *Pacific*, and *Baltic*.[8] Women were most likely attended by maids in their cabin, like the protagonist in the short story "My Blonde Wig" (1876).[9] A young brunette woman, referred to as Kitty, loses her hair due to a fever and buys a blond wig from a French saleswoman at a hair store on Broadway in New York. To pass the time until her hair grows back and to have a change of scenery, she takes a steamship to Panama. She finds the steamer's salon and rooms comfortable, but the wig is unbearably hot in the evenings in her cabin. She turns away the stewardess's attempts to help her undress her hair, not wanting her and the captain, with whom she has fallen in love, to learn that she is bald beneath the wig. Her description of the ship and the service she receives aligns well with Jonathan Stafford's study of the great efforts made to recreate the comforts of home for wealthy white passengers aboard ships, exemplified by ornate interior decoration. This "steamship domesticity" helped assuage the discomfort of long-distance travel overseas, during which time passengers sought to minimize the experience of being in a mobile state.[10]

FIGURE 5.1

George R. Lawrence Co. (Chicago, Illinois).
[Woman Combing Her Hair in Ladies' Toilet
Room], ca. 1905. Photograph. Library of
Congress, Washington, DC.

Much more common than photographs of hair care aboard steamships or trains are depictions of women *en cheveux* at the beach. As a result of expanding railroad routes and increasing leisure time for the middle and upper classes, vacations became more common in the United States. Resorts—at Newport, Rhode Island; Saratoga, New York; Long Branch, New Jersey; and Manchester, Massachusetts—flourished and along with them the social scene by the water.[11] As in Europe, promenading on the boardwalk was a favorite pastime, and it called for a specialized wardrobe and coiffure, for which women could consult any number of fashion periodicals and catalogues (fig. 5.2). Certain hairpieces might be chosen for their promise of maintaining their curl in the sea air, as natural hair could become "limp and crimpless."[12] However, on the beach itself, when bathing costumes were worn, the rules relaxed, and so did the hair. A trade card for a Boston retailer illustrates the difference (fig. 5.3). In the image, a woman and man stroll along a beach. The woman wears a long-sleeved striped pink dress with black outlines and carries a deep pink parasol in her right hand. Her blond hair is pinned back and topped by an ornate hat. She locks her left arm with the right arm of her male companion, who wears a tailcoat, a vest, trousers, and a hat and carries a walking stick. Farther to the left, behind the couple, women and men frolic in the water. The women wear bathing costumes comprised of a long tunic top and trousers made of wool. Two wear sun hats, and one with dark hair lies hatless on the sand. She may have lost her hat to a strong wave and appears to be bracing herself. Most women were not taught how to swim until the turn of the twentieth century. Instead, they bathed, meaning that they submerged themselves in shallow water and feared the large waves that might drag them out to sea. When the trade card's flap, at right, is closed, we see the door of a wooden changing room, with the teasing words "Don't open." When the flap is opened, the interior of the shack reveals two women wearing undergarments with their blond and brown hair, respectively, unbound and uncovered. Their hats hang on pegs behind them. The brunette attempts to fix her hair with her fingers, gazing in a handheld mirror. Such teasing and tantalizing images appeared in many trade cards and magazines, with women's uncovered hair providing a focal point of interest.

A colorful poster for William S. Kimball & Company's cigarettes shows women water tobogganing at Ontario Beach, Rochester, New York (fig. 5.4). Though their efforts are unsuccessful, with two women falling off one toboggan and tumbling

FIGURE 5.2

Standard Fashion Company (U.S.). Fashion
plate, May 1896. Thomas J. Watson Library,
The Metropolitan Museum of Art, New York.
Gift of Woodman Thompson (b17509853).

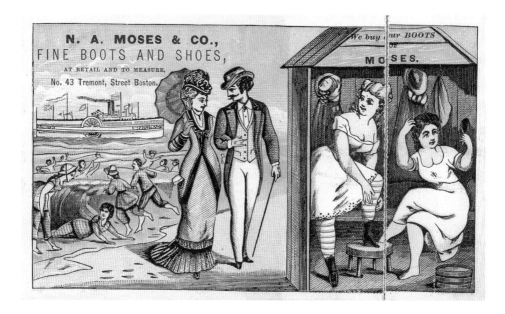

into the water, the illustration succeeds in enticing male buyers of cigarettes by showing the untethered hair and partially bare legs of five women. Another cigarette promotion depicts an even more provocative image of a young woman in a tight red, V-necked, sleeveless bathing suit, leaning on a safety rope. Head tilted down, her frizzy long hair flows behind her (fig. 5.5). A humorous *Harper's Weekly* drawing of 1858 pokes fun at the straggly hair of a rather stout woman who chaperones two young women sitting on the beach. In the background is a line of women, all loose-haired, holding a safety rope while they bathe.[13]

The beaches in the trade card above and in the *Harper's Weekly* drawing are mixed-gender, but others were segregated into women's and men's areas. Remarkably candid photographs of co-ed beaches indicate that women's uncovered hair would have been seen by men on a regular basis, something that would not have

FIGURE 5.3

N. A. Moses & Co. (Boston, Massachusetts). Trade card, 1870s–1880s. Image: Courtesy Winterthur Library.

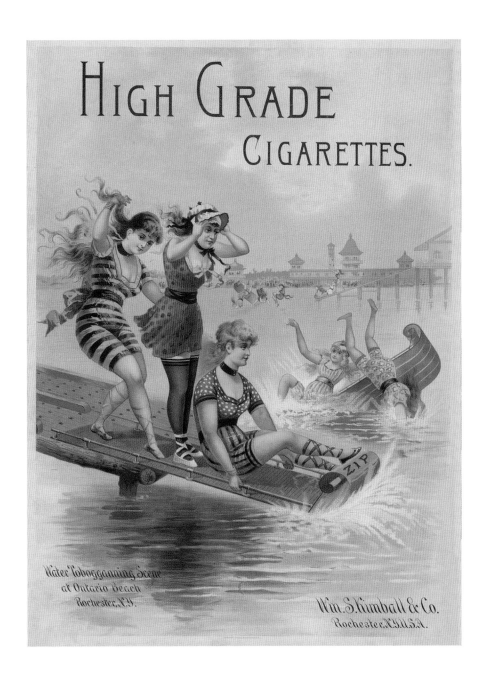

FIGURE 5.4

William S. Kimball & Company (Rochester, New York). High Grade Cigarettes poster, ca. 1887–1889. Library of Congress, Washington, DC.

been permissible in other social settings like house parties or hotels. In one from Narragansett, Rhode Island, a woman sits on a chair on the beach, her long, dark hair forward as she dries it with a towel. Her friend lies on the sand next to her, hair flowing; both are in full view of male beachgoers.[14] In a photograph from Cape May, New Jersey, a man in a tank bathing suit appears to be playfully attaching a crab to the ends of a woman's long, unbound hair (fig. 5.6). Sitting on the boardwalk below him, she turns to the camera, laughing. Wooden beach shacks line the composition at left. Hair was not always down at the beach. It might be slackly tied up or covered by a fabric bandana (figs. 5.7, 5.8), but unbound was a practical, permissible option.

ON A BICYCLE

Uncovered hair, though not totally undone, was acceptable when women were bicycling, an activity that became widespread among the upper and middle classes in the early 1890s after the invention of the drop-frame bicycle for women in the late 1880s.[15] Some women joined bicycle clubs and participated in races. Specialized magazines like *The Referee and Cycle Trade Journal* reported on the competitions, frequently noting the outfits and hats worn by women. Ankle-length skirts became necessary so that excess fabric did not catch riders' feet when they pedaled.[16] Women might wear bloomers (trousers) for ease of moving their legs while mounting and pedaling their bike. An etiquette book of 1896 praised the chicness of bloomers and their practicality in comparison to skirts on a bike.[17] As historian Kat Jungnickel writes and as photographs and drawings bear out, women were expected to retain decorum while cycling. Women in Britain, the United States, Canada, and

FIGURE 5.5

Julius Bien (U.S., b. Germany, 1826–1909), lithographer; William S. Kimball & Company, publisher. *Livorno*. In "Beautiful Bathers" series (N192), 1889. Color lithograph, sheet 9.5 × 6.4 cm. The Metropolitan Museum of Art, New York, The Jefferson R. Burdick Collection. Gift of Jefferson R. Burdick (63.350.216.192.13).

FIGURE 5.6

Cape May, New Jersey, ca. 1887. Glass
plate negative. Hagley Museum and Library,
Wilmington, Delaware (1969.002).

FIGURE 5.7

[Dorothea and Maryal Knox], ca. 1897–1898.
Silver gelatin print, 8.9 × 8.9 cm. Schlesinger
Library, Harvard Radcliffe Institute,
Cambridge, Massachusetts.

Germany submitted a number of patents for cycle wear that was functional but reserved the respectability of a skirt. Impressionist painter Mary Rogers Williams, an avid cycler, favored the Cooper Bicycle Skirt, essentially wide-legged trousers covered by a wraparound skirt panel.[18] There were also a number of skirt-holding and "trouser guard" devices to protect the fabric from getting caught in gears.[19] Another etiquette book strongly advised against wearing bloomers and yachting caps on a bicycle, associating such women riders with the unseemly acts of chewing gum and bending "their backs over handle-bars."[20] Historian Einav Rabinovitch-Fox has shown that bloomers never became universally adopted, owing to the opinions of many women and women's magazine editors that they were ugly and could hurt a single woman's chances of attracting a husband.[21] The first-round attempt at bloomers, named after activist Amelia Bloomer, in the 1850s never fully caught on either.[22] The innumerable concerns by moralists and physicians with regard to the immodesty of women wearing shorter skirts and pants have been analyzed by historians.[23] One of the chief anxieties was that women would become too masculinized, leading *Life* magazine to run a satirical cartoon in May 1896 called "The Bloomer Girl's Wedding," in which the bride and bridesmaids wear trousers, all hatless, no veils.[24] Keeping the hair neat, if not totally coiffed, while cycling was challenging. Many types of solutions were proposed. The "bicycle bang" was an unexplained chemical method of keeping the hair curled while riding.[25] In London, an enterprising hair supplier promoted the "pneumatic tube coil," a hair switch with a hidden wire to give the appearance of volume without extra weight, while riding.[26]

Choices varied for types of hats to wear when cycling. Frances E. Willard, educator and founder of the World Woman's Christian Temperance Union, wore a round straw hat with a skirt three inches from the ground, a belted tweed blouse, and walking shoes.[27] The book *Etiquette and Bicycling, for 1896* states that a certain

FIGURE 5.8

Edward Penfield (U.S., 1866–1925).
Harper's, August 1895. Harper and Brothers, publishers. Color lithograph, sheet 47.4 × 30.4 cm. The Metropolitan Museum of Art, New York. Gift of David Silve, 1936 (36.23.30).

physician counsels women to wear wool clothing and to keep the "head covering light."[28] An etiquette book published in Chicago in 1898 advises that a sailor hat may be worn, as long as it withstands wind and stays on the head.[29] The *San Francisco Call* admired more fashionable choices, like the green hat with a "scarlet bird with purple tall-feathers" worn by a Sunday rider.[30] At a Chicago race in 1895, the types ranged from fedoras and yachting caps to the "manish little cycling cap with small and big visor," and homemade cloth-covered pieces of cardboard secured to the hair with a pin.[31] Moving at a fair clip down a street, sidewalk, or boardwalk necessitated either tightly fastening one's hat or using extra pins to secure a chignon. Maria E. (Violet) Ward, author of a bicycling instruction book for women, advises that the hair should be dressed "to stand any amount of blowing about."[32]

The aforementioned May Bragdon's diaries of 1893 to 1914 chronicle her life in Rochester, New York. She worked at a patent medicine company, a manufacturing company, and her brother's architecture practice.[33] The pages are augmented by photographs of her friends and family in informal settings, as well as newspaper clippings. Bicycles figure heavily in the photographs, providing extraordinary documentation of how cycling functioned in the lives of Bragdon's co-ed circle of friends and how women dressed and tended to their hair while doing so. Assorted types of hats appear, including straw "bicycle hats" and fedoras, as well as low or high chignons without hats (fig. 5.9).

Bragdon's photographs augment the seminal, well documented, and often reproduced photographs by Alice Austen of Staten Island, New York. Beginning in 1890, Austen used glass-plate cameras and set up a darkroom in the Victorian cottage she inherited from her grandparents. A member of high society, Austen photographed her social circle in leisure activities, including bathing, tennis, and bicycling.[34] She collaborated with the aforementioned Marie E. (Violet) Ward to create photographs to illustrate Ward's instructional book, *The Common Sense of Bicycling: Bicycling for Ladies* (1896). The halftones based on her photographs show Daisy Elliott wearing a cycling suit whose skirt falls just below the knee, in various poses of mounting, pedaling, and balancing on bicycles. Her hair is pulled into a chignon at the back of the head, and she wears a fedora-type hat. Self-portraits show Austen in a similar outfit, hairstyle, and hat.[35] A less common type of image by Austen, taken in 1891, is one of her most famous. It is annotated: "Trude and I Masked, Short Skirts. 11 p.m., Thursday, Aug. 6th 1891. Gas on, flash. Stanley 35, Waterbury lense [sic], 11 ft."[36] The picture shows Alice and her friend Gertrude Eccleston wearing white masks that cover their eyes and the tops of their noses. They wear only their underclothes, dark

FIGURE 5.9

Mary Giving Con a Pansy. Cyanotype, 3.9 ×
5.2 cm. In May Bragdon diary, May 9, 1897.
Bragdon family papers, A.B81, Rare Books,
Special Collections, and Preservation, River
Campus Libraries, University of Rochester.

stockings, and shoes, and their arms are bare. They pretend to smoke cigarettes and pose as women below their station.[37] In Trude's private, curtained bedroom in the rectory of St. John's Episcopal Church where her father was the rector, the twenty-something women let down their long hair.[38]

Like Bragdon's diaries illustrated with photographs, Austen's photograph of her and Trude was not meant to be viewed outside of her family and friend circle, and loose hair is rare. Notably, relaxed hair does not appear in Bragdon's diary photographs, although she mentions it throughout the written entries. When playing basketball with women friends at the YWCA gym, she writes: "All our hairs were down."[39] On vacation in York, Maine, she bathed in the ocean and appears to have been able to swim by then—three years earlier when still learning she remained somewhat "panic-y."[40] This time, when a large wave dunked her, she "didn't mind anything but my hair."[41] Finally, one August day at the beach in Nantucket, Massachusetts, she writes, "Got my hair soaking and took a long sun-bath."[42]

Images of Black women on bicycles show a variation of hairstyles and caps. Katherine ("Kittie") Towle Knox of Boston raced competitively and was the first Black or mixed-heritage woman member of the national men's League of American Wheelmen in 1893, founded in Newport, Rhode Island (all Black members would be disallowed the following year).[43] In bloomers, she rode a bicycle without a dropped frame, and wore a cap over her pulled-back hair.[44]

Bicycle catalogues, advertisements, and decorative prints show all variations of women's hairstyles while riding (fig. 5.10). Some of the most visually captivating images leverage the effect of free-flowing hair to elicit a sense of freedom and independence for women. The promotional design for Shirk Bicycles incorporates the swirling hair of a bicycle rider into arcs conveying rapid motion (fig. 5.11). The rider appears on a curving road resembling a racetrack, two male riders behind her.

This type of all-encompassing dynamism later defined the paintings and sculpture of the Italian Futurists, a movement founded in 1909 and exemplified by members like artist Giacomo Balla. Maurice Brazil Prendergast's illustration for the cover and an interior plate of the book *On the Point* (1895) by Nathan Haskell Dole adopts a similar aesthetic. With her left hand, a fashionable woman holds down her straw hat against the wind as she gazes at the sea. Her long blond hair streams outward, its waves melding with the yellow sun (fig. 5.12). Her hat ribbons, dress bow, and pleats follow the sway. We see her from the back and are granted a full view of the swirling hair and fabrics.

FIGURE 5.10

Frederick A. Stokes Company (New York).
Riverside Drive, New York, ca. 1896. Color
lithograph, 27.9 × 21 cm. Library of Congress,
Washington, DC.

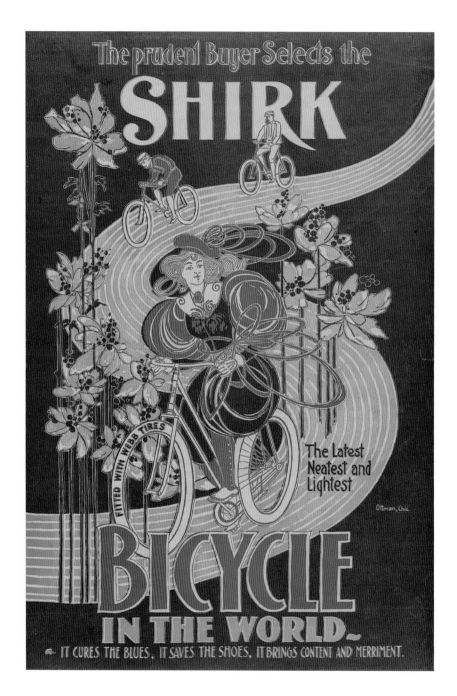

FIGURE 5.11

J. Ottmann Lithographing Company. *The Prudent Buyer Selects the Shirk*, 1893. Poster, 49.5 × 32.9 cm. Library of Congress, Washington, DC.

FIGURE 5.12

Maurice Brazil Prendergast (U.S., 1858–
1924). *On the Point, by Nathan Haskell Dole*,
1895. Poster, 42 × 29 cm. Boston Public
Library (2012.AAP.575).

A number of manufacturers utilized the word *velocipede* (referring to two-wheeled cycles from earlier in the century) for products from hair oil to tobacco, giving them the opportunity to show women cycling, hair escaping from their hats.[45] Although meant to catch the eye of customers, the visual trope of a woman's hair fluttering while riding a bicycle in U.S. visual culture was discernibly more subdued than it was in France. There, an entire genre of advertisements and posters tested boundaries, bordering on lascivious. The Gladiator and Liberator brands published several posters with women riding (sometimes nude, often in the guise of allegorical figures), their blond or red hair streaming behind them. In comparison, U.S. illustrator Charles A. Cox's poster for a bearings company—showing a six-person cycle ridden by women who pedal while reading a magazine or book, their blond, red, and black hair flying, and knees showing—appears markedly tame (see fig. 7.1).

When considered against the photographic evidence, exemplified by Bragdon's and Austen's work, as well as fashion plates and drawings, the posters and advertisements clearly represent male fantasies and anxieties. By most accounts, hair was meant to stay secured to the head, whether or not it was under a hat. A summer fashion spread for "bicycle girls" in the *San Francisco Call* in May 1898 shows a variety of hats on the four women models.[46] In March 1896, the editorial pages of the "bicycle issue" of *Vogue* show hats on all the women riders, including the two-page illustration *The Bicycle Rest*, depicting men and women gathered in a park, some seated and others standing.[47] The advertisements are more varied. Remington Bicycles on Broadway in New York shows a black-and-white stylized scene evoking a Gothic fairytale of a woman riding, hair escaping her small hat and flowing behind her.[48]

Acceptable hair was different when women were cycling than it was when they were beachgoing and bathing, where the hair might be completely undone, but both arenas unsettled previous rules of self-presentation. A satirical cartoon by William Henry Walker for *Life* in 1895 captures the anxiety of the moment (fig. 5.13). The woman at left wears a bathing ensemble with ill-matched, puffed sleeves. She wrings the water out of the skirt, and her hair falls out of its chignon. At right, a woman with hair pulled back and under a fedora, wears a blouse with overly large sleeves and bloomers. As the two talk on the boardwalk, a seemingly waterlogged child (left) and a man and woman under a parasol on the beach (center) look on. Another caricature titled *The Awful Effects of Velocipeding* (ca. 1885) depicts a woman riding a bicycle, hair and skirt fluttering behind her, as she crashes into a man on a bicycle, throwing him off. And she smokes.

FIGURE 5.13

William Henry Walker (U.S., 1871–1938).
[Two women talking on a boardwalk], *Life*,
August 29, 1895. Princeton University
Library.

The concern over wildness when women were moving through outdoor spaces was part of the reaction to the advent of the so-called New Woman, a phrase first used by British author and orator Sarah Grand in 1894.[49] The literature on the development of the New Woman type and the response to it, often an outright backlash, is broad and thorough. A brief summary will suffice here so that we may focus on what arose out of it in the world of hair. The concept and image of the New Woman took hold in the United States and England in the 1890s through illustrations, the popular press, and literature. In drawings by Howard Chandler Christy, Harrison Fisher, and especially Charles Dana Gibson for *Century*, *Collier's Weekly*, the *Ladies Home Journal*, and *Life*, the New Woman (and related Gibson Girls resulting from the specific type by Gibson), was white, middle to upper class, single, tall, and lean.[50] Gibson's models included his wife, Irene Langhorne Gibson, and dancer Evelyn Nesbit. The New Woman type was defined in the popular imagination as a woman who rode bicycles, participated in sports like tennis and field hockey, perhaps attended college and joined a profession like teaching, nursing, or social work, and advocated for political and social policies like suffrage. Many of them delayed marriage and childbearing and smoked cigarettes, an act seen as deviant and threatening to family morals, virtue, and beauty.[51] They adopted relatively roomy, comfortable clothes, a sign of their claim to agency and liberty in their daily lives. As Rabinovitch-Fox points out, the two-piece outfit of a smart-looking, yet mass-produced shirtwaist and bell-shaped skirt became the archetypal look.[52]

Magazine illustrations and posters give the false impression that all women who adopted the Gibson Girl look were white. Black women took up the shirtwaist, bell skirt, and upswept spherical hairstyle, using them to promote inclusion in middle-class life and to advance equality. As discussed in chapter 4, products aimed at providing Black women with the Eurocentric white standard of long, shiny, brushable hair were widespread later in the century. One further advertisement is useful to discuss here, as it presents the Gibson Girl style, notoriously associated with the white Anglo-Saxon women that illustrator Charles Gibson used as models, for Black women. By 1900, advertisements for an Imperial Whitener showed a bifurcated line drawing. The "before" side depicts a woman with dark skin and short, curly hair, and the "after" side shows her with light skin and wavy smooth hair pulled into a top knot evoking the Gibson Girl style.[53] Both the skin-lightening product (with the dominating word "imperial" in its name) and the use of the Gibson Girl style as the desired outcome underscore the continuous imposition of white beauty norms and the pressures to adopt them.

Photographs of Black women show how they claimed the style into their hairdressing practices as a way to visually signal their middle-class status.[54] The unidentified woman in a photograph from the 1890s wears her hair brushed forward and teased upward in a pompadour, another soft, airy hairstyle that was popular at the time (fig. 5.14). Authors Juliette Harris and Pamela Johnson make the important point that this type of hairstyle for Black women is molded but not straightened: "artfully shaped mounds of smoothed but unstraightened nappy hair."[55] The graduation portrait of Octavia C. Long (fig. 5.15) shows the full bouffant that became a recognizable symbol of middle-class, independent women in the first decade of the twentieth century (fig. 5.16) and that was expanded on during the New Negro movement and extended into the Harlem Renaissance era.[56]

The sizable counterreaction against the New Woman included men and women in the United States and abroad who perceived a threat of so-called unfeminine behavior in women. They were skeptical of "rational" clothing that was worn without corsets and petticoats and thus was more amenable to athletics.[57] They feared that women's work for social causes would disallow sufficient time to tend to husbands and children.[58] The concerns appear across general and race-specific publications alike.[59] Further, women were now handling tools to fix malfunctioning bicycles. Ward's book features chapters titled "Women and Tools" and "Tools and How to Use Them." Satirical caricatures in line with the aforementioned one of the cycling, smoking woman endangering a man's life when she crashes into him illustrated their apprehension. *Punch* magazine ran similar ones, along with snarky poems, as did *Truth* magazine in its New York and London editions.[60] Several companies issued satirical stereographs of imposing New Women in bloomers next to bicycles directing men to do their own washing and sewing.[61] One titled "New Woman Barber" shows a woman in underclothes, knees exposed, gripping the head of a frightened male client as she prepares to shave his face.[62]

Shorter, lighter hairstyles evolved with the freer lifestyle, simultaneously with the new clothing. Hairstyles associated with the New Woman in the 1890s were spherical. They were upswept from the face and fastened into a loose chignon, without fringes. Aptly, they incorporated air in a way commensurate with pneumatic tires on bicycles. It could be achieved with shorter hair than previous styles, but if one's natural hair was not long enough, a woman could buy lengths of fake hair to pile over a "rat" or postiche.[63] The culmination was a buoyant, rounded bouffant

FIGURE 5.14

[Portrait of a woman], late 1890s.
Photograph, 15.2 × 10.6 cm. Missouri State
Museum (T00.2008.008.0003nn).

FIGURE 5.15

Constant F. Squires (U.S., 1871–1916).
Octavia C. Long, 1909. Silver and
photographic gelatin on photographic
paper, 22.9 × 13.3 cm. Smithsonian National
Museum of African American History
and Culture. Gift of Naomi Long Madgett
(2011.79.10).

with the hair swirled high and wide around the front of the head (fig. 5.17). A supplemental switch or roll of hair might be added for extra volume.[64] Volume was carried to an extreme when women placed a large picture hat atop the bouffant, creating endless fodder for satirists (fig. 5.18). However, as with most satires, a truth was revealed. Hairstyles register effectively as symbols, and they take up space. The look became a signature for a number of high-profile women, two of whom are especially well documented in widely circulated images.

HAIR STORIES

IDA B. WELLS

Ida B. Wells of Mississippi was a noted civil rights activist, journalist, and educator who was famously outspoken about racial inequities and stereotypes throughout her influential career. She wrote for a number of newspapers, including *Free Speech and Headlight*, which she co-owned.[65] In her investigative journalism and activism, which took her to Memphis, New York, Chicago, and England, she exposed and

FIGURE 5.16

[Elizabeth Carter Brooks and Emma Azelia Smith Hackley], ca. 1900. Five photographs mounted on card, overall 13 × 23 cm. Library of Congress, Washington, DC (LOT 15574, no. 3).

FIGURE 5.17

Charles Dana Gibson (U.S., 1867–1944).
Bachelor's Wall Paper, 1902. Machine-
printed paper, 62.5 × 56.5 cm. Cooper
Hewitt, Smithsonian Design Museum, New
York. Gift of Philadelphia Museum of Art
(1971-58-3-a,b).

wrote about lynchings of Black people by white people and the unsubstantiated claims of crimes that led to them.[66] Broadly distributed engravings and photographs show that Wells consistently wore her natural hair pulled up into a spherical updo (fig. 5.19).

Historian Leigh Raiford has analyzed how Wells used photographs to advance her social justice work. As part of her antilynching campaign, she mobilized abject photographs of lynchings to substantiate their atrocity and defy any sense of her own fear.[67] With portraits of herself that she commissioned and circulated—she placed one on the title page of her 1892 pamphlet *Southern Horrors: Lynch Law in All Its Phases*—she used her image to symbolize justice, authority, and action.[68] Raiford and others have noted the pride of Wells's pose in these bust-length photographs and illustrations, head turned slightly to the right or left. Her interest in fine clothing, the cost of which she documented in her diaries, became part of her self-presentation.[69] Her face is turned in half profile to the right, and her natural hair, pinned at the top of her head and augmented by a hairpiece, takes up space and has a presence that is equal to that of her lacy black dress and upright pose. Her hairstyle was consistent throughout the 1890s, which was an influential decade for her, especially during the World's Columbian Exposition of 1893 when she wrote the pamphlet *The Reason Why the Colored American Is Not in the World's Columbian*

FIGURE 5.18

A Millinery Eruption, Harper's Weekly, May 17, 1902, 632.

FIGURE 5.19

Sallie E. Garrity (U.S., ca. 1862–1907).
Ida B. Wells-Barnett, ca. 1893. Albumen
silver print, image 13.9 × 9.8 cm. National
Portrait Gallery, Smithsonian Institution
(NPG.2009.36).

Exposition.[70] After the turn of the century, she kept the hair volume in the front, while adopting a full New Woman bouffant.[71] In 2019, Mattel's Barbie Inspiring Women Series issued an Ida B. Wells Barbie doll that used her signature hairstyle of the 1890s. Two years later, sculptor Andrea Lugar also used the style in her figurative bronze statue of Wells, which stands at Ida B. Wells Plaza in Memphis, Tennessee.

MINNIE MADDERN FISKE

Actress Minnie Maddern Fiske (born Marie Augusta Davey) began her stage career as a child in New Orleans, later starred in Henrik Ibsen plays, and married playwright and journalist Harrison Grey Fiske. Her long career resulted in innumerable images of her, from cartes-de-visites to portrait paintings by acclaimed artists. The images provide rare visual documentation for one woman's hairstyles, off and on the stage. In an 1893 oil-on-canvas portrait by Maximilien Colin, she sits in an unembellished studio, wearing a black dress with stylish puffed sleeves but otherwise lacking detail (fig. 5.20). She rests her feet (we see only her left boot) on a floral upholstered pillow. Its peach and orange tones blend with the wooden floor and offset her red hair. The green drapery behind her, perhaps meant to suggest a stage curtain, also complements the orangey red of her hair, which is further highlighted by the incoming light source at the upper left. Her rather intense stare and pursed lips may be meant to signal her talent at playing dramatic roles, while her unpinned bright hair, cut fairly short in the front and somewhat fluffy at the top, sides, and back, further resonates with her changing identities as an actress, though the artist shows her at rest.

More unruly looks for Fiske are shown in a profile portrait in a black-and-white carte-de-visite from 1895[72] and in a half-length portrait photograph of her in costume, draped in white chiffon, lips closed, looking attentively at the viewer.[73] In 1898, the Sarony photography studio issued a color lithograph of her in the role of Tess

FIGURE 5.20

Maximilien Colin (U.S., 1862–1894). *Minnie Maddern Fiske*, 1893. Oil on canvas, 182.5 × 122.5 cm. National Portrait Gallery, Smithsonian Institution, Washington, DC. Gift of Mr. and Mrs. Walter Schnormeier (NPG.67.19).

of the d'Urbervilles. A halo of frizzy red hair defines the representation of her in this tragic role.[74] At the turn of the century, her hair is swept up more neatly in the frontal pompadour that she wore for *Miranda of the Balcony*, along with costumes by the House of Worth, including the surviving, so-called wheat dress (fig. 5.21).[75]

Her style culminated in the spherical New Woman bouffant that Ernest Haskel's profile portrait so grandly established as her hallmark look at the time (fig. 5.22). Strands of dark swirled hair, with touches of blush pink, converge into a mass, the front sloping low onto her forehead. Originally a drawing with applied watercolor, the image was reproduced as a lithograph and circulated with press materials with the sole word "Fiske" printed on it.[76]

By the time William Merritt Chase painted her portrait in 1910, Fiske's spherical red bouffant hairstyle once again defines her look, but the conservative blacks and browns of the U.S. Impressionist painter's rendition no longer signal an upstart but portray an established performer.[77] She featured in three plays that year, taking the lead role in two of them.

The ease with which Wells and Fiske fostered a signature identity through hair and the speed with which other New Women like them tended to and arranged their hair while in transit, exercising, and bathing in the sea underscores the command women had over their self-presentation. By entering and embodying more fluid environments and spaces previously restricted to them, they actively shifted authority away from men, pushing against patriarchal allocation and control of space. This resistance and reshaping of the power structure was visually expressed in the loosening of hairstyles. Looking at how women negotiated the dynamics of liminal and newly accessible spaces deepens our understanding of how they related to different environments, a core aspect of human geographical studies. When we

FIGURE 5.21

Otto Sarony Co. studio (New York). *Minnie Maddern Fiske in "Miranda of the Balcony,"* between 1901 and 1907. Photograph mounted on cardboard, image 18.1 × 12.4 cm. University of Washington Libraries, Special Collections (JWS12918).

FIGURE 5.22

Ernest Haskel (U.S., 1876–1925). *Mrs. Fiske (Minnie Maddern Fiske)*, 1900. Lithograph, sheet 49.4 × 42.1 cm. The Metropolitan Museum of Art, New York. Gift of Abigail Aldridge, granddaughter of the artist, 2015 (2015.704.5).

consider the lived experiences of individual women—fixing their hair within the small dimensions of a railroad cabin or exposing their wet hair after a dip in the ocean—we expand our conception of how quotidian practices hold deep meaning and the potential to rebalance power dynamics. The next chapter continues the inquiry into patriarchally conceived spaces and investigates how recentering women's role in the international market for raw hair shifts the emphasis to the humanity of the people supplying and sustaining the trade.

6

THE INTERNATIONAL MARKETPLACE

As cultural geographer Nigel Thrift and others have effectively theorized, in keeping with Michel Foucault's theories of space, territory, and power, one of the main engines of empire is the patriarchal control of space.[1] If we conceive of the international hair market as a vast space, a transnational arena, then we can begin to see the systems of patriarchal imperialism that underlie its workings. This chapter first constructs the hair trade by using data available in official records. It then questions the data and points out its difficulties, especially the vexingly incomplete and inconsistent sets of figures from year to year. Finally, the chapter disrupts the archive by inserting, claiming space for, the lived experiences of women who contributed to and participated in the market. The result is a restoration of the human dimension to the machinations of the hair trade.

A generative starting point for this endeavor is the constructed place of the World's Columbian Exposition of 1893 in Chicago. Territorialization and spatial control were the organizing principles of the exposition, a celebration of the anniversary of Christopher Columbus's arrival in the Americas four hundred and one years earlier (the fair was originally planned for 1892 but was delayed by one year). Western exceptionality and the colonization of indigenous lands and peoples were on display and were sources of pride for the governing bodies that conceived and planned the exposition. The stereotypical, arbitrary, and exoticized displays of peoples and products from diverse nations can be traced in the presence and treatment of hair services and products across the fair. A number of thorough studies of colonization and racist exoticism at the exposition shrewdly examine the preoccupation with typology and the typing of peoples in the period and are worth consulting.[2]

WORLD'S COLUMBIAN EXPOSITION OF 1893, CHICAGO

Over six months in 1893, some 27 million people visited the World's Columbian Exposition in Chicago along Lake Michigan (fig. 6.1). The massive, immersive display of about 65,000 exhibits was meant to express U.S. power and ingenuity on a global level. From the first Ferris wheel and moving sidewalk to the Edison tower of light in the Electrical Building, the fair was large and commanding and achieved its organizers' goals.

As scholars have shown, the fair also was rife with nativist, racist attitudes and methods. For instance, Carolyn Schiller Johnson analyzes the problematic "public anthropology" of the so-called villages erected on the Midway to display the cultures of Native Americans and colonized peoples.[3] Recent studies have worked to restore the agency of women, peoples of various heritages, and organizations to the fair. Judith K. Brodsky and Ferris Olin write about Bertha Honoré Palmer's leadership of the Woman's Building, which included a wealth of works of art made by women and a vast library of books written by women over several centuries.[4] In turn, Anna R. Paddon, Sally Turner, and John McCluskey elucidate the contributions of Black people like Ida B. Wells and Frederick Douglass to the fair, despite exclusionary efforts by multiple figures, including Palmer.[5] Julie K. Brown's fascinating study of identification photographs of food service employees at the fair sheds light on the experiences of laborers.[6]

The event and its extant publications, souvenirs, and photographs provide a wellspring of documentation for the U.S. zeitgeist in the last years of the nineteenth century. Historian Timothy J. Gilfoyle has cleverly called it an "interpretive smorgasbord" for scholars, with good reason.[7] For hair studies, we return to the well once more, finding extraordinary, distilled documentation for the multiple levels on which hair figured at the exposition. Many souvenir and "reminiscence" books describe the hair of women, men, and children in the national exhibits.[8] The novelty of the so-called Cairo barbers drew men seeking a shave and an anecdote to bring home.[9] As for onsite amenities for visitors and staff, a barbershop was run by Rosensteel & Purcell, presumably a Chicago team, which grossed more than $12,000 over the run of the exposition.[10] From the commercial standpoint,

FIGURE 6.1

William Charles Hughes (British, 1844–1908).
*Manufactures and Liberal Arts Building,
World's Columbian Exposition, Chicago,
1893.* Hand-colored glass lantern slide,
7.1 × 7.2 cm. National Gallery of Victoria,
Melbourne (2014.736).

manufacturers and merchants from Italy, Germany, Spain, and the United States exhibited "hair work, coiffures and accessories of the toilet" in department H of the Manufactures and Liberal Arts Building (fig. 6.2). These included coiffures, wigs, switches, hats, barber's and hairdresser's tools and appliances, and combs and brushes (figs. 6.3, 6.4).[11]

Tiffany & Company's extensive display of jeweled objects (fig. 6.5) included thirteen hair ornaments, tiaras, and a "toilet table worth $9,000."[12] Archival sketches for some of the pieces bear out a writer's description of "riotous" amounts of diamonds and gems (fig. 6.6).[13] The company also designed more restrained combs, an enormous product category, and advertised the affordability of its products in middle-class print publications.[14]

Near the Tiffany exhibit was the German display, replete with toupees, switches, combs, and brushes.[15] The Austrian display is documented as including combs, but it seems likely that it may also have shown wax figures with real hair, as Vienna was known for exporting them to the trade in London, Paris, and New York.[16] A hair curler by K. A. P. Electric Novelty Co. in LaCrosse, Wisconsin, was featured in the Electricity Building, and Nichols and Co. of Chicago showed its curling irons with wooden handles, which protected users' hands from the burns that commonly were caused by iron tongs.[17] Exhibitors from Canada (listed under "Great Britain"), the United States, Mexico, and Argentina won awards for hairwork, both ornaments made out of hair and hairpieces for coiffures.[18] Wigs, bangs, curls, puffs, and more were displayed on a "ventilated hair foundation" (no photographs exist). Hair product merchants like Hoosier Curling Fluid Manufacturing Co. of Chicago advertised in the many newspapers, pamphlets, and souvenir books that circulated for visitors planning their trips or returning home.[19]

Hair was related to other raw goods at the exposition. Jute, hemp, and flax were among the "animal and vegetable fibers" on view in the Agricultural Building.[20] At times when human hair supplies were low, these materials, although rougher, "ropy," and less desirable, might be substituted in hairpieces.[21] Wool or goat's hair might also be used in "puffs" and "rats" and could be half as expensive as the same pieces made with human hair.[22] Human hair was so closely related to the enormous trade in animal hair and its manufactures that some official reports do not separate the categories in yearly totals. For a sense of scale, nonhuman hair and its manufactures in 1891 totaled about $2.2 million, ranking it among the top forty agricultural imports.[23] Animal hair from horses, cows, and hogs was used to stuff mattresses and upholstered chairs and to make various types of brushes, and some

FIGURE 6.2

Interior of Manufactures and Liberal Arts Building, World's Columbian Exposition, Chicago, 1893. From J. W. Buel, *The Magic City* (St. Louis: Historical Publishing Co., 1894). Photographic reproduction, 20.3 × 25.4 cm. Image: Northern Illinois University Libraries.

FIGURE 6.3

Gorham Manufacturing Company
(Providence, Rhode Island, founded 1831).
Hair brush, ca. 1890. Silver, L. 10.2 cm.
RISD Museum, Providence, Rhode Island,
The Gorham Collection. Gift of Textron Inc.
Courtesy of the RISD Museum, Providence,
RI (1991.126.239).

FIGURE 6.4

Mlle. Louise (Brooklyn, New York). Hat, ca.
1890. Bast fiber, cotton, birds, feathers.
Brooklyn Museum Costume Collection at
The Metropolitan Museum of Art, Gift of
the Brooklyn Museum, 2009. Gift of Pratt
Institute, 1943 (2009.300.1777).

FIGURE 6.5

Charles Dudley Arnold (U.S., 1844–1927),
[Tiffany & Company exhibit, World's
Columbian Exposition, Chicago], 1893.
Platinum print on board, image 19.1 ×
22.3 cm. Chicago Public Library, C. D. Arnold
Photographic Collection (B012_V006_P014).

FIGURE 6.6

Tiffany & Company (U.S., 1837–present).
Sketch of hair piece, 1893. Watercolor and
ink on paper. Copyright Tiffany Archives,
New York.

was used for haircloth in garments.[24] There were also periodic rumors that animal hair, such as Angora rabbit hair, was mixed with human hair in some hairpieces.[25] Animals were housed in the Live Stock Exhibit, and fruits and their manufactures were located in the Horticulture Building.[26] Pomatums, or pomades, for human hair at one point were made with bear's grease, and some contained apples as a perfuming agent.[27] Later in the century, pomades sometimes were made with a combination of lard, beef or mutton suet, wax, and oil (perhaps castor, coconut, or olive), though as demonstrated by the individual purveyors of hair products, there were no universal recipes or standards.[28]

As a result of the fair's concept of anthropologically typing peoples from throughout the world, many exhibitions of different cultures included dubious presentations and explanations of hair practices. The crafting of hair ornaments was commonly demonstrated in the exposition's so-called villages, including Ceylon (present-day Sri Lanka) and Lapland in Finland.[29] Descriptions in official fair publications and illustration captions provide a sense of the extent of the racism and exoticism in play. In the documentary photograph book published in 1895 with images taken by a government photographer, a typical page shows a young man from southeast Africa and a young woman from Egypt under the heading "The Pride of the Desert." The text explains that the man's "plaits and fine ringlets are made possible by the lavish use of cocoanut oil."[30] Such objectifying language is used throughout the publications, which notably included guides for children, thus perpetuating a Western-centric viewpoint and tone of superiority.[31] The report by the Congress of Women uses this style in its descriptions written by white U.S. women (their portraits are provided at the top of each article) of Samoan, Japanese, and Spanish women's hairdressing.[32] Historian Rachel Boyle makes the important point that the majority of images from the fair were mediated by the administration of the exposition. There were two main photographers of the grounds and for souvenir books—Charles Dudley Arnold and J. J. Gibson.[33]

National newspapers and souvenir albums also produced images, but it is difficult to counterbalance those publications with the viewpoints of visitors, as personal photographs from the fair remain scarce in public collections. However, admiration for the pavilions and displays by countries like Norway and Sweden, which for decades had been esteemed for their "hardy fair-haired races" in ethnographic and phrenological texts, is amply evident in photographs and texts.[34] Poet Celia Thaxter from New Hampshire creates an image of a Norwegian woman in one of her letters: "Anethe, everybody says, was a regular fair beauty, young and strong, with splendid thick yellow hair, so long she could sit on it."[35] Sweden's 12,000-square-foot cathedralesque wooden building was rivaled in reputation by Norway's functional reproduction of a Viking ship.[36] Women from Scandinavian countries or local women of Nordic descent were undoubtedly included in the "World's Congress of Beauty" exhibit on the Midway Plaisance, sponsored by the International Dress and Costume Company. A banner on the building reads: "40 Ladies from 40 Nations," but the countries from which the women purportedly hailed are not well documented.[37] The exhibit was mainly an attraction for men to ogle at women, who either sat on display or danced. As Boyle observes, the beauty of white women from European countries, including Denmark, Sweden, Scotland, and Greece, was exalted at the fair. A souvenir album shows images of women representing the United States, Ireland, Scotland, and "Fatima, the Oriental Beauty" wearing what the organizers conceived as traditional hairstyles and headwear.[38]

GEOGRAPHIC AND ECONOMIC SCOPE OF THE HUMAN HAIR TRADE

It is not yet possible to draw a complete picture of the hair trade in the nineteenth century. Even in the period, writers pointed out how little the average consumer knew about this "staple article."[39] By 1907, in Marseille, France, one of the centers of hair commerce, it was still referred to as "an unusual trade."[40] Study of its commerce is hampered by limited documentation, which as Johanna Wassholm and Anna Sundelin note, was a "mobile petty trade" in many regions.[41] The most thorough overviews from the period are by Mark Campbell and Ellen Bacon. The oft-cited Campbell was a Chicago-based hair dealer and hairdresser who was active from the 1860s through the late 1870s (fig. 6.7).[42] His best-known book is *Self-Instructor in the Art of Hair Work: Hair Braiding and Jewelry of Sentiment* (1867 and 1875 editions). Much of the information appears to derive from an article in *The London Review* of September 1865, which was subsequently reprinted in the middle-class U.S. magazine *Godey's Lady's Book and Magazine* in 1866.[43]

Campbell's book, articles in popular magazines like *Godey's* and *Scientific American*, and medical, scientific, and physical culture publications appear to be the main sources of how hair trade information circulated in the mid- to late century. However, it is necessary and worthwhile to fact-check and correct Campbell's and Bacon's information with that given in economic reports whenever possible.

In *Self-Instructor*, Campbell explains that length, texture, and color determined value, with prices ranging from $15 to $200 per pound in 1867.[44] He lists the main sources of hair as France, Italy, Russia, Germany, Norway, and Sweden.[45] This register of countries matches those given in the U.S. Treasury report for imports, with the exception of Russia.[46] The Treasury report includes additional countries (Prussia, Holland, England, Scotland, Canada, and Cuba) from which hair was imported in varying amounts. The total value was $255,238 (about $5,107,709.03 in 2022).[47] It is productive to fill in more of the global picture by using supplemental records. At about this time, the press cites Paris as the center of the trade (fig. 6.8), with further

FIGURE 6.7

"Retail Department." From Mark Campbell,
*Self-Instructor in the Art of Hair Work: Hair
Braiding and Jewelry of Sentiment*, 1867, 266.

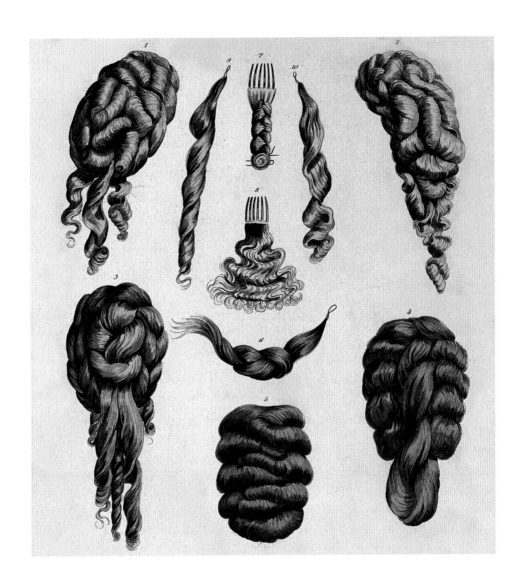

FIGURE 6.8

Revue de la coiffure, May 1, 1875. Colored
engraving, image 20 × 16.5 cm. Wellcome
Library, London (31446i).

locations in France (Marseille, Lyon, Caen, Guibray, and Beaucaire) also involved in the supply. Among other highlighted countries are Holland, Spain, Scotland, Ireland, Belgium, and Poland.[48]

In 1877, the *New York Times* confirmed Marseille as a center for hair commerce, claiming that imports had increased from fifty tons in 1873 to eighty tons in 1875, though those figures cannot be verified.[49] Historian Steven Zdatny cites the figure of 80,000 kilograms (approximately eighty-eight tons) of raw hair in the French marketplace each year in the 1880s.[50] He also identifies the Maison Patte, a French dealer in hair that sent agents to rural villages.[51] Italy and China reportedly provided the largest quantities to Marseille, followed by Turkey and Japan. Minor amounts were said to come from Egypt, India, Germany, and Algeria.[52] In 1880, the *London Telegraph* praised the glossy, long hair obtained from Limoges and cited the United States and Great Britain as the largest customers of France's hair trade.[53] In 1894, *Scientific American* refers to Limousin, Brittany, Normandy, and Beauce as providing the most desirable hair. It also notes that hair from India and China continued to be imported into France.[54]

Ellen D. Bacon's 1901 article titled "Hair" prefaces the section on hairwork awards in the *Report of the Committee on Awards of the World's Columbian Commission*, published eight years after the closing of the exposition, reflecting the fair's initiatives to categorize and quantify peoples and products across nations.[55] Her article appears to be an attempt to create an official publication on the hair industry. It begins with a typically Eurocentric and pseudoscientific text about hair throughout Western history and continues with a description of hair harvests, wholesale merchants, and traveling hair merchants in rural Europe.[56] Bacon then presents a chart purporting to show imports of manufactured and unmanufactured hair into France from European and Asian countries by kilograms, with their values in francs for the early 1890s.[57]

The information in the Bacon article is inaccurate, however, and does not match the U.S. government's annual report of foreign commerce.[58] Because Bacon's figures are off by several thousands of dollars, they are not reprinted here. Instead, correct data for 1891 is presented. The total in 1891 for all imported dutiable human hair (clean and drawn hair was dutiable at 20 percent, and manufactured hair was dutiable at 35 percent) was $82,866.51. The total in 1891 for all imported duty-free human hair (raw, uncleaned, and not drawn) was $76,318.00. The grand total of imported human hair was $159,184.51. Only dollar amounts are provided, without quantities in pounds or tons, making it challenging to fact-check accounts beyond the one by Bacon in newspapers and magazines, such as the figure of five million tons per year cited in an 1853 article or twelve million pounds per year cited in one from 1897.[59] Precise quantities were likely too difficult to produce due to lack in documentation from people who worked in the industry.

In addition to the years mentioned by Campbell and by Bacon, a few other representative years are discussed here, rather than an attempt at an annual accounting, to offer a sense of the size and trajectory of the trade. Various early sources help in this project. For instance, hair dealers and manufacturers are listed in New York directories before midcentury, and U.S. newspapers began reporting on the international trade in the mid-1850s.[60] Alexander Rowland's book *The Human Hair, Popularly and Physiologically Considered with Special Reference to Its Preservation, Improvement and Adornment, and the Various Modes of Its Decoration in All Countries* (1853) helps to situate Holland as a key, early participant by referring to a company of Dutch farmers that collected hair annually in Germany.[61] In 1859, a U.S. magazine corroborated this statement about Holland, stating that London hair merchants imported some five tons per year and that a Dutch company served as intermediary.[62] With regard to the economic scope of the trade, in 1869, *Scientific American* asserted, without a source, that the "total annual crop of the globe is at present about one million pounds."[63] In 1875, the *New York Times* alleged to quote the U.S. Bureau of Statistics stating that "human hair and its manufactures" was among the forty-five leading commodities imports.[64] The claim cannot be substantiated in the Treasury report for that year, which does not appear to include a list of the leading imports. In other years that do include such a list, all types of hair are grouped together, without separating human hair from animal hair, the size of which sometimes landed it in the top forty imports. Nonetheless, it is possible to obtain import values for human hair for the year 1875, when the grand total was $584,772:

1. Cleaned or drawn (duty 30 percent): value of import, $303,053.35
2. Manufactured (duty 40 percent): value of import, $27,684.00
3. Uncleaned (duty 20 percent): value of import, $254,035.00[65]

Due to the variables in how commodities were divided into categories and due to inconsistencies in reporting from year to year, it is difficult to select a commodity to regularly compare to raw human hair and to manufactured human hair. However, the following materials have clear information for the year 1875 and can provide a useful point of comparison for a raw commodity (hemp yarn) and for manufactures using that raw commodity of hemp yarn (utilitarian bags and bagging manufactured with hemp):

Hemp yarn (duty five cents per pound): value of import, $68,136.00
Hemp, jute, and other fiber not otherwise specified, and manufactures of bags, cotton bags, and bagging (duty 40 percent): value of import, $1,179,723.51[66]

It is evident that all categories of human hair (at a total of $584,772 for 1875) sit well below the grand total of raw hemp and its manufactures that year (at $1,247,859.50).[67] Totaling about 46 percent of such a utilitarian material, however, human hair maintained a sizable presence in the marketplace. Probing the sources of the supply provides further information.

The top three countries providing human hair to the United States for the fiscal year ending June 30, 1875, were England ($350,560), France ($219,087), and Germany ($200,792). They were followed by Belgium ($18,548), Scotland ($8,485), the Netherlands ($5,215), Canada ($4,215), and China ($4,058). The next tier of supplies came in from Italy ($234), Japan ($192), Ireland ($95), Portugal ($80), Sweden and Norway ($75), Cuba ($40), Mexico ($36), the West Indies ($9), Austria ($5), and Spain ($4). These figures are for direct imports. The United States received quantities of hair from some of these places, especially Sweden and Norway, indirectly through England, France, and Germany. This specification explains why Sweden and Norway appear prominently in newspaper accounts, despite the low figure in the report cited here.[68]

These figures support statements that hair commerce was high in the early and mid-1870s when fashions for women's hairstyles required substantial amounts of supplemental pieces.[69] In the 1880s, the commerce was lower but fluctuated. For the fiscal year ending on June 30, 1881, the total imports into the United States were valued at $304,670. Substantive amounts (more than $1,000 worth) came in from France, Germany, England (the same top three as in 1875), Hong Kong, and Italy.[70] In 1882, the total value of imports increased to $454,150, with the main countries listed as Austria, France, Russia, Switzerland, Belgium, Denmark, England, and Scotland. What we can extrapolate from the years of data is that human hair held a constant presence in U.S. imports and that the providing countries could change significantly, depending on supply. This finding supports the various countries named in the press throughout the decades. The publications that reported on the hair trade and the countries with which the United States was dealing range from national to regional newspapers and from general interest to fashion magazines like *Harper's Bazar*. The diversity provided an indication that how and from where human hair was obtained and how the supply affected prices each year were of concern to a vast swath of readers across the country.

PRICING

How much of their expendable income were people spending on hair? As with quantities, hair prices are not given in official reports, but advertisements and articles provide a sense of fees and their fluctuations. In fall 1872, C. S. Dyer and Son of Cincinnati, Ohio, importers of human hair and manufacturers of human hair goods, issued pricing by the dozen for finished curls, switches, chignons, French twists, top and side frizzettes, wool puffs and rats, and hair puffs and rats, ranging from $1.75 to $250, depending on the item.[71] However, for prepared curled hair and straight hair by the pound, the firm provide prices only by request due to the weekly changes. For contextual purposes, in 1870, a woman working as a clerk or bookkeeper in the United States might earn between $5 and $30 per week. A public schoolteacher in a sizable city might earn $500 per year.[72] Because a purchase of one or two hair items could comprise a week's salary for a middle-class woman, it was undoubtedly a well-considered, planned purchase.

The value of certain colors of hair shifted based on which color was in style at a given time.[73] When visiting a London hair warehouse in the early 1870s, British writer James Greenwood observed that the value of German hair was up in the market due to the popularity of blond ("yellow").[74] A medical guidebook of 1881 states that "golden hair" was valued most highly in the English market, as high as $2 per ounce.[75] Campbell provides further information: "Hair of the ordinary colors range in price from $15 to $100 per pound, but that of gray and white from $100 to $200 per pound."[76] He explains the high price of gray and white hair derived from the manual labor needed to separate white strands from gray ones.[77] Gray and white hair were in consistent demand for court wigs in Europe and for older women's wigs from at least the 1850s into the 1890s.[78] *The American Hairdresser* noted when it was in especially low supply, a sign of thriving business.[79]

In its frequent advertisements in *Hairdressers' Weekly Journal*, British hair dealer Osborne, Garrett, and Company highlighted the availability of "pure white hair."[80] The premium prices bear out Campbell's statement with regard to its desirability. So, too, does a sales pamphlet by Mrs. C. Thompson of New York from 1883 (fig. 6.9). Thompson ran a robust business in hairpieces, both at her headquarters near

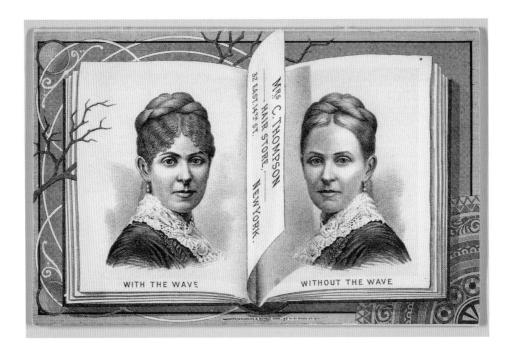

Union Square and by mail (she did not use agents out of a concern that they might copy her patented waves). The text explains that the Thompson Wave will always cost more in white and have longer wait times because white hair was difficult to procure.[81] White hair's most valuable characteristic was that it absorbed dyes more easily than other colors, which required a preliminary step of bleaching.[82]

Following white and gray, blond is the third most frequently mentioned shade in reports on the market and pricing. Wassholm and Sundelin's study of the trade in Nordic states between 1870 and 1914 is the most thorough study of any regional or international hair trade before the twentieth century and provides useful context

FIGURE 6.9

"With the Wave, without the Wave," *Mrs. C. Thompson, Importer and Manufacturer of Wigs, Hair Jewelry* (New York: Mrs. C. Thompson, 1883).

for what was shown at the World's Columbian Exposition and the machinations of procuring a supply of a desired hair color.[83] Their findings support the period accounts given above that cite Germany, Norway, and Sweden as providers of blond hair, adding Finland, Belgium, and the Netherlands.[84] They pinpoint a boom in the Nordic market in the 1870s when elaborate hairstyles with large chignons became popular in urban centers. Part of the value of blond hair there was that women protected it from the sun, which appeared in limited hours during parts of the year, by wearing a head covering.[85] In an effort to glean insights into the working methods of itinerant peddlers and the women who sold them their hair, the authors find that German "cutters," most likely Jewish, were prevalent.[86] Others came from Russia and traded in northern Scandinavia.[87] Wassholm and Sundelin ascertain that the Nordic hair trade was national and transnational—for example, within Sweden, between Sweden and Germany, or between Finland and Great Britain.[88] As stated above, reports from the United States around this time confirm the inclusion of Norway (and Italy and Denmark) as an exporter of hair to the United States.[89]

Wassholm and Sundelin were also able to determine the gender roles within the trade. Hair exchanges were made between male peddlers and local women. In literature and the press, the men were associated with dishonesty and trickery, while the women might be morally condemned for selling their hair.[90] On the whole, however, women retained the most power. They were responsible for growing healthy hair, and they decided whether to cut and sell it. Anthropologist Emma Tarlo makes the incisive point that growing long hair takes significant amounts of time and planning. At least two years would be required to grow a length long enough for use in a wig or switch.[91] Agents might even pay advances to women for the future growth of their hair.[92] When a community of women adopts new standards of beauty after attaining higher benchmarks of living, like preferring a fashionable hairstyle instead of a traditional cap, as did rural Nordic women circa 1880, they could put into motion a shift of an entire trade.[93] Toward the end of the century, women across Europe slowed the practice of selling their hair, causing a rise in cost for European hair well into the twentieth century, especially blond.[94] The market then turned toward importing Asian hair.[95] The power that women, even the most poor, had within the workings of an international market becomes abundantly clear.

Finally, a note on exports is required. The amount of hair that businesses in the United States obtained from its own citizens and used domestically as well as the amount it exported is difficult to determine. As mentioned above, Treasury reports did not consistently separate human from animal hair, and so evidence must be pieced together. A newspaper article of 1870 states that the United States exported hair from citizens within its own borders to Europe and "the East."[96] This may have been an impact of the Franco-Prussian War, which interrupted the supply of European hair on the market.[97] More commonly, however, sources claim that the hair of U.S. women did not grow as quickly as that of European women.[98] An article from 1889 cites a hair dealer in New York who obtained a supply from a local hair harvest but states that the United States could not meet its own demand.[99] Notably, the dealer boasts about the large size of the U.S. industry ("over five thousand importers, manufacturers and dealers of hair") and says that it would have a display at the forthcoming World's Columbian Exposition.[100] It seems most likely that exports comprised hair products rather than raw hair. Madame Lefevre of Philadelphia shipped goods from her five-story building to clients in Jamaica, the West Indies, Switzerland, and Italy, as well as to the U.S. trade.[101]

HUMANIZING THE HAIR TRADE

The data for the sprawling hair trade is overly generalized, inconsistent, and riddled with racial stereotypes. However, acknowledging the limitations of the archive and setting aside the frustrations of working with it can yield new insights. Layering the human dimension onto the archival data brings visibility to the women defining and engaging in the market. The aim is to address corporeality and materiality— the heads of hair, moving hands, and scissors behind the data points charted in official records.

Numerous steps were involved between when the hair was initially harvested and when it became ready for the market, all of which become more meaningful when we consider the haptic and aural human aspects of it, an effective way of countering the stereotypes rampant in the trade. During Greenwood's visit to the warehouse in London, he observed bales of hair and was disturbed by the "tightly packed tails."[102] The owner of the business acquired the stock from hair cutters and peddlers who traveled throughout the European countryside. There was a long tradition of peasant women in Brittany and the Auvergne providing their hair for payment, and hair-shearing scenes became sentimentalized spectacles in midcentury works of literature by such writers as Thomas Adolphus Trollope.[103] Stories recounted that before and after they sold their hair, either in exchange for money or goods like a piece of jewelry, women wore a traditional bonnet.[104] Parisian

photographer Charles Géniaux was fascinated by a hair harvest in Brittany. The village scenes, replete with patronizing captions, accompanied his article titled "The Human Hair Harvest in Brittany," published in *Wide World Magazine* in 1900 (figs. 6.10, 6.11, 6.12).[105]

It is worthwhile to engage with the photographs on their own account, extracting them from the condescending, primitivizing text of Géniaux's article and from the photograph captions that revel in pity and contempt for the villagers and hair shearers. Out of the article's nine photographs, three are discussed here, chosen for the clarity of their images and the visibility of the girls' and women's faces. The photographs are repositioned as a new tool toward envisioning the human dimension of the trade.

FIGURE 6.10

Charles Géniaux (French, 1870–1931). "The Human Hair Harvest in Brittany," *Wide World Magazine*, February 1900, 431.

FIGURE 6.11

Charles Géniaux. "The Human Hair Harvest
in Brittany," *Wide World Magazine*, February
1900, 434.

FIGURE 6.12

Charles Géniaux. "The Human Hair Harvest in Brittany," *Wide World Magazine*, February 1900, 435.

In the foreground of the first photograph, the faces of seven girls and women can be ascertained, either in profile or looking directly at the camera (see fig. 6.10). A young woman nearly at center is seen with her blond hair loose, without a bonnet. She talks in a circle with two women about her age and an older woman at right. Géniaux identifies the older woman as the "wife of the chief hair-shearer," a claim that cannot be verified. The blond woman's hair is not especially long, as it rests on her shoulders, raising the question of whether she has just had her hair cut, in which case the sentimentalized accounts of "shearing" are rendered overdramatized. On the whole, the scene forefronts activity between women in a rural setting. Two men wearing hats observe in the background, where at least one horse and four carts are also visible.

In the next photograph, a man in a cape, identified in the article as Monsieur Gérard, lifts a portion of a girl's brown hair, perhaps in the midst of cutting it (see fig. 6.11). How many inches will be cut? How much money might the girl earn, and what might she use it for? Were there consequences if she refused to have her hair cut? Other women gather in front of her. A young woman at right, turned in profile, watches the action, perhaps anticipating her own turn or waiting for her companion so they may leave together. The third photograph shows a young girl with a bonnet, another girl with her wavy blond hair exposed, a woman bent over the girl, seemingly helping her tie a kerchief, perhaps to form a head covering, while three older women look toward the photographer (see fig. 6.12).

This process of reading the photographs on their own terms brings the Breton women and girls to the center of the story, adding faces, emotion, and even a sense of color (blond, brunette) to the archive of the hair trade, disrupting and augmenting the dry facts and figures of the unreliable annual reports. With some creative imagining, the photographs enrich the picture of the workings of the supply side of the trade.

Accounts of how the hair was processed after cutting are rather clinical and reflect the exoticism and biases that were on display at the World's Columbian Exposition. When received at the warehouse, hair was painstakingly cleaned to remove dirt and oil, and in some cases, it was dyed and bleached.[106] The cleanliness of hair was a strong selling point during a time when hygiene was of the utmost cultural importance. There was concern that diseases like ringworm, parasites like lice, or organisms like mildew traveled in the hair.[107] Racism and classism are rampant in accounts of the origins of hair stock, which was informed by medical and scientific publications. *Scientific American* claimed that the hair of women in Brittany and Italy was especially prone to carrying lice eggs.[108] Charles Henri Leonard, a physician and the author of *The Hair: Its Growth, Care, Diseases and Treatment* (1881), warns against "musky smells" and "ammoniacal odors" from the hair of some nations, including China, that could lead to disease.[109] In 1880, a U.S. reporter disparaged Chinese hair until it is converted into matching "Caucasian" hair: "The Chinese hair is mostly used for switches on account of its length, and after being bleached cannot be told from ordinary women's hair."[110] They say that the price is cheaper for Chinese hair: fifty cents to $1 per pound versus "ordinary hair," which would sell between $8 and $100 per pound.[111] There were reports that lengths of hair came from the severed queues of male Chinese prisoners.[112] Tarlo makes the point that this hair came into the United States well after the Chinese Exclusion Act of 1882 prohibited Chinese laborers from entering the country and excluded Chinese immigrants already in the United States from becoming citizens. The queue was also a target of racially motivated violence against Chinese immigrants.[113]

The United States had been importing Chinese hair since the late 1860s, and there was an increase in the early 1870s.[114] By 1910, the United States bought nearly $700,000 worth from Hong Kong, which became a center of trade.[115] Hair from Italy, Mexico, China, India, and Japan (a late holdout in joining the trade) was often pillorized as too coarse and too dark, requiring intensive stripping of the color with chemicals like nitric acid before it could be redyed in lighter colors.[116] *Scientific American* claimed that workers who cleaned hair from China and India contracted diseases.[117] Prejudice does not seem to have slowed the desire for imports, though, especially when supplies ran low from European countries or when dark hair had a popular turn over blond.[118] In 1884, there was concern that the Sino-French War might constrict the supply of Chinese hair to the U.S. market.[119] Whether there was actually a decline is difficult to ascertain, as the Treasury reports once again did not separate human hair from animal hair. There was equal disdain for hair obtained in undesirable ways in parts of Europe. Scavenging cast-off hair from drainage gutters was a known practice.[120] There were also rumors of dealers illicitly obtaining "churchyard hair" from graveyards.[121]

After hair was cleaned and deals were made, importers in the United States were required to pay tariffs on the commodity. As shown in the information above for 1875, unprocessed hair was less expensive to import than prepared pieces and switches, but tariff rates were high. In 1869, *Scientific American* stated, "The cost of hair nearly quadruples from the time it is cut until it gets into the hands of the retailer." It explains that the preparation for hair to be sold as attachable ringlets or curls would entail rolling it about four inches long, covering it with paper, boiling, and then drying it in an oven.[122] After all processes and safeguards were attended to, hair products entered the marketplace, sold to buyers by independent store owners throughout the United States, department stores like Stern Brothers in New York, and national mail-order catalogue companies like Sears, Roebuck & Company. An instruction book for hairdressers explains that significant cleaning in hot water with soap and baking soda might still be needed after the hair was received, followed by sun drying.[123] In 1872, the firm of J. W. and K. Chisholm in New York reportedly employed one hundred workers to prepare hair for selling.[124] They provided raw hair for hairwork and hair jewelry, wigs for women who lost hair due to illness, and adornments and supplements like "waterfalls" (hair wrapped around cotton intended to adorn and add volume), side braids, back braids, curls attached to a comb, and more (fig. 6.13).[125]

At the other end of the spectrum from Chisholm's large operation were individual practitioners who made their living working closely with clients. Using extant letters, it is possible to piece together how they conducted business, navigated the ups and downs of the market, and relied on postal services. The business of Addie L. Contrelli of Chicago is an instructive example showing the mobility and expansiveness of the hair business. Letters indicate that Contrelli purchased small quantities of hair from suppliers when she needed to bolster the sample hair provided to her by customers for the hairpieces she crafted for them in Chicago.[126] A series of letters to her client Lenette E. Wilson of Algona, Iowa, documents the braids and waves she was commissioned to make for Wilson and her friends. They also record Contrelli's financial concerns and her desire for more orders. She worked from her rented home but greatly wished to rent a store in Mason City, Iowa, and expand her offerings. It was too burdensome for her to do so in Chicago: "a person cannot start here in business unless they have money of their own."[127] Contrelli appears to have been a widow who was caring for herself and Birdie, likely her daughter. To make ends meet, she occasionally traveled to women's homes to shampoo their hair.[128] She writes of aiming to please her customers as best as she could, conscientiously agreeing to redo a braid she made for Wilson, which was deemed an incorrect shade that did not correspond to the sample of Wilson's hair that she had mailed to Contrelli.[129] Providing samples of one's hair was standard practice, but inevitably some natural and false hair would not be perfect matches. Notably, the transactions and fulfillment of orders were done entirely by mail, even after Contrelli succeeded in relocating to Mason City (some fifty-five miles east of Algona) by January 1884.[130] To

FIGURE 6.13

Set of human hair curls, 1850s–1880s.
Victoria and Albert Museum, London
(AP.24–1889).

invoke mobilities theorists Kevin Hannam, Mimi Sheller, and John Urry's themes of the relationship of dwellings to the concept of stability, Contrelli's work in the hair business lacked stability both in job orders and in a fixed place from which to work.[131] She wrote to Wilson that her rented home in Chicago was subject to change, and it was best to address her letters to the post office.[132]

———

The movement of Contrelli's letters and hair samples through the postal mail and the final delivery of hairwork resonate with mobilities theorists' emphasis on the "travel of material things within everyday life."[133] Observing which material things traded across great distances accentuates how those materials held meaning and value to the communities at either end. Photographs and letters by women involved in the business animate the still-evolving picture of the global hair trade. This chapter has foregrounded the lived experiences of women in the trade—what their daily lives were like, how they might have felt, and what challenges they undertook. It has been necessary to interrogate the imperialist displays and subsequent reports by the World's Columbian Exposition and the biased text and photograph captions by Géniaux in his article for *Wide World Magazine*. If left unexamined, those sources would perpetuate the false premise that the supplies and workings of hair adhered to the arbitrarily demarcated boundaries of imperially conceived venues, whether a constructed so-called village at the exposition or the rows and columns of data in governmental annual reports. The experiences of women in the market, from the Breton village gatherings to Contrelli's mailing of hand-fashioned braids and fringes to her clients, expose and destabilize the unreliable archive. Their contributions allow the robust, potent space of the international hair market to reclaim its domain in the historical record.

7

CONCLUSION: GROUNDING THE EPHEMERAL

When we consider the prominence of a mirrored vanity table in a woman's bedroom and ask what structures and systems lie beyond it, the concept of hair as a site of critical meaning in society becomes grounded and measurable. The places and spaces of hair care and hairdressing help answer the question of how a matter so seemingly ephemeral as hair was doing so much cultural work in the mid- to late nineteenth century. *Beyond Vanity* has mapped buildings that housed hair businesses and looked at the photographs and writings of people who owned and patronized the enterprises and who moved through and personalized those places with family names on storefront signs and pictures on salon walls. The solidity of porcelain sinks and iron-clad reclining chairs speaks to the cultural attitude of the longevity and profitability of hair services. A topic such as modernized plumbing becomes especially noteworthy when we recognize that running water allowed proprietors to offer the amenity of wet shampooing. Taken together, furnished hair salons, barbershops, and stores embody what cultural geographer Yi-Fu Tuan so poignantly terms "centres of felt value."[1]

Beyond Vanity takes seriously the expenditure of time spent on hair practices and the amounts of money invested in cleaning and buying supplemental hair, the stakes of which increased in the performative arenas of parties, theatrical stages, and portrait studios. The distinctive hairstyles and headwraps chosen by enslaved peoples who had been displaced from their homes contributed to broader cultural expressions that superseded the places from which they emerged. Likewise, the negotiations women made with themselves and their employers as to how they

FIGURE 7.1

Charles A. Cox (British, 1829–1901).
Bearings, 1896. Relief print, 46 × 33.5 cm.
Boston Public Library (2012.AAP.7).

would wear their hair come into sharper focus. The management of hair led several Black entrepreneurs to enter the market with custom-made products and tested the limits of a marketplace initially constructed by white people in positions of authority. The care and expression of Black hair held the power to push against boundaries that were constructed according to white Euro-American standards of beauty. Tracing the changes in the treatment and perception of women's hair that arose in relation to open-air spaces like a beach or bicycle path foregrounds its role in symbolizing newfound mobility and independence (fig. 7.1). The revelation of the vast trade in raw hair casts light on the international exchange of a commodity that held value for different peoples across Europe, the United States, and parts of Asia. The scope of the trade was enormous, although archival documentation is elusive and defies quantification. Tons of switches of hair crossed borders, sometimes multiple times as handlers navigated export and import systems, claiming and paying duties. Charting the course of hair's movement across countries as a commodity demonstrates not only its mobility but also its substantiality as a cultural force worthy of business transactions, taxes, and advertising campaigns. By interrogating the data and infusing it with the lived experiences of women who participated in the trade—who gave their hair cuttings to it and made an income from it—this book has restored the humanity to what was called an "unusual trade."[2]

Reflections in a looking glass of a woman dressing her hair are but one plane of the overall prism of the hair picture. *Beyond Vanity* has considered three-dimensional shops and two-dimensional representations of them in promotional trade cards that circulated so broadly that they made their way into museum collections several states away from their origin. Critical readings of advertising imagery cast nuance onto the constantly shifting tastes in hair color and the synthetic dyes that were available to meet demand. Some frivolity attached to hair in the period is undeniable, and rightfully so. Women's letters and diaries express joy in trying out a new style, frustration when a curl will not hold, or envy when their hair will not achieve what a friend's hair will. But as shown here, the previous tendency to overlook hair in favor of intrinsically more valuable or lasting materials has detracted from our acknowledgment of it as a matter worthy of rich, critical discourse. Recasting hair in terms of place, space, and time grants new appreciation for its saliency in society.

ACKNOWLEDGMENTS

I extend my gratitude to dear mentors, colleagues, friends, and devoted supporters Young Bae, Fran Gormley, Pamela Workman Hilton, Jane McAllister and Steve Speil, Sarah McFadden, Sarah Elizabeth Mesle, Kevin D. Murphy, Adam Paget, Benjamin Patino, Jonathan Michael Square, and Mieka F. Wick. I am deeply grateful to Victoria Hindley at the MIT Press for her extraordinary foresight, guidance, and wisdom. Heartfelt thanks are due to Deborah Cantor-Adams, Maya Carlisle-Swedberg, Gabriela Bueno Gibbs, Katie Lewis, Jessica Pellien, Mary Reilly, and Rosemary Winfield at the Press for their expertise, creativity, and patience. Research funding was generously granted by the David Jaffee Fellowship in Visual and Material Culture at the American Antiquarian Society, Worcester, Massachusetts, and the Winterthur Research Fellowship Program, Delaware.

Essential support for this publication was provided by FEKKAI and Bastide Aix-en-Provence and the MIT Press Cooper Memorial Design Fund.

NOTES

CHAPTER 1

1. Brian Connolly and Marisa Fuentes, "Introduction: From Archives of Slavery to Liberated Futures?," *History of the Present* 6, no. 2 (2016): 105.

2. Anna Arabindan-Kesson, *Black Bodies, White Gold: Art, Cotton, and Commerce in the Atlantic World* (Durham, NC: Duke University Press, 2021); Jennifer L. Morgan, *Reckoning with Slavery: Gender, Kinship, and Capitalism in the Early Black Atlantic* (Durham, NC: Duke University Press, 2021).

3. Geraldine Biddle-Perry, ed., *A Cultural History of Hair*, 6 vols. (London: Bloomsbury Academic, 2019).

4. Aileen Ribeiro, *Facing Beauty: Painted Women and Cosmetic Art* (New Haven, CT: Yale University Press, 2011); Susan J. Vincent, *Hair: An Illustrated History* (London: Bloomsbury Visual Arts, 2018); Victoria Sherrow, *Encyclopedia of Hair: A Cultural History* (Westport, CT: Greenwood Press, 2006); Caroline Cox, *Good Hair Days: A History of British Hairstyling* (London: Quartet Books, 1999).

5. "Hair," ed. Bernadette Fort, special issue, *Eighteenth-Century Studies* 38, no. 1 (Fall 2004).

6. Richard Corson, *Fashions in Hair: The First Five Thousand Years*, 6th ed. (London: P. Owens, 1980), first published 1965 by Hastings House (New York).

7. Neil R. Storey and Fiona Kay, *Victorian Fashions for Women* (Havertown, PA: Pen & Sword History, 2022).

8. Steven Zdatny, "Fashion and Class Struggle: The Case of Coiffure," *Social History* 18, no. 1 (1993): 53–72; Steven Zdatny, *Hairstyles and Fashion: A Hairdresser's History of Paris, 1910–1920* (Oxford: Berg, 1999); Steven Zdatny, *Fashion, Work, and Politics in Modern France* (Basingstoke, UK: Palgrave Macmillan, 2015).

9. Galia Ofek, *Representations of Hair in Victorian Literature and Culture* (Farnham, UK: Ashgate, 2009); Carol de Dobay Rifelj, *Coiffures: Hair in Nineteenth-Century French Literature and Culture* (Newark: University of Delaware Press, 2010). See also Elisabeth G. Gitter, "The Power of Women's Hair in the Victorian Imagination," *Publications of the Modern Language Association of America* 99, no. 5 (October 1984): 936–954; Royce Mahawatte, "Hair and Fashioned Femininity in Two Nineteenth-Century Novels," in *Hair: Styling, Culture and Fashion*, ed. Geraldine Biddle-Perry and Sarah Cheang (Oxford: Berg, 2008), 193–204.

10. Jasmine Nichole Cobb, *New Growth: The Art and Texture of Black Hair* (Durham, NC: Duke University Press, 2022), 27.

11. Tameka N. Ellington, Joseph L. Underwood, and Sarah Rogers-Lafferty, eds., *Textures: The History and Art of Black Hair* (Kent, OH: Kent State University Museum, 2020).

12. Shane White and Graham White, "Slave Hair and African American Culture in the Eighteenth and Nineteenth Centuries," *Journal of Southern History* 61, no. 1 (February 1995): 45–76; Shane White and Graham White, *Stylin': African American Expressive Culture from Its Beginnings to the Zoot Suit* (Ithaca, NY: Cornell University Press, 1998), 39–62, 169–172; Paul Dash, "Black Hair Culture, Politics and Change," *International Journal of Inclusive Education* 10, no. 1 (2006): 27–37.

13. Tameka N. Ellington, ed., *Black Hair in a White World* (Kent, OH: Kent State University Press, 2023).

14. Lyzette Wanzer, ed., *Trauma, Tresses, and Truth: Untangling Our Hair through Personal Narratives* (Chicago: Chicago Review Press, 2023).

15. Noliwe M. Rooks, *Hair Raising: Beauty, Culture, and African American Women* (New Brunswick, NJ: Rutgers University Press, 1996); Julie A. Willett, *Permanent Waves: The Making of the American Beauty Shop* (New York: New York University Press, 2000). For example, Ayana D. Byrd and Lori L. Tharp, *Hair Story: Untangling the Roots of Black Hair in America*, rev. ed. (New York: St. Martin's Press, 2014), first published 2001; Tiffany M. Gill, *Beauty Shop Politics: African American Women's Activism in the Beauty Industry* (Champaign: University of Illinois Press 2010); Tabora A. Johnson and Teiahsha Bankhead, "Hair It Is: Examining the Experiences of Black Women with Natural Hair," *Open Journal of Social Sciences* 2, no. 1 (January 2014): 86–100; Cheryl Thompson, "Black Women, Beauty, and Hair as a Matter of Being," *Women's Studies* 38, no. 8 (October 15, 2009): 831–856.

16. Kobena Mercer, "Black Hair/Style Politics," in *Out There: Marginalization and Contemporary Cultures*, ed. Russell Ferguson, Martha Gever, Trinh T. Minh-ha, and Cornel West (Cambridge, MA: MIT Press, 1990), 247–264.

17. Anna-Mari Almila, "What Is 'Space' for Dress? Theoretical Considerations of a Spatial Turn for Fashion Studies," *International Journal of Fashion Studies* 8, no. 1 (April 2021): 7.

18. Alla Myzelev and John Potvin, *Fashion, Interior Design and the Contours of Modern Identity* (Farnham, UK: Ashgate, 2010), 4.

19. Heidi Brevik-Zender, *Fashioning Spaces: Mode and Modernity in Late-Nineteenth-Century Paris* (Toronto: University of Toronto Press, 2015); John Potvin, ed., *The Places and Spaces of Fashion, 1800–2007* (New York: Routledge, 2009), 5.

20. Brevik-Zender, *Fashioning Spaces*: 205; Elizabeth L. Block, *Dressing Up: The Women Who Influenced French Fashion* (Cambridge, MA: MIT Press, 2021), 135–168.

21. Louise Crewe, *The Geographies of Fashion: Consumption, Space, and Value* (London: Bloomsbury Academic, 2017), 2.

22. Sarah Cheang and Geraldine Biddle-Perry, "Conclusion: Hair and Human Identity," in *Hair: Styling, Culture and Fashion*, ed. Geraldine Biddle-Perry and Sarah Cheang (Oxford: Berg, 2008), 252.

23. Kim Smith, "From Style to Place: The Emergence of the Ladies' Hair Salon in the Twentieth Century," in *Hair: Styling, Culture and Fashion*, ed. Geraldine Biddle-Perry and Sarah Cheang (Oxford: Berg, 2008), 55.

24. Ruth Holliday and John Hassard, eds., *Contested Bodies* (London: Routledge, 2001), 147–149; Kim Smith, "From Style to Place: The Emergence of the Ladies' Hair Salon in the Twentieth

Century," in *Hair: Styling, Culture and Fashion*, ed. Geraldine Biddle-Perry and Sarah Cheang (Oxford: Berg, 2008), 55–65.

25. Yi-Fu Tuan, *Space and Place: The Perspective of Experience* (Minneapolis: University of Minnesota Press, 1977), 164–165.

26. Tuan, *Space and Place*, 136.

27. Tuan, *Space and Place*, 4.

28. Tuan, *Space and Place*, 184.

29. Henri Lefebvre, *The Production of Space* (Oxford: Blackwell, 1991), 154.

30. Tuan, *Space and* Place, 4.

31. Nigel Thrift, "Space," *Theory, Culture & Society* 23, no. 2/3 (2006): 139–146.

32. Thrift, "Space," 139–146.

33. Kevin Hannam, Mimi Sheller, and John Urry, "Editorial: Mobilities, Immobilities and Moorings," *Mobilities* 1, no. 1 (March 1, 2006): 1, 9–10.

34. Michel Foucault, *Security, Territory, Population: Lectures at the Collège de France, 1977–78*, ed. Michel Senellart, trans. Graham Burchell (Basingstoke, UK: Palgrave Macmillan, 2014).

35. Setha M. Low, "Spatializing Culture: An Engaged Anthropological Approach to Space and Place," in *The People, Space and Place Reader*, ed. Jack Gieseking, William Mangold, Cindi Katz, Setha Low, and Susan Saegert (London: Routledge, 2014), 37; Setha M. Low, *Spatializing Culture: The Ethnography of Space and Place* (London: Routledge, 2017), 128.

36. Low, *Spatializing Culture*, 95.

37. Helen Sheumaker, *Love Entwined: The Curious History of Hairwork in America* (Philadelphia: University of Pennsylvania Press, 2007).

38. Rebecca M. Herzig, *Plucked: A History of Hair Removal* (New York: New York University Press, 2015).

39. Michael Kwass, "Big Hair: A Wig History of Consumption in Eighteenth-Century France," *American Historical Review* 111, no. 3 (2006): 634; Margaret K. Powell and Joseph Roach, "Big Hair," *Eighteenth-Century Studies* 38, no. 1 (Fall 2004): 80.

40. Karin Calvert, "The Function of Fashion in Eighteenth-Century America," in *Of Consuming Interests: The Style of Life in the Eighteenth Century*, ed. Cary Carson, Ronald Hoffman, and Peter J. Albert (Charlottesville: Published for the United States Capitol Historical Society by the University Press of Virginia, 1994), 263–270; Lynn Festa, "Fashion and Adornment," in *A Cultural History of Hair in the Age of Enlightenment*, ed. Margaret K. Powell and Joseph Roach (London: Bloomsbury Academic, 2019), 58; Lynn Festa, "Personal Effects: Wigs and Possessive Individualism in the Long Eighteenth Century," *Eighteenth-Century Life* 29, no. 2 (April 1, 2005): 69.

41. Marcia R. Pointon, *Hanging the Head: Portraiture and Social Formation in Eighteenth-Century England* (New Haven, CT: Yale University Press, 1993), 46, 54.

42. Kwass, "Big Hair," 635–641.

43. Pointon, *Hanging the Head*, 121; Festa, "Personal Effects," 59.

44. Kwass, "Big Hair," 644–647.

45. Kwass, "Big Hair," 648; Pointon, *Hanging the Head*, 117–120.

46. Carolyn L. White, "The Fall of Big Hair: Hair Curlers as Evidence of Changing Fashions," in *The Importance of British Material Culture to Historical Archaeologies of the Nineteenth Century*, ed. Alasdair Brooks (Lincoln: University of Nebraska Press, 2015), 178; Pointon, *Hanging the Head*, 107–111.

47. See Kate Haulman, *The Politics of Fashion in Eighteenth-Century America* (Chapel Hill: University of North Carolina Press, 2011), 47–80.

48. Laura J. Galke, "Tressed for Success: Male Hair Care and Wig Hair Curlers at George Washington's Childhood Home," *Winterthur Portfolio* 52, no. 2/3 (June 1, 2018): 86.

49. Galke, "Tressed for Success," 99–100.

50. Douglas W. Bristol Jr., *Knights of the Razor: Black Barbers in Slavery and Freedom* (Baltimore, MD: Johns Hopkins University Press, 2009), 16; White and White, "Slave Hair and African American Culture in the Eighteenth and Nineteenth Centuries," 62–63, 66; White and White, *Stylin'*, 51–52.

51. See Louisa Cross, "Fashionable Hair in the Eighteenth Century: Theatricality and Display," in *Hair: Styling, Culture and Fashion*, ed. Geraldine Biddle-Perry and Sarah Cheang (Oxford: Berg, 2008), 18–23; Harriet Stroomberg, *High Heads: Spotprenten Over Haarmode in De Achttiende Eeuw* (Enschede: Rijksmuseum Twenthe, 1999).

52. Aileen Ribeiro, *Dress in Eighteenth-Century Europe, 1715–1789* (New Haven, CT: Yale University Press, 2002), 211; see also Amelia Rauser, "Hair, Authenticity, and the Self-Made Macaroni," *Eighteenth-Century Studies* 38, no. 1 (Fall 2004): 101–117.

53. Festa, "Fashion and Adornment," 75–78.

54. John Potvin, "The Velvet Masquerade: Fashion, Interior Design and the Furnished Body," in *Fashion, Interior Design and the Contours of Modern Identity*, ed. Alla Myzelev and John Potvin (Farnham, UK: Ashgate, 2010), 10.

55. Powell and Roach, "Big Hair," 87–93; Rauser, "Hair, Authenticity, and the Self-Made Macaroni," 101–117, 103; Ribeiro, *Dress in Eighteenth-Century Europe*, 236.

56. *The Vis-a-vis Bisected, or the Ladies Coop*, 1776. Print. Published by Matthias Darly. The British Museum, London, J,5.128.

57. Peter McNeil, "Ideology, Fashion and the Darlys' 'Macaroni' Prints," in *Dress and Ideology: Fashioning Identity from Antiquity to the Present*, ed. Shoshana-Rose Marzel and Guy D. Stiebel (London: Bloomsbury, 2014), 111–136.

58. Susan J. Vincent, *The Anatomy of Fashion: Dressing the Body from the Renaissance to Today* (Oxford: Berg, 2009), 1–34.

59. See Kimberly Chrisman-Campbell, *Fashion Victims: Dress at the Court of Louis XVI and Marie-Antoinette* (New Haven, CT: Yale University Press, 2015), 20–31; Caroline Weber, *Queen of Fashion* (New York: Henry Holt, 2006), 94–130.

60. Rauser, "Hair, Authenticity, and the Self-Made Macaroni," 114.

61. Morag Martin, *Selling Beauty: Cosmetics, Commerce, and French Society, 1750–1830* (Baltimore, MD: Johns Hopkins University Press, 2009), 155–173.

62. Martin, *Selling Beauty*, 1–2.

63. Festa, "Personal Effects," 74.

64. Festa, "Personal Effects," 79; Martin, *Selling Beauty*, 156–160.

65. Richard Wrigley, "Mistaken Identities: Disguise, Surveillance, and the Legibility of Appearances," in *The Politics of Appearances: Representations of Dress in Revolutionary France* (Oxford: Berg, 2002), 229–258.

66. Festa, "Personal Effects," 79–82.

67. Martin, *Selling Beauty*, 170–171.

68. Bristol, *Knights of the Razor*, 12–13; Cross, "Fashionable Hair in the Eighteenth Century," 20; Vincent, *The Anatomy of Fashion*, 1–34.

69. Bristol, *Knights of the Razor*, 26.

70. Corson, *Fashions in Hair*, 361–362.

CHAPTER 2

1. Nigel Thrift, "Space," *Theory, Culture & Society* 23, no. 2/3 (2006): 141; Yi-Fu Tuan, *Space and Place: The Perspective of Experience* (Minneapolis: University of Minnesota Press, 1977), 183.

2. See Kevin Hannam, Mimi Sheller, and John Urry, "Editorial: Mobilities, Immobilities and Moorings," *Mobilities* 1, no. 1 (March 1, 2006): 13.

3. Thrift, "Space," 142.

4. Ellen M. Plante, *Women at Home in Victorian America: A Social History* (New York: Facts on File, 1997), 133–134; Caroline Cox, *Good Hair Days: A History of British Hairstyling* (London: Quartet Books, 1999), 17; Victoria Sherrow, *Encyclopedia of Hair: A Cultural History* (Westport, CT: Greenwood Press, 2006), 386; Kim Smith, "From Style to Place: The Emergence of the Ladies' Hair Salon in the Twentieth Century," in *Hair: Styling, Culture and Fashion*, ed. Geraldine Biddle-Perry and Sarah Cheang (Oxford: Berg, 2008), 57.

5. The liquid was comprised of 97 percent alcohol, 1.5 percent castor oil, and 1 percent tincture of catharides (Spanish fly). Sherrow, *Encyclopedia of Hair*, 175.

6. See [Rear view of woman, possibly Martha Matilda Harper, with hair reaching down near her ankles], ca. 1914. Photographic print. Library of Congress, LC-USZ62–76323; Jane R. Plitt, *Martha Matilda Harper and the American Dream: How One Woman Changed the Face of Modern Business* (Syracuse, NY: Syracuse University Press, 2000), 48–50.

7. Historian Ferdinand Meyer V has documented that the seven daughters of Fletcher and Mary Sutherland—Sarah, Victoria, Isabella, Grace, Naomi, Dora, and Mary—were born between 1851 and 1865. Ferdinand Meyer V, "The Amazing 7 Sutherland Sisters," Peachridge Glass, February 10, 2013, https://www.peachridgeglass.com/2013/02/the-amazing-7-sutherland-sisters.

8. [Seven women], 1890. Photograph. Maine Historical Society, no. 413-67.

9. Fashion plates, *Godey's Lady's Book*, September 1858, 259.

10. Bessie [Elizabeth D.] Wood [Kane] ALS to Bessie [Elizabeth Kane], May 12, 1852, Kane family papers, William L. Clements Library, University of Michigan.

11. Jennie [last name unknown] to Mattie Tackitt, Buffalo, New York, December 10, 1867, Women's History Collection, William L. Clements Library, The University of Michigan.

12. Royce Mahawatte, "Hair and Fashioned Femininity in Two Nineteenth-Century Novels," in *Hair: Styling, Culture and Fashion*, ed. Geraldine Biddle-Perry and Sarah Cheang (Oxford: Berg, 2008), 195; Vincent, *Hair*, 62–64.

13. "The Modern Coiffure an Art," *Evening World* (New York), July 16, 1894: 2.

14. "First-Class Help, Females," *The Sun* (New York), February 5, 1899, 1, 11; "Situations Wanted," *Evening World*, July 16, 1894, 2.

15. See, for example, Franz Hanfstaengl, after Caspar Netscher, *A Woman with a Dog on Her Knee Having Her Hair Dressed by a Female Assistant*, between 1800 and 1899. Lithograph. Wellcome Collection, London, Wellcome Library no. 31202i.

16. The longevity of this theme is evidenced by the late date of the steel engraving. Although the print was made toward the end of the century, the scene is a nostalgic view of the 1860s.

17. For a period image of a bedroom, see [Boudoir], undated. Stereograph. Library of Congress, Washington, DC, LC-DIG-stereo-1s08180.

18. Gail Caskey Winkler and Roger W. Moss, *Victorian Interior Decoration: American Interiors, 1830–1900* (New York: H. Holt, 1986), 138–139.

19. Hans Heinrich (Henry) Bebie (Swiss, 1824–1888). *The Toilette*, undated. Probably oil on canvas. Location unknown. See https://americangallery.wordpress.com/2010/12/15/henry-bebie-1824-1888.

20. See Joanna Pitman, *On Blondes* (London: Bloomsbury, 2003), 144–145.

21. For example, Edgar Degas. *Toilette of a Woman*, 1889. Pastel and charcoal. State Hermitage Museum, St. Petersburg, OP-43788.

22. Edmond de Goncourt and Jules de Goncourt, *Journal: Mémoires de la vie littéraire*, vol. 4 (Paris: Fasquelle, Flammarion, 1956), 674.

23. For example, Edgar Degas. *Young Woman at Her Toilet*, undated. Etching. Bibliothèque Nationale de France, Paris, 924913 (Reed-Shapiro 28–1); Edgar Degas. *Woman Having Her Hair Combed*, ca. 1886–1888. Pastel on light green woven paper. The Metropolitan Museum of Art, New York, H. O. Havemeyer Collection, Bequest of Mrs. H. O. Havemeyer, 1929, 29.100.35.

24. For example, Henri de Toulouse-Lautrec. *Combing Their Hair*, 1896. Lithograph printed in two colors. The Metropolitan Museum of Art, New York, Bequest of Scofield Thayer, 1982, 1984.1203.170.

25. For example, James Carroll Beckwith. *Woman Seated at Vanity, Braiding Her Hair*, 1890s. Graphite, watercolor, pastel, and crayon on ivory paper. New-York Historical Society, 1935.85.3.132; George Bellows. *Girl Fixing Her Hair*, 1923–1924. Lithograph. Columbus Museum of Art, Museum Purchase with funds provided by Eloise Bragdon, by exchange, 2012.022.

26. Griselda Pollock, "Modernity and the Spaces of Femininity," in *Vision and Difference: Femininity, Feminism, and Histories of Art* (London: Routledge, 1988), 56–66.

27. Gib Prettyman. "The Serial Illustrations of *A Hazard of New Fortunes*," *Resources for American Literary Study* 27, no. 2 (2001): 179–195.

28. For the European context, see Vincent, *Hair*, 66.

29. Will Bashor, *Marie Antoinette's Head: The Royal Hairdresser, the Queen, and the Revolution* (Guilford, CT: Lyons Press, 2013), 5; Cox, *Good Hair Days*, 66; Sherrow, *Encyclopedia of Hair*, 163; Smith, "From Style to Place," 55; Zdatny, *Fashion, Work, and Politics in Modern France*, 1.

30. "Hairdressing," *Vogue*, June 22, 1899, ii; Byron Company, *Hotel Martin*, 1896. Photograph. Museum of the City of New York, 93.1.1.6400.

31. Zdatny, *Hairstyles and Fashion*, 20–22.

32. Sherrow, *Encyclopedia of Hair*, 162.

33. Arlene Alpert, Margrit Altenburg, Diane Carol Bailey, Letha Barnes, and Lisha Barnes, *Milady's Standard Cosmetology* (Boston: Cengage Learning, 2007), 9.

34. Geraldine Biddle-Perry and Sarah Cheang, "Introduction: Thinking about Hair," in *Hair: Styling, Culture and Fashion*, ed. Geraldine Biddle-Perry and Sarah Cheang (Oxford: Berg, 2008), 6; Smith, "From Style to Place," 56; Sherrow, *Encyclopedia of Hair*, 201. For a humorous British etching, see *A Woman Having Her Hair Cut by a Male Hair-Dresser*, undated. Wellcome Collection, London, Wellcome Library no. 31384i.

35. Cecil Beaton, *The Glass of Fashion* (Garden City, NY: Doubleday, 1954), 44–45.

36. Louisa May Alcott, *Little Women: or, Meg, Jo, Beth, and Amy* (Boston: Roberts Brothers, 1890), 183.

37. Louisa May Alcott, *Little Women: or, Meg, Jo, Beth, and Amy* (Boston: Roberts Brothers, 1880), 203. The same illustration is shown in Louisa May Alcott, *Little Women: or, Meg, Jo, Beth, and Amy* (Boston: Little, Brown, 1896), 203.

38. Louisa May Alcott, *Little Women: A Story for Girls* (London: Religious Tract Society, 1912), between pp. 224–225. I thank Abby Yochelson for her assistance locating this volume.

39. Louisa May Alcott, *Little Women: or, Meg, Jo, Beth, and Amy* (Boston: Little, Brown, and Co., 1918), 205.

40. Alcott, *Little Women* (1880), 32.

41. Virginia Penny, *The Employments of Women: A Cyclopaedia of Woman's Work* (Boston: Walker, Wise & Co., 1863), 278–280.

42. Penny, *The Employments of Women*, 278–279.

43. Penny, *The Employments of Women*, 279.

44. I thank Natalie Burclaff, Library of Congress, for her research assistance.

45. *Wilson's Business Directory of New York City* (New York: Trow City Directory Company, 1867), 255–256.

46. *Boyd's Business Directory of the State of Maryland* (Washington, DC: William H. Boyd, 1875), 195, 241.

47. For example, Hugh P. Wood of Boston: "Centerdale," *Olneyville Times* (Providence, RI), April 26, 1895, 5.

48. Eliza Frances Andrews diary, 1870–1872, August 15, 1870, Andrews Family Papers, University of Tennessee at Chattanooga Special Collections, MS-004-02-08.

49. Nora C. Usher, "Some Things I Learnt in America," *Work and Leisure: A Magazine Devoted to the Interests of Women*, August 1, 1892, 218–220.

50. Vincent, *Hair*, 72–73. See also, for example, Gertrude G. de Aguirre, *Women in the Business World; or, Hints and Helps to Prosperity* (Boston: Arena Publishing Co., 1894), 185–186; "Detroit's Pretty Barber," *Milwaukee Daily Sentinel*, November 21, 1877, 3.

51. "Women Make Good Barbers," *American Hairdresser*, February 1896, 28; "The New Woman's Newest Idea," *American Hairdresser*, December 1896, 12.

52. Juliet E. K. Walker, ed., *Encyclopedia of African American Business History* (Westport, CT: Greenwood Press, 1999), 282.

53. Quincy T. Mills, *Cutting along the Color Line: Black Barbers and Barber Shops in America* (Philadelphia: University of Pennsylvania Press, 2013), 23; Juliet E. K. Walker, *The History of Black Business in America: Capitalism, Race, Entrepreneurship* (New York: Macmillan, 1998), 109.

54. Mills, *Cutting along the Color Line*, 23.

55. Mills, *Cutting along the Color Line*, 25, 53.

56. Douglas W. Bristol Jr., *Knights of the Razor: Black Barbers in Slavery and Freedom* (Baltimore, MD: Johns Hopkins University Press, 2009), 8–70.

57. Penny, *The Employments of Women*, 279.

58. Penny, *The Employments of Women*, 279–280.

59. Frances E. Willard Journals, May 25, 1870, Journal 42, 14, Frances E. Willard Journal Transcription, https://willard.historyit.com/public-sites/home/transcripts.

60. Xiomara Santamarina, *Belabored Professions: Narratives of African American Working Womanhood* (Chapel Hill: University of North Carolina Press, 2005), 109–115; Eliza Potter, *A Hairdresser's Experience in High Life* (Cincinnati, OH: Privately printed, 1859), 73.

61. Lawrence Graham, *The Senator and the Socialite: The True Story of America's First Black Dynasty* (New York: Harper Perennial, 2007), 369.

62. Trade card, Hawx's Hair Cutting Rooms, Hotel St. Stephens (*sic*), New York, undated. Museum of the City of New York, F2012.99.555.

63. Stanley Turkel, *Built to Last: 100+ Year-Old Hotels in New York* (Bloomington, IN: AuthorHouse, 2011), 9–18; Anthony W. Robins, "Hotel Albert" (New York City), http://thehotelalbert.com/photos.html.

64. Elizabeth L. Block, *Dressing Up: The Women Who Influenced French Fashion* (Cambridge, MA: MIT Press, 2021), 40–47, 52–60.

65. K. C. Spier, *Universal Exposition Paris, 1889: J. C. Conolly's Illustrated Guide for the Use of English and American Visitors* (Liverpool, UK: J. C. Conolly, 1889), *passim*.

66. "The Bradley Martin Fete," *New York Times*, February 10, 1897, 7.

67. Penny, *The Employments of Women*, 278.

68. Collection of the author.

69. The *Providence, Rhode Island, City Directory* (Polk City Directories) for 1910 lists it under "barbers."

70. For more on mixed-gender barbershops, see Mills, *Cutting along the Color Line*, 26.

71. For example, Wards's "Bargain Column," *Herald and Review* (Decatur, IL), May 14, 1896, 7.

72. Frank C. Bridgeford, *Barber Instructor and Toilet Manual* (Kansas City, MO: Frank C. Bridgeford, 1900), unpaginated.

73. "French Ideas about Hairdressing," *The Sun* (New York), October 15, 1899, 4; "Shampooing in the American and French Styles," *New York Herald* (Paris ed.), December 21, 1893.

74. Jessica P. Clark, *The Business of Beauty: Gender and the Body in Modern London* (London: Bloomsbury Visual Arts, 2020), 112, 118n35.

75. For example, "Formulary," *Pharmaceutical Era* 5 (April 1, 1891): 206; "Wash for the Hair," *Evening Star* (Washington, DC), March 23, 1895, 16.

76. L. Howard Jones, *The Barbers' Manual* (McComb, OH: Gospel Way and Food Print, 1898), 52.

77. Theodore A. Kochs, *Price List and Barbers' Purchasing Guide of Barbers' Chairs, Furniture, and Barbers' Supplies* (Chicago: Skeen & Stuart Stationery Co., 1884), 36–39.

78. Hiram Streitenberger, *Streitenberger's Manual and Barbers' Hand Book of Formulas* (Chillicothe, OH: Hiram Streitenberger, 1887), 21.

79. Evelyn Welch, "Art on the Edge: Hair and Hands in Renaissance Italy," *Renaissance Studies* 23, no. 3 (2009): 244.

80. Steven Zdatny, *Hairstyles and Fashion: A Hairdresser's History of Paris, 1910–1920* (Oxford: Berg, 1999), 19; Caroline Cox, *Good Hair Days: A History of British Hairstyling* (London: Quartet Books, 1999), 32–34; "The Dangers of Hairdressing," *The Hospital: A Journal of the Medical Sciences and Hospital Administration* 22, no. 566 (July 31, 1897): 295–296.

81. For instructions on singeing, see Jones, *The Barbers' Manual*, 56–57. For an illustration, see Arthur Bass Moler, *The Manual on Barbering, Hairdressing, Manicuring, Facial Massage, Electrolysis and Chiropody as Taught in the Moler System of Colleges* (New York: Arthur Bass Moler, 1906), 53. See "Dry Shampoo," *Sterling Standard* (Sterling, IL), August 13, 1896, 1; Kochs, *Price List and Barbers' Purchasing Guide*, 85.

82. "A Queer Place to Drown," *Evening Times* (Washington, DC), November 18, 1897, 4.

83. Kochs, *Price List and Barbers' Purchasing Guide*, 20–21.

84. Kochs, *Price List and Barbers' Purchasing Guide*, 8–9.

85. Kochs, *Price List and Barbers' Purchasing Guide*, 8.

86. Katherine C. Grier, *Culture and Comfort: Parlor Making and Middle-Class Identity, 1850–1930* (Washington, DC: Smithsonian Institution Press, 1997), 32–43.

87. Grier, *Culture and Comfort*, 33–38.

88. See "Hard Times Token" from Phalon's Hair Cutting, 1837. Copper. New-York Historical Society, INV.13767.

89. "Phalon's Saloon," *Gleason's Pictorial Drawing-Room Companion*, February 12, 1853, 112. For more on Phalon, see Manuel J. Vieira, *Tonsorial Art Pamphlet* (Indianapolis: Press of the Publishing House, 1877), 10–12.

90. Lyman H. Low, "Hard Times Tokens," *American Journal of Numismatics* (July 1899): 20.

91. See *Phalon's Bower of Perfume, in the Crystal Palace, New York*, 1853. Photograph. New York Public Library Digital Collections, The Miriam and Ira D. Wallach Division of Art, Prints and Photographs: Picture Collection, The New York Public Library.

92. "Phalon and Son's Cocoine," *Harper's Weekly*, February 12, 1859, 112; "Phalon's Cocin" (*sic*), *Harper's Weekly*, December 31, 1859, 842; "The 'Cocoaine' Trade-mark Case," *New York Times*, October 24, 1860, 2.

93. *The Ladies Guide and City Directory for Shopping, Travel, Amusements, etc., in the City of New York* (New York: G. P. Putnam's Sons, 1885), 119.

94. For example, Gustav Knecht Manufacturing Co., *Price List and Barbers' Reference Book of Gust. Knecht M'f'g Co.* (Chicago: Goes & Quensel, 1888–1889), 32.

95. [Interior view of E. J. Dutra's Barber Shop, 1210 Market Street, Oakland, California], undated. Photograph. Oakland Museum of California, H69.196.3; [Beehive Barber Shop, Rochester, Minnesota], ca. 1896. Photograph. Olmsted County Historical Society, 1952.771.0019. For barbershop interiors, see Bristol, *Knights of the Razor*, 61–63.

96. Gustav Knecht Manufacturing Co., *Price List and Barbers' Reference Book*.

97. For example, [Dick Russell Barber Shop in Rochester, Minnesota], 1890. Photograph. Olmsted County Historical Society, 1976.082.0011; [Lemuel W. Tozier Hairdresser room], ca. 1888. Photographic print. New Hampshire Historical Society; gift of May Nutter, 1974.045.

98. Kochs, *Price List and Barbers' Purchasing Guide*, 95.

99. "Go to G. H. Henderson's Lady Barber Shop," *State Capital* (Springfield, IL), June 6, 1891, 4.

100. Claire Zalc, "Trading on Origins: Signs and Windows of Foreign Shopkeepers in Interwar Paris," *History Workshop Journal* 70 (Autumn 2010): 133.

101. [View of Eastport and vicinity], ca. 1880. Photographic print. Maine Historical Society, Maine Memory Network, item 1214.

102. "Business Woman Taken by Death," *Detroit Free Press*, January 22, 1911, A10; "Mrs. Richard W. Allen," *Detroit Free Press*, January 22, 1911, A10

103. [Mrs. R. W. Allen's Wig Making and Hair Goods, at 175 Woodward Avenue]. Sepia-toned photograph. Detroit Historical Society, 1953.067.039.

104. [Sarah Jane Allen's Hair Dressing Store at 175 Woodward Avenue]. Mounted sepia-toned photograph. Detroit Historical Society, 1953.067.025.

105. Advertisement, *American Hairdresser*, February 1896), 1–2.

106. "The Real Estate Record: A Good Average Week for the Season," *Detroit Free Press*, January 29, 1893, 19.

107. "Trade Notes," *American Perfumer* (February 1922): 537. Note that Mrs. S. A. Allen of New York, manufacturer of Mrs. S. A. Allen's World's Hair Restorer since at least 1840 and of Mrs. S. A. Allen's Zylobalsamum, appears to be unrelated to the Mrs. R. W. Allen businesses of Detroit.

108. Trade card, Alfred Greenwood & Co., 303 Canal St., New York, Joseph Downs Collection of Manuscripts and Printed Ephemera, Winterthur Library, Winterthur, Delaware, no. 72x218.

109. [Schmoele and Company, 1204 Chestnut Street, Philadelphia]. Photograph. Free Library of Philadelphia, pdcto0156.

110. Bay Bottles, "Mike's Glass Bottle Collection and Their History," https://baybottles.com/tag/l-shaw.

111. Bay Bottles, "Mike's Glass Bottle Collection and Their History"; L. Shaw advertisement, *Munsey's Magazine*, March 1905, advertising section, unpaginated; *Trow's New York City Directory* (New York: Trow City Directory Co., 1876), 1252.

112. J. W. Schwartz, "Mrs. L. Shaw," *Printer's Ink*, October 25, 1899, 3–5.

113. Schwartz, "Mrs. L. Shaw," 3–5.

114. Schwartz, "Mrs. L. Shaw," 3–5.

115. Bay Bottles, "Mike's Glass Bottle Collection and Their History."

116. "Miss M. C. Rooney," *Olneyville Times* (Providence, RI), October 9, 1891, 2.

117. For example, Annie Jenness Miller, *Physical Beauty: How to Obtain and How to Preserve It* (New York: C. L. Webster & Co., 1892), 110; Philip G. Hubert Jr. et al, *The Woman's Book, Dealing Practically with the Modern Conditions of Home-Life, Self-Support, Education, Opportunities, and Every-Day Problems*, vol. 2 (New York: Charles Scribner's Sons, 1894), 352.

118. Frank G. Carpenter, *Carp's Washington* (New York: McGraw-Hill, 1960), 101–102.

119. See, for example, "Well-Paying Work," *Olneyville Times* (Providence, RI), June 30, 1888, 4.

120. Olivia Gruber Florek, "'I Am a Slave to My Hair': Empress Elisabeth of Austria, Fetishism, and Nineteenth-Century Austrian Sexuality," *Modern Austrian Literature* 42, no. 2 (June 2009): 8.

121. For example: Dressing jacket. U.S., 1885–1890. Silk, cotton. The Metropolitan Museum of Art, New York, Brooklyn Museum Costume Collection at The Metropolitan Museum of Art; gift of the Brooklyn Museum, 2009; gift of Lillian E. Glenn Peirce, 1946, 2009.300.121.

122. "Combing Cape," *Godey's Lady's Book*, August 1890, 168.

123. Frances Ann Kemble, *Records of a Girlhood*, 2nd ed. (New York: Henry Holt and Co., 1883), 132; Frances Ann Kemble, *Further Records 1848–1883: A Series of Letters by Frances Ann Kemble* (New York: Henry Holt and Co., 1891), 247.

124. May Bragdon Diaries, April 23, 1893, Rare Books, Special Collections and Preservation Rush Rhees Library, University of Rochester, New York.

125. May Bragdon Diaries, April 16, 1893.

126. May Bragdon Diaries, June 4, 1895.

127. May Bragdon Diaries, June 17, 1893.

128. May Bragdon Diaries, June 17, 1893.

129. May Bragdon Diaries, January 31, 1897.

130. May Bragdon Diaries, February 2, 1896.

131. May Bragdon Diaries, June 14, 1897.

132. Mme Hygeia, "Beauty Talks: The Care of the Hair," *San Francisco Call*, February 12, 1899, 27; A. T. W., "What to Do with Oily Hair," *Good Housekeeping*, October 12, 1889, 283; see "A Sun Bath after a Shampoo with Packer's Tar Soap," *The Chautauquan*, October 1899, 107.

133. "Shampoo Parties," *Abbeville Press and Banner* (Abbeville, SC), October 8, 1890, 11.

134. "Shampoo Parties," 11.

135. Sarah Heaton, "Introduction: Empires of Hair and Their Afterlives," in *A Cultural History of Hair in the Age of Empire*, ed. Sarah Heaton (London: Bloomsbury Academic, 2019), 15; Walter Barlow Stevens, *St. Louis, the Fourth City, 1764–1909* (Chicago: S. J. Clarke Publishing Co., 1909), 560.

136. See Elizabeth L. Block, *Dressing Up: The Women Who Influenced French Fashion* (Cambridge, MA: MIT Press, 2021), fig. 3.4, for an 1893 example on wheels.

137. "Hair Dressing Parlor," *Deadwood Evening Independent*, June 1, 1897, 3.

138. For example, "Hairdressing Parlors," *Emporia Daily Republican* (Emporia, KS), October 28, 1898, 4; "Ingersoll's Mechanical Brush," *Scientific American*, June 15, 1861, 384.

CHAPTER 3

1. Yi-Fu Tuan, *Space and Place: The Perspective of Experience* (Minneapolis: University of Minnesota Press, 1977), 8–11.

2. Nigel Thrift, "Space," *Theory, Culture & Society* 23 (no. 2/3) (2006): 144.

3. James Dabney McCabe, *Lights and Shadows of New York Life; or, The Sights and Sensations of the Great City. A Work Descriptive of the City of New York in All Its Various Phases . . .* (Philadelphia: National Publishing Co., 1872), 573.

4. Aileen Ribeiro, *Facing Beauty: Painted Women & Cosmetic Art* (New Haven, CT: Yale University Press, 2011), 247.

5. Frances E. Willard, *Glimpses of Fifty Years: The Autobiography of an American Woman* (Chicago: Woman's Temperance Publication Association, 1889), 69.

6. See Florence Hartley, *The Ladies' Book of Etiquette, and Manual of Politeness* (Boston: G. W. Cottrell, 1860), 28.

7. C. S. Snyder, *Decorum: A Practical Treatise on Etiquette and Dress of the Best American Society* (Chicago: J. A. Ruth & Co., 1877), 270.

8. Hartley, *The Ladies' Book of Etiquette*, 152.

9. Hartley, *The Ladies' Book of Etiquette*, 167.

10. Hartley, *The Ladies' Book of Etiquette*, 47.

11. Emily Edson Briggs, *The Olivia Letters* (New York: Neale Publishing Co., 1906), 392.

12. Frank G. Carpenter, *Carp's Washington* (New York: McGraw-Hill, 1960), 101.

13. "Forget-Me-Notes," *Sunday Herald and Weekly National Intelligencer* (Washington, DC), August 24, 1890, 4.

14. "'Diana' Knots and Mauve Gowns," *Hocking Sentinel* (Logan, OH), November 1, 1894, 1.

15. "Concerning Back Hair," *Arizona Republican*, September 18, 1891, 3.

16. "Concerning Back Hair," 3. See Fernand Paillet (French, 1850–1918), *Amy Bend*, 1889, watercolor on ivory, New-York Historical Society; gift of the Estate of Peter Marié, 1905.18.

17. Carol Rifelj, *Coiffures: Hair in Nineteenth-Century French Literature and Culture* (Newark: University of Delaware Press, 2010), 63–66, 91–92.

18. Rifelj, *Coiffures*, 58–59.

19. "A Modern Masquerade," *Munsey's Magazine*, April–September 1897, 195–196; "Periwigs and Guinea Pigs," *New-York Tribune*, November 23, 1897, 5.

20. John Singer Sargent. *Ellen Terry as Lady Macbeth*, 1889. Oil on canvas. Tate Britain, N02053.

21. "How Women Wear Their Hair," *Wichita Eagle*, January 3, 1890, 8; Katharine De Forest, "Our Paris Letter," *Harper's Bazar*, June 27, 1896, 542; "Sarah Bernhardt's Hair," *American Hairdresser*, August 1896, 15.

22. "How Women Wear Their Hair," 8.

23. Théobald Chartran. *Sarah Bernhardt in "Gismonda,"* after 1896. Oil on canvas. Musée Carnavalet, Paris, P2697.

24. "A New Coiffure: The Gismonda," *Evening World* (New York), February 2, 1900, 6.

25. See Sarony. *Maude Adams as Juliet in "Romeo and Juliet,"* 1899. Cabinet photograph. Museum of the City of New York, 63.148.1.

26. Alphonse Mucha. *Maude Adams as Joan of Arc*, 1909. Oil on canvas. The Metropolitan Museum of Art, New York; gift of A. J. Kobler, 1920, 20.33.

27. "False Hair," *St. Louis Republic*, September 15, 1901, magazine section, 47.

28. "A Chapter on Actresses," *Abbeville Press and Banner* (Abbeville, SC), January 18, 1893, 2.

29. "Missing Links," *Mineral Point Tribune* (Mineral Point, WI), April 1, 1886, 5.

30. "Current Notes," *Lippincott's Monthly Magazine*, November 1890, 727.

31. Michael Cooper, "Overlooked No More: Sissieretta Jones, a Soprano Who Shattered Racial Barriers," *New York Times*, August 15, 2018, D8.

32. Addison N. Scurlock, *Sissieretta Jones*, ca. 1911. Photograph. H. Lawrence Freeman Collection, Rare Book & Manuscript Library, Columbia University, no accession number.

33. All photographs are in the Costume Ball Photograph Collection, PR 223, Department of Prints, Photographs, and Architectural Collections, New-York Historical Society.

34. "The Color of Their Tresses," *Morning Call* (San Francisco), January 17, 1892, 11.

35. Jessie M. Wood, "The Actress," *Life*, March 26, 1896, 233.

36. McCabe, *Lights and Shadows of New York Life*, 794.

37. Joanna Pitman, *On Blondes* (London: Bloomsbury, 2003), 139, 143–144.

38. Edith Snook, "Beautiful Hair, Health, and Privilege in Early Modern England," *Journal for Early Modern Cultural Studies* 15, no. 4 (Fall 2015): 25.

39. Rifelj, *Coiffures*, 136–138.

40. "The Coming Bleach," *Scientific American*, May 14, 1881, 314.

41. See American Antiquarian Society, Worcester, Massachusetts, records 149187, 149443, and 149217.

42. Snyder, *Decorum*, 293.

43. Rifelj, *Coiffures*, 129–135; Marion Roach, *The Roots of Desire: The Myth, Meaning, and Sexual Power of Red Hair* (New York: Bloomsbury, 2005), 22–24, 176.

44. Willard, *Glimpses of Fifty Years*, 11–12.

45. Willard, *Glimpses of Fifty Years*, 12.

46. Ruth Mellinkoff, "Judas's Red Hair and the Jews," *Journal of Jewish Art* 9 (1982): 46; Penny Howell Jolly, *Hair: Untangling a Social History* (Saratoga Springs, NY: Frances Young Tang Teaching Museum and Art Gallery at Skidmore College, 2004), 8, 56, 60.

47. Ribeiro, *Facing Beauty*, 270.

48. Albert Herter (U.S., 1871–1950). *Woman with Red Hair*, 1894. Oil on canvas. Smithsonian American Art Museum, Washington, DC; gift of Laura Dreyfus Barney and Natalie Clifford Barney in memory of their mother, Alice Pike Barney, 1959.15.

49. Mellinkoff, "Judas's Red Hair and the Jews," 31; Michel Pastoureau, *Red: The History of a Color* (Princeton, NJ: Princeton University Press, 2017), 102–105.

50. Kathy Lee Peiss, *Hope in a Jar: The Making of America's Beauty Culture* (New York: Metropolitan Books, 1998), 39.

51. *The Manners That Win* (Minneapolis, MN: Buckeye Publishing Co., 1886), 388.

52. Eliza Frances Andrews, *The War-Time Journal of a Georgia Girl, 1864–1865*, ed. Spencer B. King Jr. (New York: D. Appleton and Co., 1908), 133–134.

53. Andrews, *The War-Time Journal of a Georgia Girl*, 299.

54. Andrews, *The War-Time Journal of a Georgia Girl*, 299.

55. Andrews, *The War-Time Journal of a Georgia Girl*, 87, 216, 93.

56. See advertisements for Ayer's hair vigor produced by Dr. J. C. Ayer and Co., Lowell, Massachusetts: Library of Congress call no. PGA-Ayer (J. C.)-Ayer's hair vigor; and Baker Library Special Collections, Harvard Business School, Cambridge, Massachusetts, TC6246.0009:6246.

57. For example, *Harper's Bazar*, April 7, 1894, 273.

58. "Beautiful New York Women," *Yakima Herald* (Yakima, WA), June 9, 1892, 5.

59. "Mrs. Belmont Younger," *Topeka State Journal*, November 26, 1897, 4.

60. Steven Zdatny, *Hairstyles and Fashion: A Hairdresser's History of Paris, 1910–1920* (Oxford: Berg, 1999), 17.

61. "Hair Doctress," *The Liberator*, April 4, 1856, 3 (emphasis in the original).

62. "A Few Words with Our Correspondents," *Godey's Lady's Book*, October 1864, 354.

63. Frank C. Bridgeford, *Barber Instructor and Toilet Manual* (Kansas City, MO: Frank C. Bridgeford, 1900), unpaginated; Victoria Sherrow, *Encyclopedia of Hair: A Cultural History* (Westport, CT: Greenwood Press, 2006), 156.

64. Mrs. John A. Logan, *The Home Manual: Everybody's Guide in Social, Domestic and Business Life* (Philadelphia: Standard Publishing Co., 1889), 130–132; McCabe, *Lights and Shadows of New York Life*, 808.

65. Charles Henri Leonard, *The Hair: Its Growth, Care, Diseases and Treatment* (Detroit: C. Henri Leonard, Medical Book Publisher, 1881), 158–171; J. R. Stitson (pseud. for Joseph Scott Stillwell), *The Human Hair, Its Care and Preservation* (New York: Maple Publishing Co., 1900), 189–193.

66. Stitson, *The Human Hair*, 196–197.

67. "The Dangers of Hairdressing," *The Hospital: A Journal of the Medical Sciences and Hospital Administration* 22, no. 566 (July 31, 1897): 295–296; Bernarr Macfadden, *Macfadden's New Hair*

Culture: Rational, Natural Methods for Cultivating Strength and Luxuriance of the Hair (New York: Physical Culture Pub. Co., 1899), 130–131.

68. Zdatny, *Hairstyles and Fashion*, 17–18.

69. "With Hair Combed High," *Morning Times* (Washington, DC), August 16, 1896, 20.

70. Richard Ormond and Elaine Kilmurray, *John Singer Sargent: The Later Portraits* (New Haven, CT: Yale University Press, 2003), 102–104.

71. "The Modern Juggernaut," *Christian Union* (New York), December 15, 1887, 667.

72. Mia Fineman, *Faking It: Manipulated Photography before Photoshop* (New York: Metropolitan Museum of Art, distributed by Yale University Press, 2012), 206; Matthew Fox-Amato, *Exposing Slavery: Photography, Human Bondage, and the Birth of Modern Visual Politics in America* (New York: Oxford University Press, 2019), 33, 252n52, 252–253n53.

73. Jasmine Nichole Cobb, *Picture Freedom: Remaking Black Visuality in the Early Nineteenth Century* (New York: New York University Press, 2015), 1.

74. See "America and the Tintype," International Center of Photography, https://www.icp.org/browse/archive/collections/america-and-the-tintype-september-19-2008-january-14-2009?page=2.

75. Tina Brown, "Painted Backgrounds for Turn of the Century Photographers," *Unbound*, Smithsonian Libraries and Archives, https://blog.library.si.edu/blog/2018/07/19/painted-backgrounds-for-turn-of-the-century-photographers/#.YkiSI27MJhE.

76. "Accessories, Backgrounds, Drapery, and Hair," *Photographic Times and American Photographer* 9, no. 102 (December 1879): 275.

77. "Accessories, Backgrounds, Drapery, and Hair," 275.

78. Joseph Wake, "The Art of Painting on the Photographic Image," *British Journal of Photography* 24, no. 908 (September 28, 1877): 461.

CHAPTER 4

1. The term "mobile labor" is also useful here; see Cristiana Bastos, Andre Novoa, and Noel B. Salazar, "Mobile Labour: An Introduction," *Mobilities* 16, no. 2 (March 4, 2021): 155–163.

2. Setha M. Low, "Spatializing Culture: An Engaged Anthropological Approach to Space and Place," in *The People, Space and Place Reader*, ed. Jack Gieseking, William Mangold, Cindi Katz, Setha Low, and Susan Saegert (London: Routledge, 2014), 37.

3. Anne O'Hagan, "Behind the Scenes in the Big Stores," *Munsey's Magazine*, January 1900, 528–537.

4. Robert W. Twyman, *History of Marshall Field & Co., 1852–1906* (Philadelphia: University of Pennsylvania Press, 1954), 80.

5. "Saleswomen's Appearance," *Dry Goods Economist*, November 20, 1909, 44.

6. Lawrence Graham, *The Senator and the Socialite: The True Story of America's First Black Dynasty* (New York: Harper Perennial, 2007), 368–369, 451–452.

7. Compare to "Ladies' and Children's Wear Street and House Suits," *Harper's Bazar*, November 15, 1873, 728–729.

8. "Mrs. Josephine B. Bruce," *Washington Bee*, September 24, 1892, 1; "A Power at Tuskegee," *Colored American*, March 24, 1900, 1.

9. Faye E. Dudden, *Serving Women: Household Service in Nineteenth-Century America* (Middletown, CT: Wesleyan University Press; Scranton, PA: distributed by Harper & Row, 1983), 51; Renée Huggett, *Hair-Styles and Head Dresses* (London: Batsford Academic and Educational, 1982), 51. For illustrations of hairstyles for servants in 1842 and 1844, see Richard Corson, *Fashions in Hair: The First Five Thousand Years* (New York: Hastings House, 1965), 519; Elizabeth L. O'Leary, *At Beck and Call: The Representation of Domestic Servants in Nineteenth-Century American Painting* (Washington, DC: Smithsonian Institution Press, 1996), 167–168.

10. Dominique Cocuzza, "Stella Blum Grant Report: The Dress of Free Women of Color in New Orleans, 1780–1840," *Dress* 27, no. 1 (January 1, 2000): 80–82.

11. Louis Antoine Collas (French, 1775–1856). *Free Woman of Color Wearing a Tignon*, 1829. Oil on canvas, 44 × 36 in. (111.7 × 91.4 cm). New Orleans Museum of Art; Kai Mercel, "Tignon," *The Fashion and Race Database*; https://fashionandrace.org/database/tignon; Noliwe M. Rooks, "Black Hair, Self-Creation, and the Meaning of Freedom," in *Connecting Afro Futures: Fashion × Hair × Design*. ed. Claudia Banz et al. (Bielefeld, Germany: Kerber Verlag, 2019), 16; Jonathan Michael Square, "Culture, Power, and the Appropriation of Creolized Aesthetics in the Revolutionary French Atlantic," *SX Salon* 36, February 2021, http://smallaxe.net/sxsalon/discussions/culture-power-and-appropriation-creolized-aesthetics-revolutionary-french.

12. Anna Arabindan-Kesson, "Dressed Up and Laying Bare: Fashion in the Shadow of the Market," *Vestoj* 9 (undated): unpaginated.

13. Jonathan Square cites the following example worn by a white woman in the Ludlow family of New York: Evening turban, U.S., ca. 1823. Cotton. The Metropolitan Museum of Art, New York, Bequest of Maria P. James, 1910, 11.60.248. Square, "Culture, Power, and the Appropriation of Creolized Aesthetics." See also Jonathan Square, "Fashioning the Self," Instagram post, September 21, 2022.

14. Matthew Fox-Amato, *Exposing Slavery: Photography, Human Bondage, and the Birth of Modern Visual Politics in America* (New York: Oxford University Press, 2019), 35–42.

15. Fox-Amato, *Exposing Slavery*, 38–41.

16. Juliette Bowles, "Natural Hair Styling: A Symbol and Function of African-American Women's Self-Creation" (Master's thesis, College of William and Mary, 1990), 26–27; Deborah Willis and Carla Williams, *The Black Female Body: A Photographic History* (Philadelphia: Temple University Press, 2002), 128–137.

17. Arabindan-Kesson, "Dressed Up and Laying Bare," unpaginated; Shane White and Graham White, *Stylin': African American Expressive Culture from Its Beginnings to the Zoot Suit* (Ithaca, NY: Cornell University Press, 1998), 56–57.

18. Barbara Heath, "Space and Place within Plantation Quarters in Virginia, 1700–1825," in *Cabin, Quarter, Plantation: Architecture and Landscapes of North American Slavery*, ed. Clifton Ellis and Rebecca Ginsburg (New Haven, CT: Yale University Press, 2010), 156–176; Esther C. White, "The Landscape of Enslavement: His Space, Their Places," in *Lives Bound Together:*

Slavery at George Washington's Mount Vernon, ed. Susan Prendergast Schoelwer (Mount Vernon, VA: Mount Vernon Ladies Association, 2016), 89.

19. Stephanie M. H Camp, *Closer to Freedom: Enslaved Women and Everyday Resistance in the Plantation South* (Chapel Hill: University of North Carolina Press, 2006), 28.

20. Nigel Thrift, "Space," *Theory, Culture & Society* 23 (2–3) (2006): 140.

21. Thrift, "Space," 143–144.

22. Whitney Nell Stewart, "A Protected Place: The Material Culture of Home-Making for Stagville's Enslaved Residents," *Winterthur Portfolio* 54, no. 4 (December 2020): 248.

23. Frances Ann Kemble, *Journal of a Residence on a Georgian Plantation in 1838–39* (New York: Harper & Brothers, 1863), 32.

24. Eliza Ripley, *Social Life in Old New Orleans, Being Recollections of My Girlhood* (New York: D. Appleton and Co., 1912), 257.

25. Saidiya Hartman, "Venus in Two Acts," *Small Axe* 26 (June 2008): 11.

26. Helen Bradley Foster, *"New Raiments of Self": African American Clothing in the Antebellum South* (Oxford: Berg, 1997), 85–96, 110–124; Katie Knowles, "The Fabric of Fast Fashion: Enslaved Wearers and Makers as Designers in the American Fashion System," in *Black Designers in American Fashion*, ed. Elizabeth Way (London: Bloomsbury Visual Arts, 2021), 22–23; Jonathan Michael Square, "Slavery's Warp, Freedom's Weft: A Look at the Work of Eighteenth- and Nineteenth-Century Enslaved Fashion Makers and Their Legacies," in *Black Designers in American Fashion*, ed. Elizabeth Way (London: Bloomsbury Visual Arts, 2021), 32–37.

27. For example, "For Sale–A Negro Girl, well-qualified for pastry cooking, washer and ironer, and warranted to be a first-rate seamstress," *Nashville Union*, January 7, 1853, 3.

28. Tom Costa et al., "The Geography of Slavery in Virginia," University of Virginia, http://www2.vcdh.virginia.edu/gos/essays.html.

29. Jasmine Nichole Cobb, *Picture Freedom: Remaking Black Visuality in the Early Nineteenth Century* (New York: New York University Press, 2015), 118–119.

30. Elizabeth Keckley, *Behind the Scenes: or, Thirty Years a Slave, and Four Years in the White House* (New York: G. W. Carleton & Co., 1868), 88, 101, 203.

31. *Born in Slavery: Slave Narratives from the Federal Writers' Project, 1936–1938*, https://www.loc.gov/collections/slave-narratives-from-the-federal-writers-project-1936-to-1938; Works Progress Administration, *Slave Narratives: A Folk History of Slavery in the United States from Interviews with Former Slaves* (17 vols.) (Washington, DC: Library of Congress, 1941).

32. Sharon Ann Musher, "The Other Slave Narratives: The Works Progress Administration Interviews," in *The Oxford Handbook of the African American Slave Narrative*, ed. John Ernest (Oxford: Oxford University Press, 2014), 101–118.

33. Juliette Harris, "Hair and Hairstyles," in *World of a Slave: Encyclopedia of the Material Life of Slaves in the United States*, ed. Martha B. Katz-Hyman and Kym S. Rice (Santa Barbara, CA: Greenwood, 2011), 265–271. For more on the use of bandanas, see White and White, *Stylin'*, 58–61.

34. Federal Writers' Project: Slave Narrative Project, vol. 4, Georgia, pt. 2, Garey-Jones, 1936, Manuscript/Mixed Material, Library of Congress. For a measured analysis in favor of using

the materials in the Federal Writers' Project: Slave Narrative Project as primary sources, see Stephanie E. Jones-Rogers, *They Were Her Property: White Women as Slave Owners in the American South* (New Haven, CT: Yale University Press, 2019), xviii–xix.

35. Federal Writers' Project: Slave Narrative Project, vol. 4, Georgia, pt. 2, Garey-Jones, 1936, Manuscript/Mixed Material, Library of Congress; Federal Writers' Project: Slave Narrative Project, vol. 2, Arkansas, pt. 7, Vaden-Young, 1936, Manuscript/Mixed Material, Library of Congress.

36. Foster, *"New Raiments of Self,"* 252; White and White, *Stylin'*, 57.

37. Foster, *"New Raiments of Self,"* 250–251; Federal Writers' Project: Slave Narrative Project, vol. 4, Georgia, pt. 4, Telfair-Young with combined interviews of others, 1936, Manuscript/Mixed Material, Library of Congress.

38. Foster, *"New Raiments of Self,"* 250–252.

39. William H. Robinson, *From Log Cabin to the Pulpit, or, Fifteen Years in Slavery* (Eau Clair, WI: James H. Tifft, 1913), 45–46.

40. Federal Writers' Project: Slave Narrative Project, vol. 2, Arkansas, pt. 2, Cannon-Evans, 1936, Manuscript/Mixed Material, Library of Congress.

41. Yi-Fu Tuan, *Space and Place: The Perspective of Experience* (Minneapolis: University of Minnesota Press, 1977), 8–11; Thrift, "Space," 143–144.

42. [Portrait of a woman wearing a hat], 1860s. Photograph. Stephan Loewentheil Photograph Collection, #8043, Division of Rare and Manuscript Collections, Cornell University Library, SL_AFAM_0608_007.

43. For example: [Unidentified freedwoman], ca. 1865. Tintype. International Center of Photography, New York, 67.2004; [Woman], ca. 1860. Ambrotype. Stephan Loewentheil Photograph Collection, #8043, Division of Rare and Manuscript Collections, Cornell University Library; [Woman wearing a bonnet], ca. 1850. Daguerreotype, Stephan Loewentheil Photograph Collection, #8043. Division of Rare and Manuscript Collections, Cornell University Library.

44. Thomas H. Lindsey, [Small log cabin on the grounds of Biltmore House, with men, women, and children doing various jobs], 1897. Photograph. Robert Langmuir African American Photograph Collection, Stuart A. Rose Manuscript, Archives, and Rare Book Library.

45. Cobb, *Picture Freedom*, 4–6.

46. Cobb, *Picture Freedom*, 119–121.

47. The Library Company of Philadelphia, P.9719. According to a note in the catalogue: "This caricature is similar in content to the prints from the series, 'Life in Philadelphia' (London Set), and has been catalogued as a part of the series."

48. Kimberlé Crenshaw, *Defending the C.R.O.W.N.: Life, Liberty, and the Pursuit of Nappyness, Intersectionality Matters with Kimberlé Crenshaw* (podcast), https://soundcloud.com/intersectionality-matters/ep-7-defending-the-crown-life-liberty-and-the-pursuit-of-nappyness.

49. John Campbell, *Negro-Mania: Being an Examination of the Falsely Assumed Equality of the Various Races of Men* (Philadelphia: Campbell & Powers, 1851), *passim*; Peter Arrell Browne, *The Classification of Mankind, by the Hair and Wool of Their Heads: With the Nomenclature of Human Hybrids* (Philadelphia: J. H. Jones, 1852), *passim*.

50. Federal Writers' Project: Slave Narrative Project, vol. 4, Georgia, pt. 2, Garey-Jones, 1936, Manuscript/Mixed Material, Library of Congress; Federal Writers' Project: Slave Narrative Project, vol. 2, Arkansas, pt. 3, Gadson-Isom, 1936, Manuscript/Mixed Material, Library of Congress.

51. Edith Snook, "Beautiful Hair, Health, and Privilege in Early Modern England," *Journal for Early Modern Cultural Studies* 15, no. 4 (Fall 2015): 38.

52. Heather V. Vermeulen, "Race and Ethnicity: Mortal Coils and Hair-Raising Revolutions, Styling 'Race' in the Age of Enlightenment," in *A Cultural History of Hair in the Age of Enlightenment*, ed. Margaret K. Powell and Joseph Roach (London: Bloomsbury Academic, 2021), 136.

53. Snook, "Beautiful Hair, Health, and Privilege in Early Modern England," 38.

54. Sharon Block, *Colonial Complexions: Race and Bodies in Eighteenth-Century America* (Philadelphia: University of Pennsylvania Press, 2018), 77.

55. Mathelinda Nabugodi, "Afro Hair in the Time of Slavery," *Studies in Romanticism* 61, no. 1 (2022): 81–82.

56. Peter A. Browne, *Trichologia Mammalium; or, A Treatise on the Organization, Properties and Uses of Hair and Wool Together with an Essay upon the Raising and Breeding of Sheep* (Philadelphia: J. H. Jones, 1853), 65–67.

57. For example, "The Hair," *Scientific American*, April 3, 1852, 229. See Sarah Cheang, "Roots: Hair and Race," in *Hair: Styling, Culture and Fashion*, ed. Geraldine Biddle-Perry and Sarah Cheang (Oxford: Berg, 2008), 27–42.

58. For example, Federal Writers' Project: Slave Narrative Project, vol. 2, Arkansas, pt. 3, Gadson-Isom, 1936, Manuscript/Mixed Material, Library of Congress.

59. Foster, *"New Raiments of Self,"* 253.

60. Noliwe M. Rooks, *Hair Raising: Beauty, Culture, and African American Women* (New Brunswick, NJ: Rutgers University Press, 1996), 25.

61. The term *mulatto* often referred to people of mixed European, African, and Native American descent. See A. B. Wilkinson, *Blurring the Lines of Race and Freedom: Mulattoes and Mixed Bloods in English Colonial America* (Chapel Hill: University of North Carolina Press, 2020), 16–18.

62. White and White, *Stylin'*, 47.

63. Low, "Spatializing Culture," 37.

64. Louisa Picquet and Hiram Mattison, *Louisa Picquet, the Octoroon: or, Inside Views of Southern Domestic Life* (New York: Hiram Mattison, 1861), 17.

65. Jones-Rogers, *They Were Her Property*, 97.

66. Harriet A. Jacobs, *Incidents in the Life of a Slave Girl* (Boston: Published for the author, 1861), 118.

67. Last Seen: Finding Family after Slavery, Villanova University, Villanova, PA, http://informationwanted.org.

68. For descriptions of hair in missing person advertisements, see White and White, *Stylin'*, 41–45.

69. Quotation from Sharon Block, "Creating Race on Colonial American Bodies," virtual webinar, LeHigh University, March 5, 2021. See also Block, *Colonial Complexions*, 60–83.

70. Block, *Colonial Complexions*, 65.

71. "The Great African Hair Unkinker," *New York Times*, February 9, 1859, 8.

72. Martin H. Freeman, "The Educational Wants of the Free Colored People," *Anglo-African Magazine*, January 1859, 116–117.

73. Sojourner Truth, Olive Gilbert, and Frances W. Titus, *Narrative of Sojourner Truth . . .* (Battle Creek, MI: For the author, 1878), vii.

74. "Value of Your Hair," *Washington Bee*, November 17, 1888, 1.

75. "The Negro His Own Enemy," *Washington Bee*, April 28, 1894, 2.

76. "Shall We Continue in the Old Ruts?," *State Capital* (Springfield, IL), September 5, 1891, 1.

77. Advertisements: *Washington Bee*, September 18, 1897, 7 (Kinkara, Hairoline); *Washington Bee*, December 31, 1898, 4 (Angeline); *Washington Bee*, July 22, 1899, 8 (Lee's Take-Out Kink); "Beauty Conquers All," *Richmond Planet*, December 10, 1898, 2 (Osiline); *Richmond Planet*, October 27, 1900, 2 (Straightine).

78. Tiffany M. Gill, *Beauty Shop Politics: African American Women's Activism in the Beauty Industry* (Champaign: University of Illinois Press 2010), 18.

79. For example, "Hair-Dressing," *State Capital* (Springfield, IL), August 29, 1891, 3, reprinted from *New York Ledger*.

80. "Fashion Notes," *Washington Bee*, April 16, 1892, 3; "It Is Fashionable," *Washington Bee*, December 7, 1895, 8.

81. "Imperial Hair Coloring," *Washington Bee*, December 20, 1890, 4.

82. Beverly Lowry, *Her Dream of Dreams: The Rise and Triumph of Madam C. J. Walker* (New York: Knopf Doubleday, 2011), 119–120. See "Rebecca E. Elliott," *The Freeman* (Indianapolis), May 24, 1890, 7.

83. "Mrs. George Birdsong Is the Agent for Mrs. Rebecca Elliott's Hair Pomade and Hair Grower," *State Capital* (Springfield, IL), June 6, 1891, 4.

84. "Boston Chemical Company," *Colored American*, October 1900, 332.

85. "Hartona Remedy Company," *Colored American*, November 1901, 82. Noliwe M. Rooks analyzes a similar advertisement by Crane and Company, Richmond, Virginia in Rooks, *Hair Raising*, 27–29.

86. "Hartona Remedy Company," *Colored American*, January 1903, 242.

87. "Madame Delmore's Hair Vigor," *Colored American*, November 1901, 1.

88. Dessilin Carteaux's death year is unknown, but he is not listed with Christiana Carteaux in the 1850 Census.

89. "Improvement in Champooing (*sic*) and Hair Dyeing, 'Without Smutting,'" *The Liberator*, December 19, 1862, 3.

90. "Hair Doctress," *Boston Evening Transcript*, July 23, 1885, 6.

91. T. Thomas Fortune, "Artist Bannister," *Providence News*, November 10, 1896, 2.

92. Juanita Holland, "'Co-Workers in the Kingdom of Culture': Edward Mitchell Bannister and the Boston Community of African-American Artists, 1848–1901" (PhD diss., New York, Columbia University, 1998), 14n4, 257, 345, chronology in appendix.

93. William Wells Brown, *The Black Man: His Antecedents, His Genius, and His Achievements* (New York: Thomas Hamilton, 1863), 216; Holland, "'Co-Workers in the Kingdom of Culture,'" 164; Juanita Holland, "To Be Free, Gifted, and Black: African American Artist Edward Mitchell Bannister," *International Review of African American Art* 12, no. 1 (1995): 4–25, 12; Aston Gonzalez, *Visualizing Equality: African American Rights and Visual Culture in the Nineteenth Century* (Chapel Hill: University of North Carolina Press, 2020), 183.

94. George W. Forbes, "E. M. Bannister with Sketch of Earlier Artists," 8, Edward Mitchell Bannister and George W. Forbes letters and manuscripts, Rare Books and Manuscripts Division, Boston Public Library.

95. Edward Mitchell Bannister. *Portrait of Christiana Carteaux Bannister*, ca. 1860. Oil on panel. RISD Museum, Providence, Rhode Island; gift of the Edward M. Bannister Foundation, 2016.38.1. Sculptor Pablo Eduardo based his bust-length clay portrait (2002; Rhode Island State House) of her on the painting.

96. "Improved Method of Champooing and Hair-Dyeing," *The Liberator*, February 3, 1854, 4.

97. "Champooing and Hair-Dyeing Saloon," *The Liberator*, November 30, 1855, 4.

98. E. M. Bannister probably to C. H. Brainerd, April 8, 1880, Boston Public Library, Rare Books and Manuscripts Division, Ch.F.6.77.

99. "Hair Doctress, Madame Carteaux," *Boston Evening Transcript*, January 12, 1874, 6; "Hair Doctress, Mme Carteaux," *Boston Evening Transcript*, July 31, 1875, 3.

100. "Madam (*sic*) Carteaux," *Boston Evening Transcript*, April 21, 1883, 5.

101. "Madame Carteaux," *Providence Journal*, April 10, 1879, n.p.

102. Forbes, "E. M. Bannister with Sketch of Earlier Artists"; "Oberlin Rescuers; Meeting of Colored Citizens of Boston," *The Liberator*, June 10, 1859, 2. See also Naurice Frank Woods Jr., *Insuperable Obstacles: The Impact of Racism on the Creative and Personal Development of Four Nineteenth-Century African-American Artists* (Cincinnati, OH: Union Institute, 1993), 149; Martin Henry Blatt, Donald Yacovone, and Thomas J. Brown, eds., *Hope and Glory: Essays on the Legacy of the Fifty-Fourth Massachusetts Regiment* (Amherst: University of Massachusetts Press, 2001), 98; Gonzalez, *Visualizing Equality*, 184.

103. Gonzalez, *Visualizing Equality*, 184.

104. "Emancipation Day," *The Liberator*, December 25, 1863, 3. See also Gonzalez, *Visualizing Equality*, 184–185.

105. Sarah Josepha Hale to Christiana Carteaux, Philadelphia, January 13, 1852, Rare Books and Manuscripts Division, Ms. Am. 516, Boston Public Library.

106. Untitled, *The Liberator*, January 20, 1860, 11.

107. Barbara McCaskill and Caroline Gebhard, eds., *Post-Bellum, Pre-Harlem: African American Literature and Culture, 1877–1919* (New York: New York University Press, 2006), 64; "Sanitary Fair of Colored Ladies," *The Liberator*, October 21, 1864, 3–4, Edward Mitchell Bannister Papers, Archives of American Art, Smithsonian Institution.

108. Jane Lancaster, "I Would Have Made Out Very Poorly Had It Not Been for Her," *Rhode Island History* 59, no. 4 (2001): 107; Jane Lancaster, "At Long Last, A Tribute to Bannister," *Providence Journal*, 2002, G1, 8; Aston Gonzalez, *Visualizing Equality: African American Rights and Visual Culture in the Nineteenth Century* (Chapel Hill: University of North Carolina Press, 2020), 185.

109. Forbes, "E. M. Bannister with Sketch of Earlier Artists," 8.

110. For the increase in women's salons in the 1920s, see Kim Smith, "From Style to Place: The Emergence of the Ladies' Hair Salon in the Twentieth Century," in *Hair: Styling, Culture and Fashion*, ed. Geraldine Biddle-Perry and Sarah Cheang (Oxford: Berg, 2008), 55–65.

111. "Bannister House (93 Benevolent Street)," Art in Ruins, https://artinruins.com/property/bannister-house-pvd.

112. JerriAnne Boggis, Eve Allegra Raimon, and Barbara A. White, eds., *Harriet Wilson's New England: Race, Writing, and Region* (Durham, NH: University of New Hampshire Press and Hanover, NH: University Press of New England, 2007), 131; Karsonya Wise Whitehead, "Sarah Parker Remond," in *Encyclopedia of African American History*, ed. Leslie M. Alexander and Walter C. Rucker, vol. 1 (Santa Barbara, CA: ABC-CLIO, 2010), 512–514; Ayana D. Byrd and Lori L. Tharps, *Hair Story: Untangling the Roots of Black Hair in America* (New York: St. Martin's Press, 2014, first published 2001), 75–76.

113. Byrd and Tharps, *Hair Story*, 75–76.

114. For example, see Untitled, *The Liberator*, June 10, 1859, 91; Ruth Bogin, "Sarah Parker Remond: Black Abolitionist from Salem," *Essex Institute Historical Collections* 110, no. 22 (April 1974): 120–150; Dorothy Sterling, ed., *We Are Your Sisters: Black Women in the Nineteenth Century* (New York: W. W. Norton, 1984), 175–180.

115. Ruth Bogin also notes that Caroline Remond Putnam was listed in the Salem Directory as a partner with "Mrs. C. Babcock" as "hairwork manufacturer." Bogin, "Sarah Parker Remond: Black Abolitionist from Salem," 148. The Remond Family papers are located at the Phillips Library at the Peabody Essex Museum, Salem, Massachusetts, MSS 271. According to the finding aid, the papers contain no mention of Carteaux Bannister or Bannister.

116. "Madame Carteaux's Nieces," *Boston Evening Transcript*, July 14, 1885, 6.

117. "Madame Carteaux's Root & Herb Hair Preparation," *Providence Journal*, June 17, 1901, n.p.

118. "Madame Carteaux Bannister's Niece," *Boston Evening Transcript*, February 14, 1903, 24.

119. P. Gabrielle Foreman and Katherine Flynn, "Mrs. H. E. Wilson, Mogul?," *Boston Globe*, February 15, 2009, n.p.

120. P. Gabrielle Foreman, "Recovered Autobiographies and the Marketplace: *Our Nig*'s Generic Genealogies and Harriet Wilson's Entrepreneurial Enterprise," in *Harriet Wilson's New England*, ed. JerriAnne Boggis, Eve Allegra Raimon, and Barbara A. White (Durham: NH: University of New Hampshire Press and Hanover, NH: University Press of New England, 2007), 128–130; "Use Mrs. Wilson's Hair Regenerator and Hair Dressing," *Methodist Quarterly* 20 (1860), unpaginated (approx. p. 715).

121. Harriet E. Wilson, *Our Nig: or, Sketches from the Life of a Free Black in a Two-Story White House, North* (Boston: G. C. Rand & Avery, 1859), 72.

122. Foreman, "Recovered Autobiographies and the Marketplace," 128–130.

123. Foreman and Flynn, "Mrs. H. E. Wilson, Mogul?"

124. Foreman and Flynn, "Mrs. H. E. Wilson, Mogul?"

125. Davarian L. Baldwin, *Chicago's New Negroes: Modernity, the Great Migration, and Black Urban Life* (Chapel Hill: University of North Carolina Press, 2007), 56–57.

126. Rooks, *Hair Raising*, 42–50.

127. A'Lelia Perry Bundles, *On Her Own Ground: The Life and Times of Madam C. J. Walker* (New York: Scribner, 2001), 67.

128. "Poro College," Annie Malone Historical Society, https://www.anniemalonehistoricalsociety .org/poro-college.html.

129. Baldwin, *Chicago's New Negroes*, 69–70. For the interrelated histories of Malone's and Walker's businesses, see Gill, *Beauty Shop Politics*, 18–31.

130. Baldwin, *Chicago's New Negroes*, 75.

131. Baldwin, *Chicago's New Negroes*, 76–77.

CHAPTER 5

1. Yi-Fu Tuan, *Space and Place: The Perspective of Experience* (Minneapolis: University of Minnesota Press, 1977), 183.

2. Kevin Hannam, Mimi Sheller, and John Urry, "Editorial: Mobilities, Immobilities and Moorings," *Mobilities* 1, no. 1 (March 1, 2006): 13.

3. The term "dwellings-in-motion" is from Hannam, Sheller, and Urry, "Editorial: Mobilities, Immobilities and Moorings," 13.

4. George R. Lawrence Co., "Dressing Child in Compartment," ca. 1905. Photograph. Library of Congress, reproduction no. LC-USZ62–33524.

5. For example, Byron Company, "Erie R.R. Car Interior," 1899. Silver gelatin print. Museum of the City of New York, 93.1.1.4068.

6. Mia Bay, *Traveling Black: A Story of Race and Resistance* (Cambridge, MA: Belknap Press, 2021), 42, 44, 113–118, 146.

7. Mia Bay, *To Tell the Truth Freely: The Life of Ida B. Wells* (New York: Farrar, Straus and Giroux, 2010), 45–54.

8. "An American Steamship Line," *Patriot*, April 15, 1891, 3; F. Chadwick, J. Kelley, Ridgely Hunt, John H. Gould, William H. Rideing, and A. E. Seaton, *Ocean Steamships: A Popular Account of Their Construction, Development, Management and Appliances* (New York: C. Scribner's Sons, 1891); Philip Sutton, "Maury and the Menu: A Brief History of the Cunard Steamship Company," *New York Public Library Blog*, June 30, 2011, https://www.nypl.org/blog/2011/06/30 /maury-menu-brief-history-cunard-steamship-company.

9. Kate Virginia Peyton, "My Blonde Wig," *Peterson's Magazine*, November 1876, 318.

10. Jonathan Stafford, "Home on the Waves: Domesticity and Discomfort Aboard the Overland Route Steamship, 1842–1862," *Mobilities* 14, no. 5 (September 3, 2019): 578–595.

11. See Elizabeth L. Block, "Winslow Homer and Women's Bathing Practices in *Eagle Head, Manchester, Massachusetts (High Tide)*," *American Art* 32, no. 2 (June 2018): 100–115.

12. Mrs. C. Thompson, ed., *Mrs. C. Thompson, Importer and Manufacturer of Wigs, Hair Jewelry, Ornamental Hair Work . . .* (New York: Mrs. C. Thompson, 1883), 7, 10–11.

13. Illustration, *Harper's Weekly*, September 18, 1858, 608.

14. W. B. Davidson, *After the Bath*, ca. 1898. Photograph. Library of Congress, reproduction no. LC-USZ62–70876.

15. Margaret Guroff, *The Mechanical Horse: How the Bicycle Reshaped American Life* (Austin: University of Texas Press, 2016), 35–39; Einav Rabinovitch-Fox, *Dressed for Freedom: The Fashionable Politics of American Feminism* (Urbana: University of Illinois Press, 2021), 35.

16. Guroff, *The Mechanical Horse*, 40; Rabinovitch-Fox, *Dressed for Freedom*, 39.

17. Maud C. Cooke, *Social Life: or, The Manners and Customs of Polite Society, Containing the Rules of Etiquette for All Occasions* (Philadelphia: Co-operative Publishing Co., 1896), 349.

18. Eve Kahn, *Forever Seeing New Beauties: The Forgotten Impressionist Mary Rogers Williams, 1857–1907* (Middletown, CT: Wesleyan University Press, 2019), 86–87, 108–109.

19. Kat Jungnickel, *Bikes and Bloomers: Victorian Women Inventors and Their Extraordinary Cycle Wear* (London: Goldsmiths Press, 2018), 96–114; "To Keep the Skirts and Trousers in Trim," *The Herald* (Los Angeles), June 2, 1895, 7.

20. *Etiquette for Americans by a Woman of Fashion* (Chicago: H. S. Stone and Co., 1898), 188.

21. Rabinovitch-Fox, *Dressed for Freedom*, 37–38.

22. Rabinovitch-Fox, *Dressed for Freedom*, 38.

23. For example, Guroff, *The Mechanical Horse*, 43–44; Jungnickel, *Bikes and Bloomers*, 31–54; Rabinovitch-Fox, *Dressed for Freedom*, 37.

24. "The Bloomer Girl's Wedding," May 21, 1896. Drawing. William H. Walker Cartoon Collection, MC068, Public Policy Papers, Department of Special Collections, Princeton University Library.

25. "Wheelmen and Their Wheels," *Evening Star* (Washington, DC), August 28, 1897, 19.

26. Jungnickel, *Bikes and Bloomers*, 41.

27. Frances E. Willard, *A Wheel within a Wheel: How I Learned to Ride the Bicycle, with Some Reflections by the Way* (New York: F. H. Revell Co., 1895), 74.

28. John Wesley Hanson, *Etiquette and Bicycling, for 1896* (Chicago: American Publishing House, 1896), 366.

29. *Etiquette for Americans by a Woman of Fashion*, 187. For an example, see Sailor hat, 1883, straw and silk, The Metropolitan Museum of Art, Brooklyn Museum Costume Collection at the Metropolitan Museum of Art, New York, 2009.300.2091.

30. "Bicycle Girls and Their Summer Road Gowns," *San Francisco Call*, May 29, 1898, 27.

31. "Thousands Were in Line," *Referee and Cycle Trade Journal*, May 31, 1895, unpaginated.

32. Maria E. Ward, *The Common Sense of Bicycling: Bicycling for Ladies* (New York: Brentano's, 1896), 97.

33. May Bragdon, May Bragdon Diaries, Rare Books, Special Collections and Preservation, Rush Rhees Library, University of Rochester, https://maybragdon.lib.rochester.edu/about.

34. For example, Alice Austen, [Daisy Elliott on a bicycle], ca. 1895. Photograph. Alice Austen Photograph Collection, Historic Richmond Town, 50.015.2513. See Bonnie Yochelson, *Miss Alice Austen and Staten Island's Gilded Age: A Biography in Photographs*, digital exhibit, 2021, Gotham Center for New York City History, https://www.gothamcenter.org/exhibits/alice-austen.

35. See Alice Austen, *E.A.A. & Bicycle*, 1893–1897. Glass plate negative. Historic Richmond Town, 50.015.5197.

36. Alice Austen, *Trude & I Masked, Short Skirts*, 1891. Glass plate negative. Historic Richmond Town, 50.015.5462.

37. See Yochelson, "Alice Austen, Satirist," in *Miss Alice Austen and Staten Island's Gilded Age*, https://www.gothamcenter.org/exhibits/alice-austen/alice-austen-satirist.

38. See Yochelson, "Alice Austen, Satirist."

39. May Bragdon Diaries, December 17, 1896.

40. May Bragdon Diaries, August 28, 1893.

41. May Bragdon Diaries, July 22, 1896.

42. May Bragdon Diaries, August 3, 1900.

43. Andrew Ritchie, "The League of American Wheelmen, Major Taylor and the 'Color Question' in the United States in the 1890s," *Culture, Sport, Society* 6, no. 2/3 (June 1, 2003): 25.

44. Anya Jabour, "How Bicycles Liberated Women in Victorian America," Commonplace, fig. 3, accessed May 10, 2022, http://commonplace.online/article/how-bicycles-liberated-women-in-victorian-america.

45. For example, Hatch Lith. Co. Velocipede Tobacco, ca. 1874. Photograph. Library of Congress (call. no. LOT 10618-30 [P&P]); Velocipede Hair Oil, ca. 1869. Photograph. Library of Congress, call. no. LOT 10632–3 [item] [P&P].

46. "Bicycle Girls and Their Summer Road Gowns," *San Francisco Call*, May 29, 1898, 27.

47. *The Bicycle Rest. Vogue*, March 12, 1896, 190–191 (illus.).

48. "Remington Bicycles," *Vogue*, March 12, 1896, xiv.

49. Sally Ledger, "The New Woman and Feminist Fictions," in *The Cambridge Companion to the Fin de Siècle*, ed. Gail Marshall (Cambridge, UK: Cambridge University Press, 2007), 153.

50. Carolyn L. Kitch, *The Girl on the Magazine Cover: The Origins of Visual Stereotypes in American Mass Media* (Chapel Hill: University of North Carolina Press, 2001), 37–46; Rabinovitch-Fox, *Dressed for Freedom*, 13–21.

51. Dolores Mitchell, "The 'New Woman' as Prometheus: Women Artists Depict Women Smoking," *Woman's Art Journal* 12, no. 1 (Spring/Summer 1991): 3.

52. Rabinovitch-Fox, *Dressed for Freedom*, 15–16.

53. "Imperial Whitener," *Richmond Planet*, June 9, 1900, 8.

54. Rabinovitch-Fox, *Dressed for Freedom*, 22–25.

55. Juliette Harris and Pamela Johnson, eds., *Tenderheaded: A Comb-Bending Collection of Hair Stories* (New York: Pocket Books, 2001), 154.

56. Rabinovitch-Fox, *Dressed for Freedom*, 22–25.

57. Patricia Marks, *Bicycles, Bangs, and Bloomers: The New Woman in the Popular Press* (Lexington: University Press of Kentucky, 1990), 147.

58. Ledger, "The New Woman and Feminist Fictions," 154; Marks, *Bicycles, Bangs, and Bloomers*, 147.

59. For example, "A Pointer on the Side," *Washington Bee*, March 28, 1896, 7.

60. Tracy J. R. Collins, "Athletic Fashion, 'Punch,' and the Creation of the New Woman," *Victorian Periodicals Review* 43, no. 3 (2010): 309–335; Marks, *Bicycles, Bangs, and Bloomers*, 165–166.

61. Keystone View Company. *The New Woman—Wash Day*, ca. 1901. Photograph. Library Company of Philadelphia, P.9998; *Sew on Your Own Buttons, I'm Going for a Ride*, ca. 1899. Photograph. Library Company of Philadelphia, P.9897.

62. William Herman Rau, *The New Woman Barber*, ca. 1897. Photograph. The Library Company of Philadelphia, P.2008.9.

63. Victoria Sherrow, *Encyclopedia of Hair: A Cultural History* (Westport, CT: Greenwood Press, 2006), 138.

64. William A. Woodbury, *Hair Dressing and Tinting: A Text-Book of the Fundamental Principles Showing the Ready Adaptability of the Ever Changing Mode of Wearing the Hair, for Professional and Private Use* (New York: G. W. Dillingham Co., 1915), 13.

65. Bay, *To Tell the Truth Freely*, 76.

66. Bay, *To Tell the Truth Freely*, 82–108.

67. Leigh Raiford, "Ida B. Wells and the Shadow Archive," in *Pictures and Progress: Early Photography and the Making of African American Identity*, ed. Maurice O. Wallace and Shawn Michelle Smith (Durham, NC: Duke University Press, 2012), 303–310.

68. Ida B. Wells, *Southern Horrors: Lynch Law in All Its Phases* (New York: The New York Age Print, 1892).

69. Raiford, "Ida B. Wells and the Shadow Archive," 314.

70. Ida B. Wells, *The Reason Why the Colored American Is Not in the World's Columbian Exposition* (Chicago: Ida B. Wells, 1893).

71. See *Ida B. Wells-Barnett with Her Four Children*, 1909. Photograph. Hanna Holborn Gray Special Collections Research Center, University of Chicago Library.

72. Minnie Fiske in "Magda." Photograph. National Museum of American History, Smithsonian Institution, 234377.

73. Fred Holland Day, *Minnie Maddern Fiske*, 1898. Photograph. Library of Congress, Washington, DC, PH-Day (F.H.), no. 686 (A size) [P&P].

74. *Mrs. Fiske: Tess of the d'Urbervilles*, ca. 1898. Lithograph by Strobridge Lithographing Co., after photograph by Napoleon Sarony. Jay T. Last Collection, The Huntington Library, San Marino, California.

75. House of Worth, Paris, "Wheat Dress," 1901. National Museum of American History, Smithsonian Institution, Washington, DC; gift of Olive Kooken, 234377.

76. See Ernest Haskell (U.S., 1876–1925). *Fiske*, 1900. Drawing by Haskell. Color lithograph by J. Ottmann Lithographing Company, Library of Congress Prints and Photographs Division, Washington, DC, digital ID var 0422 (no reproduction number), http://hdl.loc.gov/loc.pnp/var.0422.

77. William Merritt Chase (U.S. 1849–1916). *Minnie Maddern Fiske*, 1910. Oil on canvas. Museum of the City of New York, Bequest of Daniel Frohman, Esq., 41.50.1325.

CHAPTER 6

1. Nigel Thrift, "Space," *Theory, Culture & Society* 23, no. 2/3 (2006): 143–144; Michel Foucault, *Security, Territory, Population: Lectures at the Collège de France, 1977–78*, ed. Michel Senellart, trans. Graham Burchell (Basingstoke, UK: Palgrave Macmillan, 2014), *passim*.

2. See, for example, Norm Bolotin and Christine Laing, *The World's Columbian Exposition: The Chicago World's Fair of 1893* (Champaign: University of Illinois Press, 2002); Christopher Robert Reed, *All the World Is Here! The Black Presence at White City* (Bloomington: Indiana University Press, 2002); Rachel Boyle, "Types and Beauties: Evaluating and Exoticizing Women on the Midway Plaisance at the 1893 Columbian Exposition," *Journal of the Illinois State Historical Society* 108, no. 1 (2015): 18–19.

3. Carolyn Schiller Johnson, "Public Anthropology 'at the Fair': 1893 Origins, 21st-Century Opportunities," *American Anthropologist* 113, no. 4 (2011): 644–646.

4. Judith K. Brodsky and Ferris Olin, *Junctures in Women's Leadership: The Arts* (New Brunswick, NJ: Rutgers University Press, 2018), 1–21; Paul Greenhalgh, *Ephemeral Vistas: The Expositions Universelles, Great Exhibitions, and World's Fairs, 1851–1939* (Manchester, UK: Manchester University Press, 1988), 178.

5. Anna R. Paddon and Sally Turner, "African Americans and the World's Columbian Exposition," *Illinois Historical Journal* 88, no. 1 (1995): 19–36; John McCluskey, "Journey to Frederick Douglass's Chicago Jubilee: Colored American Day, August 25, 1893," in *Roots of the Black Chicago Renaissance: New Negro Writers, Artists, and Intellectuals, 1893–1930*, ed. Richard A. Courage and Christopher Robert Reed (Urbana: University of Illinois Press, 2021), 42–56.

6. Julie K. Brown, "Missing Persons: Identity Photography and Workers at the 1893 Chicago World's Columbian Exposition," *History of Photography* 44, no. 1 (November 2020): 36–49.

7. Timothy J. Gilfoyle, "White Cities, Linguistic Turns, and Disneylands: The New Paradigms of Urban History," *Reviews in American History* 26, no. 1 (1998): 175.

8. For example, J. W. Buel, *The Magic City: A Massive Portfolio of Original Photographic Views of the Great World's Fair and Its Treasures of Art, Including a Vivid Representation of the Famous Midway Plaisance* (St. Louis, MO: Historical Publishing Co., 1894), *passim*; Teresa Dean, *White City Chips* (Chicago: Warren Publishing Co., 1895), *passim*.

9. Benjamin Cummings Truman, *History of the World's Fair, Being a Complete and Authentic Description of the Columbian Exposition from Its Inception* (New York: E. B. Treat, 1893), 553.

10. *Report of the President to the Board of Directors of the World's Columbian Exposition: Chicago, 1892–1893* (Chicago: Rand, McNally & Co., 1898), 485. There does not appear to have been a hairdresser for women on the fairgrounds.

11. Moses P. Handy, *The Official Directory of the World's Columbian Exposition* (Chicago: W. B. Conkey Co., 1893), 234; Willard A. Smith, ed., *World's Columbian Exposition, 1893: Official Catalogue, Part VII. Transportation Exhibits Building, Annex, Special Building and the Lagoon* (Chicago: W. B. Conkey Co., 1893), 39. There do not appear to be any extant images of the display of hair work, coiffures, and accessories of the toilet in the Manufactures and Liberal Arts Building.

12. *Catalogue of Tiffany & Co's Exhibit* (New York: Tiffany & Co., 1893), 16–17; John Loring, *Tiffany Jewels* (New York: Harry N. Abrams, 1999), 122–143.

13. Truman, *History of the World's Fair*, 219.

14. For types of functional and ornamental combs, see Jen Cruse, *The Comb: Its History and Development a Book by Jen Cruse* (London: Robert Hale & Co., 2007).

15. *World's Columbian Exposition 1893. Official Catalogue: Exhibition of the German Empire* (Berlin: Imperial Commission, 1893), 200–201.

16. "Austria on Display at the Chicago World's Columbian Exposition, 1893: A Collection of Sources," *Journal of Austrian-American History* 1, no. 2 (July 2017): 117–127; Untitled, *American Hairdresser*, June 1896, 14.

17. Ellen D. Bacon, "Hair," in *Report of the Committee on Awards of the World's Columbian Commission* (Washington, DC: Government Printing Office, 1901), 742; Trumbull White and William Igleheart, *The World's Columbian Exposition, Chicago, 1893* (St. Louis: P. W. Ziegler & Co., 1893), 19.

18. Bacon, "Hair," 737–738. Mr. E. Burnham, owner of a large firm in Chicago, was the winner for the United States.

19. *World's Columbian Exposition Illustrated*, April 1893, xiv.

20. Richard J. Murphy, *Authentic Visitors' Guide to the World's Columbian Exposition and Chicago.* (Chicago: Union News Co., 1893), 13, 62, 63.

21. "The Hair Trade: Making Merchandise of the Glory of Woman," *New York Times*, May 15, 1870: 8; "Substitute for Hair," *Houston Daily Union*, November 18, 1870. "A Few Objections to the Use of False Hair," *Manufacturer and Builder: A Practical Journal*, 1873, 163.

22. Broadside for C. S. Dyer and Son, Cincinnati, Ohio, fall 1872. Cincinnati Museum (no accession number); "Imitation of Human Hair," *The Sun* (New York), February 8, 1871.

23. United States Bureau of the Census, *The Foreign Commerce and Navigation of the United States* (Washington, DC: Government Printing Office, 1891/1892), lxii. The calculation: all hair imports (human and nonhuman) $2,408,733; subtracted $159,184 for only human hair.

24. "A Brooklyn Industry," *Brooklyn Eagle*, July 4, 1886, 13; George S. Cole, *A Complete Dictionary of Dry Goods and History of Silk, Cotton, Linen, Wool and Other Fibrous Substances* (Chicago: W. B. Conkey Co., 1892), 173.

25. "Wigs and Wigmakers," *Otsego Farmer* (Otsego, NY), June 30, 1888, 7.

26. White and Igleheart, *The World's Columbian Exposition, Chicago, 1893*, 171, 191–205.

27. Helen Cowie, *Victims of Fashion: Animal Commodities in Victorian Britain* (Cambridge, UK: Cambridge University Press, 2022), 170–173; "Pomades and Oils," *Scientific American*, June 13, 1868, 370.

28. "Pomades and Oils," 370.

29. Halsey Cooley Ives, *The Government Collection of Original Views of the World's Columbian Exposition* (Chicago: Preston Publishing Co., 1895), unpaginated; Mrs. Potter Palmer (Bertha Palmer) et al., *Rand, McNally & Co.'s Handbook of the World's Columbian Exposition* (Chicago: Rand, McNally & Co., 1893), 212.

30. Ives, *The Government Collection of Original Views of the World's Columbian Exposition*, unpaginated.

31. For example, Tudor Jenks, *The Century World's Fair Book for Boys and Girls; Being the Adventures of Harry and Philip with Their Tutor, Mr. Douglass, at the World's Columbian Exposition* (New York: Century Co., 1893).

32. Mary Kavanaugh Oldham Eagle, ed., *The Congress of Women Held in the Woman's Building, World Columbian Exposition, Chicago, U.S.A., 1893 with Portraits, Biographies, and Addresses* (Philadelphia: S. I. Bell, 1894), 518, 558, 592, 598.

33. Boyle, "Types and Beauties," 12–13.

34. "Human Hair," *Eclectic Magazine of Foreign Literature*, June 1853, 207.

35. Celia Thaxter to Elizabeth D. Pierce, March 11, 1873, in Celia Thaxter, *Letters of Celia Thaxter*, ed. Annie Fields and Rose Lamb (Boston: Houghton Mifflin Co., 1895), 45.

36. John Joseph Flinn, *The Best Things to Be Seen at the World's Fair* (Chicago: Columbia Guide Co., 1893), 65, 143–144.

37. C. D. Arnold and H. D. Higinbotham, *Official Views of the World's Columbian Exposition* (Chicago: Press Chicago Photo-gravure Co., 1893), plate 92.

38. John Joseph Flinn, *Official Guide to Midway Plaisance* (Chicago: Columbian Guide Co., 1893), 6–8.

39. "A Harvest of Human Hair," *Walker Lake Bulletin* (Hawthorne, NV), October 13, 1897, 1.

40. Aimé Bouis, "Cheveux et postiches," *Le livre d'or de Marseille, de son commerce et de ses industries* (Marseille: A. Ged, 1907), 256.

41. Johanna Wassholm and Anna Sundelin, "Gendered Encounters in Mobile Trade: Human Hair as a Commodity in the Nordics, 1870–1914," *History of Retailing and Consumption* 6, no. 2 (May 2020): 123.

42. Helen Sheumaker, *Love Entwined: The Curious History of Hairwork in America* (Philadelphia: University of Pennsylvania Press, 2007), 97–99.

43. "False Hair: Where It Comes From," *London Review*, September 23, 1865, 328–330, reprinted in "False Hair, and Where It Comes From," *Godey's Lady's Book and Magazine*, June 1866, 510.

44. Mark Campbell, *Self-Instructor in the Art of Hair Work: Dressing Hair, Making Curls, Switches, Braids, and Hair Jewelry of Every Description* (New York: M. Campbell, 1867), 261.

45. Campbell, *Self-Instructor*, 261.

46. United States Bureau of the Census, *The Foreign Commerce and Navigation of the United States* (Washington, DC: Government Printing Office, 1866/1867), 116.

47. The United States reexported a small amount of uncleaned hair ($1,823 worth) to Bremen, Germany, and to England. United States Bureau of the Census, *The Foreign Commerce and Navigation of the United States* (1866/1867), 100.

48. "Human Hair Trade," *Brooklyn Daily Eagle*, May 18, 1866, 12; "The Trade in Human Hair," *Scientific American*, March 27, 1869, 198; "The Trade in Locks," *Brooklyn Daily Eagle*, June 21, 1869, 12.

49. "The Trade in Human Hair," *New York Times*, May 6, 1877, 9.

50. Zdatny, *Fashion, Work, and Politics in Modern France*, 7.

51. Zdatny, *Fashion, Work, and Politics in Modern France*, 7.

52. "The Trade in Human Hair," *New York Times*, May 6, 1877, 9.

53. "The Trade in Human Hair," *New York Times*, December 13, 1880, 2.

54. "The Human Hair Industry in Paris," *Scientific American*, April 28, 1894, 259.

55. *Report of the Committee on Awards of the World's Columbian Commission* (Washington, DC: Government Printing Office, 1901), 731–737.

56. *Report of the Committee on Awards of the World's Columbian Commission*, 738–740.

57. *Report of the Committee on Awards of the World's Columbian Commission*, 739.

58. United States Bureau of the Census, *The Foreign Commerce and Navigation of the United States* (1891/1892), lxii, 732. I thank Gulnar Nagashybayeva for assistance with this information.

59. "Human Hair," 207; "A Harvest of Human Hair," *Walker Lake Bulletin* (Hawthorne, NV), October 13, 1897: 1.

60. *Doggett's New-York City Directory* (New York: J. Doggett Jr., 1845/1846), *passim*. See, for example, "Human Hair," *Perrysburg Journal* (Perrysburg, OH), May 20, 1854, 1.

61. Alexander Rowland, *The Human Hair, Popularly and Physiologically Considered with Special Reference to Its Preservation, Improvement and Adornment, and the Various Modes of Its Decoration in All Countries* (London: Piper Brothers Co., 1853), 158.

62. "Human Hair as an Article of Trade," *Southern Planter*, February 1859, 107.

63. "The Trade in Human Hair," 198.

64. "Home and Foreign Trade," *New York Times*, August 16, 1875, 5.

65. United States Bureau of the Census, *The Foreign Commerce and Navigation of the United States* (Washington, DC: Government Printing Office, 1874/1875, published in 1876), 700.

66. United States Bureau of the Census, *The Foreign Commerce and Navigation of the United States*, 739–740.

67. United States Bureau of the Census, *The Foreign Commerce and Navigation of the United States*, 700.

68. United States Bureau of the Census, *The Foreign Commerce and Navigation of the United States*.

69. "A Few Objections to the Use of False Hair," 163.

70. United States Department of the Treasury, Bureau of Statistics. *Annual Report and Statements of the Chief of the Bureau of Statistics on the Commerce and Navigation of the United States for the Fiscal Year Ended 1882* (Washington, DC: Government Printing Office, 1882), 58.

71. Broadside for C. S. Dyer and Son, importers of human hair, 1872, Cincinnati Museum, no accession number.

72. "Professions for Women," *Harper's Bazar*, October 8, 1870, 647.

73. Campbell, *Self-Instructor*, 261; "False Hair, and Where It Comes From," 508–510.

74. James Greenwood, *In Strange Company; Being the Experiences of a Roving Correspondent* (London: Henry S. King & Co., 1873), 145.

75. Charles Henri Leonard, *The Hair: Its Growth, Care, Diseases and Treatment* (Detroit, MI: C. Henri Leonard, Medical Book Publisher, 1881), 10.

76. Campbell, *Self-Instructor*, 261.

77. "Buying Human Hair," *Weekly Messenger* (St. Martinsville, LA), March 23, 1895, 2; Campbell, *Self-Instructor*, 261.

78. "False Hair: Where It Comes From," *London Review*, September 23, 1865, 330; "Human Hair Trade," *Brooklyn Daily Eagle*, May 18, 1866, 12; "Market for Human Hair," *Kootenai Herald* (Kootenai, ID), July 25, 1891, 1; Rowland, *The Human Hair*, 158.

79. Untitled, *American Hairdresser*, December 1896, 3.

80. Osborne, Garrett, and Co., *Hairdressers' Weekly Journal*, July 28, 1883, 491.

81. Mrs. C. Thompson, ed., *Mrs. C. Thompson, Importer and Manufacturer of Wigs, Hair Jewelry, Ornamental Hair Work . . .* (New York: Mrs. C. Thompson, 1883), 42.

82. "The Hair Trade:" Making Merchandise of the Glory of Woman," *New York Times*, May 15, 1870: 8; Cole, *A Complete Dictionary of Dry Goods and History of Silk, Cotton, Linen, Wool and Other Fibrous Substances*, 174.

83. Wassholm and Sundelin, "Gendered Encounters in Mobile Trade," 118–136.

84. Wassholm and Sundelin, "Gendered Encounters in Mobile Trade," 123.

85. Wassholm and Sundelin, "Gendered Encounters in Mobile Trade," 123.

86. Wassholm and Sundelin, "Gendered Encounters in Mobile Trade," 120.

87. Wassholm and Sundelin, "Gendered Encounters in Mobile Trade," 121.

88. Wassholm and Sundelin, "Gendered Encounters in Mobile Trade," 123–124.

89. For example, *Monthly Report of the Deputy Special Commissioner of the Revenue, in Charge of the Bureau of Statistics, Treasury Department*, September 1869, 134, Warshaw Collection of Business Americana, Category Commission Merchants box 3, folder 6, National Museum of American History, Smithsonian Institution.

90. Sheumaker, *Love Entwined*, 151–152; Wassholm and Sundelin, "Gendered Encounters in Mobile Trade," 124–125.

91. Emma Tarlo, *Entanglement: The Secret Lives of Hair* (London: Oneworld Publications, 2016), 42.

92. Tarlo, *Entanglement*, 41.

93. Sheumaker, *Love Entwined*, 154; Wassholm and Sundelin, "Gendered Encounters in Mobile Trade," 126; Zdatny, *Fashion, Work, and Politics in Modern France*, 8.

94. Tarlo, *Entanglement*, 50–51; Zdatny, *Fashion, Work, and Politics in Modern France*, 7–8.

95. Wassholm and Sundelin, "Gendered Encounters in Mobile Trade," 128.

96. "The Hair Trade: Making Merchandise of the Glory of Woman," 8.

97. "Gleanings and Gossip," *Hartford Daily Courant*, October 26, 1870.

98. "Human Hair—A Trade and Its Tricks," *Phrenological Journal and Science of Health* (June 1873): 56. I thank Kathy Woodrell for her assistance locating this article.

99. "Human Hair Market," *Daily Independent* (Elko, NV), November 16, 1889, 2.

100. "Human Hair Market," 2.

101. Untitled, *American Hairdresser*, January 1896, 20–21.

102. Greenwood, *In Strange Company*, 143–144.

103. Rowland, *The Human Hair*, 159–160.

104. "Mercantile Miscellanies: Economy and Liberality," *Merchants' Magazine and Commercial Review*, March 1, 1863, 267; "The Trade in Human Hair," 198.; "Gathering Human Hair in France," *New York Times*, August 25, 1882, 3.

105. Charles Géniaux, "The Human Hair Harvest in Brittany," *Wide World Magazine*, February 1900), 430–436.

106. Campbell, *Self-Instructor*, 261–262; "False Hair: Where It Comes From," 510; Alf Hiltebeitel and Barbara D. Miller, eds., *Hair: Its Power and Meaning in Asian Cultures* (Albany: State University of New York Press, 1998), 144; "The Human Hair Industry in Paris," 259.

107. "A Few Objections to the Use of False Hair," 163; Hiltebeitel and Miller, *Hair*, 145; "The Trade in Human Hair," 198.

108. "The Trade in Human Hair," 198.

109. Leonard, *The Hair*, 10.

110. "Where False Hair Is Obtained," *Russellville Democrat* (Russellville, AR), December 9, 1880, 1; "Human Hair from Canton," *New York Times*, September 28, 1890, 17.

111. "Where False Hair Is Obtained," 1.

112. "False Bangs," *Salt Lake Herald*, April 24, 1883, 2.

113. Tarlo, *Entanglement*, 56–59.

114. "The Chinese Trade in Human Hair," June 27, 1877, 5, in United States Bureau of the Census, *The Foreign Commerce and Navigation of the United States* (1874/1875), 78.

115. "Chinese Hair in Puffs: Big Trade Grows Up under Demand of American Women," *New York Times*, May 15, 1909, 7; "Decline of a Strange Trade," *New York Times*, October 15, 1916, SM18.

116. For coarse hair, "L. Shaw," *New York Herald*, July 13, 1873, 1; for Mexican hair, "The Commerce in Human Hair," *Times* (London), October 10, 1868, 4.

117. "The Human Hair Industry in Paris," 259.

118. "Blonde Hair and Other," *New York Times*, September 28, 1890, 8; "Human Hair Supplies," *Dodgeville Chronicle* (Dodgeville, WI), January 15, 1875, 4; "The Trade in False Hair," *New York Times*, July 19, 1882, 3.

119. "Back Hair," *New York Times*, October 9, 1884, 4.

120. "Human Hair Supplies: An Impending Crisis in the Market," *New York Times*, December 13, 1874, 4.

121. "False Hair: Where It Comes From," 329.

122. "The Trade in Human Hair," 198.

123. Edwin Creer and Alfred M. Sutton, *Boardwork; or, The Art of Wigmaking* (London: R. Hovenden, 1903), 24–25.

124. "Local Items," *Daily Phoenix* (Columbia, SC), June 5, 1872, 2.

125. For hairwork and jewelry, see Sheumaker, *Love Entwined, passim.*

126. Addie L. Contrelli to Lenette E. Wilson, October 22, 1883, Addie L. Contrelli Letters, 1883–1884, The Newberry Library, Chicago.

127. Addie L. Contrelli to Lenette E. Wilson, August 29, 1883.

128. Addie L. Contrelli to Lenette E. Wilson, October 1, 1883.

129. Addie L. Contrelli to Lenette E. Wilson, August 29, 1883.

130. Addie L. Contrelli to Lenette E. Wilson, January 9, 1884.

131. Kevin Hannam, Mimi Sheller, and John Urry, "Editorial: Mobilities, Immobilities and Moorings," *Mobilities* 1, no. 1 (March 1, 2006): 5.

132. Addie L. Contrelli to Lenette E. Wilson, August 29, 1883.

133. James Faulconbridge and Allison Hui, "Traces of a Mobile Field: Ten Years of Mobilities Research," *Mobilities* 11, no. 1 (January 1, 2016): 5; Hannam, Sheller, and Urry, "Editorial: Mobilities, Immobilities and Moorings," 1.

CHAPTER 7

1. Yi-Fu Tuan, *Space and Place: The Perspective of Experience* (Minneapolis: University of Minnesota Press, 1977), 4.

2. Aimé Bouis, "Cheveux et postiches," *Le livre d'or de Marseille, de son commerce et de ses industries* (Marseille: A. Ged, 1907), 256.

BIBLIOGRAPHY

"Accessories, Backgrounds, Drapery, and Hair." *Photographic Times and American Photographer* 9, no. 102 (December 1879): 275.

Alcott, Louisa May. *Little Women: A Story for Girls*. London: Religious Tract Society, 1912.

Alcott, Louisa May. *Little Women: or, Meg, Jo, Beth, and Amy*. Boston: Roberts Brothers, 1880.

Alcott, Louisa May. *Little Women: or, Meg, Jo, Beth, and Amy*. Boston: Roberts Brothers, 1890.

Alcott, Louisa May. *Little Women: or, Meg, Jo, Beth, and Amy*. Boston: Little, Brown, 1896.

Alcott, Louisa May. *Little Women: or, Meg, Jo, Beth, and Amy*. Boston: Little, Brown, 1918.

Alexander, Leslie M., and Walter C. Rucker. *Encyclopedia of African American History*. Vol. 1. Santa Barbara, CA: ABC-CLIO, 2010.

Almila, Anna-Mari. "What Is 'Space' for Dress? Theoretical Considerations of a Spatial Turn for Fashion Studies." *International Journal of Fashion Studies* 8, no. 1 (April 2021): 7–23.

"A Modern Masquerade." *Munsey's Magazine*, April–September 1897, 195–196.

Alpert, Arlene, Margrit Altenburg, Diane Carol Bailey, Letha Barnes, and Lisha Barnes. *Milady's Standard Cosmetology*. Boston: Cengage Learning, 2007.

Andrews, Eliza Frances. Diary, 1870–1872, August 15, 1870. Andrews Family Papers, University of Tennessee at Chattanooga Special Collections, MS-004-02-08.

Andrews, Eliza Frances. *The War-Time Journal of a Georgia Girl, 1864–1865*. Edited by Spencer B. King Jr. New York: D. Appleton and Co., 1908.

Arabindan-Kesson, Anna. *Black Bodies, White Gold: Art, Cotton, and Commerce in the Atlantic World*. Durham, NC: Duke University Press, 2021.

Arabindan-Kesson, Anna. "Dressed Up and Laying Bare: Fashion in the Shadow of the Market." *Vestoj* 9 (undated): unpaginated.

Arnold, C. D., and H. D. Higinbotham. *Official Views of the World's Columbian Exposition*. Chicago: Press Chicago Photo-gravure Co., 1893.

"Austria on Display at the Chicago World's Columbian Exposition, 1893: A Collection of Sources." *Journal of Austrian-American History* 1, no. 2 (2017): 117–127.

Bacon, Ellen D. "Hair." In *Report of the Committee on Awards of the World's Columbian Commission*. Washington, DC: Government Printing Office, 1901.

Baldwin, Davarian L. *Chicago's New Negroes: Modernity, the Great Migration, and Black Urban Life*. Chapel Hill: University of North Carolina Press, 2007.

Bashor, Will. *Marie Antoinette's Head: The Royal Hairdresser, the Queen, and the Revolution*. Guilford, CT: Lyons Press, 2013.

Bastos, Cristiana, Andre Novoa, and Noel B. Salazar. "Mobile Labour: An Introduction." *Mobilities* 16, no. 2 (March 4, 2021): 155–163.

Bay, Mia. *To Tell the Truth Freely: The Life of Ida B. Wells*. New York: Farrar, Straus and Giroux, 2010.

Bay, Mia. *Traveling Black: A Story of Race and Resistance*. Cambridge, MA: Belknap Press, 2021.

Beaton, Cecil. *The Glass of Fashion*. Garden City, NY: Doubleday & Co., 1954.

The Bicycle Rest. *Vogue*, March 12, 1896, 190–191 (illus.).

Biddle-Perry, Geraldine, ed. *A Cultural History of Hair*. 6 vols. London: Bloomsbury Academic, 2019.

Biddle-Perry, Geraldine, and Sarah Cheang, eds. *Hair: Styling, Culture and Fashion*. Oxford: Berg, 2008.

Blatt, Martin Henry, Donald Yacovone, and Thomas J. Brown, eds. *Hope and Glory: Essays on the Legacy of the Fifty-Fourth Massachusetts Regiment*. Amherst: University of Massachusetts Press, 2001.

Block, Elizabeth L. *Dressing Up: The Women Who Influenced French Fashion*. Cambridge, MA: MIT Press, 2021.

Block, Elizabeth L. "Winslow Homer and Women's Bathing Practices in *Eagle Head, Manchester, Massachusetts (High Tide)*." *American Art* 32, no. 2 (June 2018): 100–115.

Block, Sharon. *Colonial Complexions: Race and Bodies in Eighteenth-Century America*. Philadelphia: University of Pennsylvania Press, 2018.

Boggis, JerriAnne, Eve Allegra Raimon, and Barbara A. White, eds. *Harriet Wilson's New England: Race, Writing, and Region*. Durham, NH: University of New Hampshire Press and Hanover, NH: University Press of New England, 2007.

Bogin, Ruth. "Sarah Parker Remond: Black Abolitionist from Salem." *Essex Institute Historical Collections* 110, no. 22 (April 1974): 120–150.

Bolotin, Norm, and Christine Laing. *The World's Columbian Exposition: The Chicago World's Fair of 1893*. Champaign: University of Illinois Press, 2002.

Bouis, Aimé. "Cheveux et postiches." *Le livre d'or de Marseille, de son commerce et de ses industries*. Marseille: A. Ged, 1907.

Bowles, Juliette. "Natural Hair Styling: A Symbol and Function of African-American Women's Self-Creation." Master's thesis, College of William and Mary, 1990.

Boyd's Business Directory of the State of Maryland. Washington, DC: William H. Boyd, 1875.

Boyle, Rachel. "Types and Beauties: Evaluating and Exoticizing Women on the Midway Plaisance at the 1893 Columbian Exposition." *Journal of the Illinois State Historical Society* 108, no. 1 (2015): 10–31.

Bragdon, May. May Bragdon Diaries. Rare Books, Special Collections and Preservation, Rush Rhees Library, University of Rochester. https://maybragdon.lib.rochester.edu/about.

Brevik-Zender, Heidi. *Fashioning Spaces: Mode and Modernity in Late-Nineteenth-Century Paris*. Toronto: University of Toronto Press, 2015.

Bridgeford, Frank C. *Barber Instructor and Toilet Manual*. Kansas City, MO: Frank C. Bridgeford, 1900.

Briggs, Emily Edson. *The Olivia Letters*. New York: Neale Publishing Co., 1906.

Bristol Jr., Douglas Walter. *Knights of the Razor: Black Barbers in Slavery and Freedom*. Baltimore, MD: Johns Hopkins University Press, 2009.

Brodsky, Judith K., and Ferris Olin. *Junctures in Women's Leadership: The Arts*. New Brunswick, NJ: Rutgers University Press, 2018.

Brown, Julie K. "Missing Persons: Identity Photography and Workers at the 1893 Chicago World's Columbian Exposition." *History of Photography* 44, no. 1 (November 2020): 36–49.

Brown, William Wells. *The Black Man: His Antecedents, His Genius, and His Achievements*. New York: Thomas Hamilton, 1863.

Browne, Peter A. *The Classification of Mankind, by the Hair and Wool of Their Heads: With the Nomenclature of Human Hybrids*. Philadelphia: J. H. Jones, 1852.

Browne, Peter A. *Trichologia Mammalium; or, A Treatise on the Organization, Properties and Uses of Hair and Wool Together with an Essay upon the Raising and Breeding of Sheep*. Philadelphia: J. H. Jones, 1853.

Buel, J. W. *The Magic City: A Massive Portfolio of Original Photographic Views of the Great World's Fair and Its Treasures of Art, Including a Vivid Representation of the Famous Midway Plaisance*. St. Louis, MO: Historical Publishing Co., 1894.

Bundles, A'Lelia Perry. *On Her Own Ground: The Life and Times of Madam C. J. Walker*. New York: Scribner, 2001.

Byrd, Ayana D., and Lori Tharps. *Hair Story: Untangling the Roots of Black Hair in America*. New York: St. Martin's Press, 2014. First published 2001.

Calvert, Karin. "The Function of Fashion in Eighteenth-Century America." In *Of Consuming Interests: The Style of Life in the Eighteenth Century*, edited by Cary Carson, Ronald Hoffman, and Peter J. Albert, 263–270. Charlottesville: Published for the United States Capitol Historical Society by the University Press of Virginia, 1994.

Camp, Stephanie M. H. *Closer to Freedom: Enslaved Women and Everyday Resistance in the Plantation South*. Chapel Hill: University of North Carolina Press, 2006.

Campbell, John. *Negro-Mania: Being an Examination of the Falsely Assumed Equality of the Various Races of Men*. Philadelphia: Campbell & Powers, 1851.

Campbell, Mark. *Self-Instructor in the Art of Hair Work: Dressing Hair, Making Curls, Switches, Braids, and Hair Jewelry of Every Description*. New York: M. Campbell, 1867.

Carpenter, Frank G. *Carp's Washington*. New York: McGraw-Hill, 1960.

Carson, Cary, Ronald Hoffman, and Peter J. Albert, eds. *Of Consuming Interests: The Style of Life in the Eighteenth Century*. Charlottesville: Published for the United States Capitol Historical Society by the University Press of Virginia, 1994.

Catalogue of Tiffany & Co's Exhibit. New York: Tiffany & Co., 1893.

Chadwick, F., J. Kelley, Ridgely Hunt, John H. Gould, William H. Rideing, and A. E. Seaton. *Ocean Steamships: A Popular Account of Their Construction, Development, Management and Appliances*. New York: C. Scribner's Sons, 1891.

Cheang, Sarah. "Roots: Hair and Race." In *Hair: Styling, Culture and Fashion*, edited by Geraldine Biddle-Perry and Sarah, 27–42. Oxford: Berg, 2008.

Cheang, Sarah, and Geraldine Biddle-Perry. "Conclusion: Hair and Human Identity." In *Hair: Styling, Culture and Fashion*, edited by Geraldine Biddle-Perry and Sarah Cheang, 252. Oxford: Berg, 2008.

Chrisman-Campbell, Kimberly. *Fashion Victims: Dress at the Court of Louis XVI and Marie-Antoinette*. New Haven, CT: Yale University Press, 2015.

Clark, Jessica P. *The Business of Beauty: Gender and the Body in Modern London*. London: Bloomsbury Visual Arts, 2020.

Cobb, Jasmine Nichole. *New Growth: The Art and Texture of Black Hair*. The Visual Arts of Africa and Its Diasporas. Durham, NC: Duke University Press, 2022.

Cobb, Jasmine Nichole. *Picture Freedom: Remaking Black Visuality in the Early Nineteenth Century*. America and the Long Nineteenth Century. New York: New York University Press, 2015.

Cocuzza, Dominique. "Stella Blum Grant Report: The Dress of Free Women of Color in New Orleans, 1780–1840." *Dress* 27, no. 1 (January 1, 2000): 78–87.

Cole, George S. *A Complete Dictionary of Dry Goods and History of Silk, Cotton, Linen, Wool and Other Fibrous Substances*. Chicago: W. B. Conkey Co., 1892.

Collins, Tracy J. R. "Athletic Fashion, 'Punch,' and the Creation of the New Woman." *Victorian Periodicals Review* 43, no. 3 (2010): 309–335.

"Combing Cape." *Godey's Lady's Book*, August 1890, 168.

"The Coming Bleach." *Scientific American* 44, no. 20, May 14, 1881, 314.

Connolly, Brian, and Marisa Fuentes. "Introduction: From Archives of Slavery to Liberated Futures?" *History of the Present* 6, no. 2 (2016): 105–116.

Contrelli, Addie L. Addie L. Contrelli Letters, 1883–1884. The Newberry Library, Chicago.

Cooke, Maud C. *Social Life: or, The Manners and Customs of Polite Society, Containing the Rules of Etiquette for All Occasions*. Philadelphia: Co-operative Publishing Co., 1896.

Corson, Richard. *Fashions in Hair: The First Five Thousand Years*. 6th ed. London: P. Owen, 1980. First published 1965 by Hastings House (New York).

Cowie, Helen. *Victims of Fashion: Animal Commodities in Victorian Britain*. Cambridge, UK: Cambridge University Press, 2022.

Cox, Caroline. *Good Hair Days: A History of British Hairstyling*. London: Quartet Books, 1999.

Creer, Edwin, and Alfred M. Sutton. *Boardwork; or, The Art of Wigmaking*. London: R. Hovenden, 1903.

Crenshaw, Kimberlé. *Defending the C.R.O.W.N.: Life, Liberty, and the Pursuit of Nappyness, Intersectionality Matters with Kimberlé Crenshaw*. Podcast. https://soundcloud.com/intersectionality-matters/ep-7-defending-the-crown-life-liberty-and-the-pursuit-of-nappyness.

Crewe, Louise. *The Geographies of Fashion: Consumption, Space, and Value*. London: Bloomsbury Academic, 2017.

Cross, Louisa. "Fashionable Hair in the Eighteenth Century: Theatricality and Display." In *Hair: Styling, Culture and Fashion*, edited by Geraldine Biddle-Perry and Sarah Cheang, 15–26. Oxford: Berg, 2008.

Cruse, Jen. *The Comb: Its History and Development a Book by Jen Cruse*. London: Robert Hale & Co., 2007.

"Current Notes." *Lippincott's Monthly Magazine*, November 1890, 727.

"The Dangers of Hairdressing." *The Hospital: A Journal of the Medical Sciences and Hospital Administration* 22, no. 566 (July 31, 1897): 295–296.

Dash, Paul. "Black Hair Culture, Politics and Change." *International Journal of Inclusive Education* 10, no. 1 (January 1, 2006): 27–37.

de Aguirre, Gertrude G. *Women in the Business World; or, Hints and Helps to Prosperity*. Boston: Arena Publishing Co., 1894.

Dean, Teresa. *White City Chips*. Chicago: Warren Publishing Co., 1895.

Doggett's New-York City Directory. New York: J. Doggett Jr., 1845/1846.

Dudden, Faye E. *Serving Women: Household Service in Nineteenth-Century America*. Middletown, CT: Wesleyan University Press; Scranton, PA: distributed by Harper & Row, 1983.

Eagle, Mary Kavanaugh Oldham, ed. *The Congress of Women Held in the Woman's Building, World Columbian Exposition, Chicago, U.S.A., 1893 with Portraits, Biographies, and Addresses*. Philadelphia: S. I. Bell, 1894.

Ellington, Tameka N., ed. *Black Hair in a White World*. Kent, OH: Kent State University Press, 2023.

Ellington, Tameka N., Joseph L. Underwood, Sarah Rogers-Lafferty, eds. *Textures: The History and Art of Black Hair*. Kent, OH: Kent State University Museum, 2020.

Ellis, Clifton, and Rebecca Ginsburg, eds. *Cabin, Quarter, Plantation: Architecture and Landscapes of North American Slavery*. New Haven, CT: Yale University Press, 2010.

Etiquette for Americans by a Woman of Fashion. Chicago: H. S. Stone and Co., 1898.

"False Hair, and Where It Comes From." *Godey's Lady's Book and Magazine*, June 1866, 508–510.

Faulconbridge, James, and Allison Hui. "Traces of a Mobile Field: Ten Years of Mobilities Research." *Mobilities* 11, no. 1 (January 1, 2016): 5.

Federal Writers' Project: Slave Narrative Project. Manuscript/Mixed Material, Library of Congress, 1936–1938.

Festa, Lynn. "Fashion and Adornment." In *A Cultural History of Hair in the Age of Enlightenment*, edited by Margaret K. Powell and Joseph Roach. London: Bloomsbury Academic, 2019.

Festa, Lynn. "Personal Effects: Wigs and Possessive Individualism in the Long Eighteenth Century." *Eighteenth-Century Life* 29, no. 2 (April 1, 2005): 47–90.

"A Few Objections to the Use of False Hair." *Manufacturer and Builder: A Practical Journal,* 1873, 163.

"A Few Words with Our Correspondents." *Godey's Lady's Book*, October 1864, 354.

Fineman, Mia. *Faking It: Manipulated Photography before Photoshop*. New York: Metropolitan Museum of Art, distributed by Yale University Press, 2012.

Flinn, John Joseph. *The Best Things to Be Seen at the World's Fair*. Chicago: Columbian Guide Co., 1893.

Flinn, John Joseph. *Official Guide to Midway Plaisance*. Chicago: Columbian Guide Co., 1893.

Florek, Olivia Gruber. "'I Am a Slave to My Hair': Empress Elisabeth of Austria, Fetishism, and Nineteenth-Century Austrian Sexuality." *Modern Austrian Literature* 42, no. 2 (June 2009): 1–15.

Foreman, P. Gabrielle. "Recovered Autobiographies and the Marketplace: Our Nig's Generic Genealogies and Harriet Wilson's Entrepreneurial Enterprise." In *Harriet Wilson's New England: Race, Writing, and Region*, edited by JerriAnne Boggis, Eve Allegra Raimon, and Barbara A. White. Durham, NH: University of New Hampshire Press and Hanover: Published by University Press of New England, 2007.

Fort, Bernadette, ed. "Hair." Special issue, *Eighteenth-Century Studies* 38, no. 1 (Fall 2004).

Foster, Helen Bradley. *"New Raiments of Self": African American Clothing in the Antebellum South*. Oxford: Berg, 1997.

Foucault, Michel. *Security, Territory, Population: Lectures at the Collège de France, 1977–78*. Edited by Michel Senellart. Translated by Graham Burchell. Basingstoke, UK: Palgrave Macmillan, 2014.

Fox-Amato, Matthew. *Exposing Slavery: Photography, Human Bondage, and the Birth of Modern Visual Politics in America*. New York: Oxford University Press, 2019.

Freeman, Martin H. "The Educational Wants of the Free Colored People." *Anglo-African Magazine* 1, no. 1, January 1859, 116–117.

Galke, Laura J. "Tressed for Success: Male Hair Care and Wig Hair Curlers at George Washington's Childhood Home." *Winterthur Portfolio* 52, no. 2/3 (June 1, 2018): 85–135.

Géniaux, Charles. "The Human Hair Harvest in Brittany." *Wide World Magazine*, February 1900, 430–436.

Gilfoyle, Timothy J. "White Cities, Linguistic Turns, and Disneylands: The New Paradigms of Urban History." *Reviews in American History* 26, no. 1 (1998): 175–204.

Gill, Tiffany M. *Beauty Shop Politics: African American Women's Activism in the Beauty Industry.* Women in American History. Champaign: University of Illinois Press, 2010.

Gitter, Elisabeth G. "The Power of Women's Hair in the Victorian Imagination." *Publications of the Modern Language Association of America* 99, no. 5 (October 1984): 936–954.

Goncourt, Edmond de, and Jules de Goncourt. *Journal: Mémoires de la vie littéraire.* Vol. 4. Paris: Fasquelle, Flammarion, 1956.

Gonzalez, Aston. *Visualizing Equality: African American Rights and Visual Culture in the Nineteenth Century.* Chapel Hill: University of North Carolina Press, 2020.

Graham, Lawrence. *The Senator and the Socialite: The True Story of America's First Black Dynasty.* New York: Harper Perennial, 2007.

Greenhalgh, Paul. *Ephemeral Vistas: The Expositions Universelles, Great Exhibitions, and World's Fairs, 1851–1939.* Manchester, UK: Manchester University Press, 1988.

Greenwood, James. *In Strange Company; Being the Experiences of a Roving Correspondent.* London: Henry S. King & Co., 1873.

Grier, Katherine C. *Culture and Comfort: Parlor Making and Middle-Class Identity, 1850–1930.* Washington, DC: Smithsonian Institution Press, 1997.

Guroff, Margaret. *The Mechanical Horse: How the Bicycle Reshaped American Life.* Austin: University of Texas Press, 2016.

Gustav Knecht Manufacturing Co. *Price List and Barbers' Reference Book of Gust. Knecht M'f'g Co.* Chicago: Goes & Quensel, 1888–1889.

"The Hair." *Scientific American,* April 3, 1852, 229.

"Hairdressing." *Vogue,* June 22, 1899, ii.

Hannam, Kevin, Mimi Sheller, and John Urry. "Editorial: Mobilities, Immobilities and Moorings." *Mobilities* 1, no. 1 (March 1, 2006): 1–22.

Hanson, John Wesley. *Etiquette and Bicycling, for 1896.* Chicago: American Publishing House, 1896.

Harris, Juliette. "Hair and Hairstyles." In *World of a Slave: Encyclopedia of the Material Life of Slaves in the United States,* edited by Martha B. Katz-Hyman and Kym S. Rice, 265–271. Santa Barbara, CA: Greenwood, 2011.

Harris, Juliette, and Pamela Johnson, eds. *Tenderheaded: A Comb-Bending Collection of Hair Stories.* New York: Pocket Books, 2001.

Hartley, Florence. *The Ladies' Book of Etiquette, and Manual of Politeness.* Boston: G. W. Cottrell, 1860.

Hartman, Saidiya. "Venus in Two Acts." *Small Axe* 26 (June 2008): 1–14.

Haulman, Kate. *The Politics of Fashion in Eighteenth-Century America.* Chapel Hill: University of North Carolina Press, 2011.

Heath, Barbara. "Space and Place within Plantation Quarters in Virginia, 1700–1825." In *Cabin, Quarter, Plantation: Architecture and Landscapes of North American Slavery*, edited by Clifton Ellis and Rebecca Ginsburg, 157–176. New Haven, CT: Yale University Press, 2010.

Heaton, Sarah, ed. *A Cultural History of Hair in the Age of Empire*. London: Bloomsbury Academic, 2019.

Herzig, Rebecca M. *Plucked: A History of Hair Removal*. New York: New York University Press, 2015.

Hiltebeitel, Alf, and Barbara D. Miller, eds. *Hair: Its Power and Meaning in Asian Cultures*. Albany: State University of New York Press, 1998.

Holland, Juanita. "'Co-Workers in the Kingdom of Culture': Edward Mitchell Bannister and the Boston Community of African-American Artists, 1848–1901." PhD diss., Columbia University, 1998.

Holliday, Ruth, and John Hassard, eds. *Contested Bodies*. London: Routledge, 2001.

Hubert Jr., Philip G., et al. *The Woman's Book, Dealing Practically with the Modern Conditions of Home-Life, Self-Support, Education, Opportunities, and Every-Day Problems*. 2 vols. New York: Charles Scribner's Sons, 1894.

Huggett, Renée. *Hair-Styles and Head Dresses*. London: Batsford Academic and Educational, 1982.

"Human Hair." *Eclectic Magazine of Foreign Literature* 29, no. 2, June 1853, 207.

"Human Hair—A Trade and Its Tricks." *Phrenological Journal and Science of Health* (June 1873): 56.

"The Human Hair Industry in Paris." *Scientific American*, April 28, 1894, 259.

"Ingersoll's Mechanical Brush." *Scientific American*, June 15, 1861, 384.

Ives, Halsey Cooley. *The Government Collection of Original Views of the World's Columbian Exposition*. Chicago: Preston Publishing Co., 1895.

Jabour, Anya. "How Bicycles Liberated Women in Victorian America." Commonplace. Accessed May 10, 2022.

Jacobs, Harriet A. *Incidents in the Life of a Slave Girl*. Boston: Published for the author, 1861.

Jenks, Tudor. *The Century World's Fair Book for Boys and Girls; Being the Adventures of Harry and Philip with Their Tutor, Mr. Douglass, at the World's Columbian Exposition*. New York: Century Co., 1893.

Johnson, Carolyn Schiller. "Public Anthropology 'at the Fair': 1893 Origins, 21st-Century Opportunities." *American Anthropologist* 113, no. 4 (2011): 644–646.

Johnson, Tabora A., and Teiahsha Bankhead. "Hair It Is: Examining the Experiences of Black Women with Natural Hair." *Open Journal of Social Sciences* 2, no. 1 (January 2014): 86–100.

Jolly, Penny Howell. *Hair: Untangling a Social History*. Saratoga Springs, NY: Frances Young Tang Teaching Museum and Art Gallery at Skidmore College, 2004.

Jones, L. Howard. *The Barbers' Manual*. McComb, OH: Gospel Way and Food Print, 1898.

Jones-Rogers, Stephanie E. *They Were Her Property: White Women as Slave Owners in the American South* (New Haven, CT: Yale University Press, 2019).

Jungnickel, Kat. *Bikes and Bloomers: Victorian Women Inventors and Their Extraordinary Cycle Wear*. London: Goldsmiths Press, 2018.

Kahn, Eve M. *Forever Seeing New Beauties: The Forgotten Impressionist Mary Rogers Williams, 1857–1907*. Middletown, CT: Wesleyan University Press, 2019.

Katz-Hyman, Martha B., and Kym S. Rice, eds. *World of a Slave: Encyclopedia of the Material Life of Slaves in the United States*. Santa Barbara, CA: Greenwood, 2011.

Keckley, Elizabeth. *Behind the Scenes: or, Thirty Years a Slave, and Four Years in the White House*. New York: G. W. Carleton & Co., 1868.

Kemble, Frances Ann. *Further Records 1848–1883: A Series of Letters by Frances Ann Kemble*. New York: Henry Holt and Co., 1891.

Kemble, Frances Ann. *Journal of a Residence on a Georgian Plantation in 1838–39*. New York: Harper & Brothers, 1863.

Kemble, Frances Ann. *Records of a Girlhood*. 2nd ed. New York: Henry Holt and Co., 1883, 132.

Kitch, Carolyn L. *The Girl on the Magazine Cover: The Origins of Visual Stereotypes in American Mass Media*. Chapel Hill: University of North Carolina Press, 2001.

Knowles, Katie. "The Fabric of Fast Fashion: Enslaved Wearers and Makers as Designers in the American Fashion System." In *Black Designers in American Fashion*, edited by Elizabeth Way, 13–28. London: Bloomsbury Visual Arts, 2021.

Kochs, Theodore A. *Price List and Barbers' Purchasing Guide of Barbers' Chairs, Furniture, And Barbers' Supplies*. Chicago: Skeen & Stuart Stationery Co., 1884.

Kwass, Michael. "Big Hair: A Wig History of Consumption in Eighteenth-Century France." *American Historical Review* 111, no. 3 (2006): 631–659.

"Ladies' and Children's Wear Street and House Suits." *Harper's Bazaar*, November 15, 1873, 728–729.

The Ladies Guide and City Directory for Shopping, Travel, Amusements, etc., in the City of New York. New York: G. P. Putnam's Sons, 1885.

Lancaster, Jane. "At Long Last, a Tribute to Bannister." *Providence Journal*, G1, 8, 2002.

Lancaster, Jane. "I Would Have Made Out Very Poorly Had It Not Been for Her." *Rhode Island History* 59, no. 4 (2001): 107.

Ledger, Sally. "The New Woman and Feminist Fictions." In *The Cambridge Companion to the Fin de Siècle*, edited by Gail Marshall, 153–168. Cambridge, UK: Cambridge University Press, 2007.

Lefebvre, Henri. *The Production of Space*. Oxford: Blackwell Publishing, 1991.

Leonard, Charles Henri. *The Hair: Its Growth, Care, Diseases and Treatment*. Detroit: C. Henri Leonard, Medical Book Publisher, 1881.

Logan, Mrs. John A. *The Home Manual: Everybody's Guide in Social, Domestic and Business Life*. Philadelphia: Standard Publishing Co., 1889.

Loring, John. *Tiffany Jewels*. New York: Harry N. Abrams, 1999.

Low, Lyman H. "Hard Times Tokens." *American Journal of Numismatics* (July 1899): 20.

Low, Setha M. "Spatializing Culture: An Engaged Anthropological Approach to Space and Place." In *The People, Space and Place Reader*, edited by Jen Jack Gieseking, William Mangold, Cindi Katz, Setha Low, and Susan Saegert, 34–38. London: Routledge, 2014.

Low, Setha M. *Spatializing Culture: The Ethnography of Space and Place*. London: Routledge, 2017.

Lowry, Beverly. *Her Dream of Dreams: The Rise and Triumph of Madam C. J. Walker*. New York: Knopf Doubleday, 2011.

Macfadden, Bernarr. *Macfadden's New Hair Culture: Rational, Natural Methods for Cultivating Strength and Luxuriance of the Hair*. New York: Physical Culture Publishing Co., 1899.

Mahawatte, Royce. "Hair and Fashioned Femininity in Two Nineteenth-Century Novels." In *Hair: Styling, Culture and Fashion*, edited by Geraldine Biddle-Perry and Sarah Cheang, 193–204. Oxford: Berg, 2008.

The Manners That Win. Minneapolis, MN: Buckeye Publishing Co., 1886.

Marks, Patricia. *Bicycles, Bangs, and Bloomers: The New Woman in the Popular Press*. Lexington: University Press of Kentucky, 1990.

Martin, Morag. *Selling Beauty: Cosmetics, Commerce, and French Society, 1750–1830*. Baltimore, MD: Johns Hopkins University Press, 2009.

Marzel, Shoshana-Rose, and Guy D. Stiebel, eds. *Dress and Ideology: Fashioning Identity from Antiquity to the Present*. London: Bloomsbury Publishing, 2014.

McCabe, James Dabney. *Lights and Shadows of New York Life; or, The Sights and Sensations of the Great City. A Work Descriptive of the City of New York in All Its Various Phases* . . . Philadelphia: National Publishing Co., 1872.

McCaskill, Barbara, and Caroline Gebhard, eds. *Post-Bellum, Pre-Harlem: African American Literature and Culture, 1877–1919*. New York: New York University Press, 2006.

McCluskey, John. "Journey to Frederick Douglass's Chicago Jubilee: Colored American Day, August 25, 1893." In *Roots of the Black Chicago Renaissance: New Negro Writers, Artists, and Intellectuals, 1893–1930*, edited by Richard A Courage and Christopher Robert Reed, 42–56. Urbana: University of Illinois Press, 2021.

McNeil, Peter. "Ideology, Fashion and the Darlys' 'Macaroni' Prints." In *Dress and Ideology: Fashioning Identity from Antiquity to the Present*, edited by Shoshana-Rose Marzel and Guy D. Stiebel, 111–136. London: Bloomsbury, 2014.

Mellinkoff, Ruth. "Judas's Red Hair and the Jews." *Journal of Jewish Art* 9 (1982): 31–46.

"Mercantile Miscellanies: Economy and Liberality." *Merchants' Magazine and Commercial Review* 48, no. 3 (March 1, 1863): 267.

Mercer, Kobena. "'Black Hair/Style Politics.'" In *Out There: Marginalization and Contemporary Cultures*, edited by Russell Ferguson, Martha Gere, Trinh T. Minh-ha, and Cornel West, 247–264. Cambridge, MA: MIT Press, 1990.

Meyer, Ferdinand Meyer, V. "The Amazing 7 Sutherland Sisters." Peachridge Glass, February 10, 2013. https://www.peachridgeglass.com/2013/02/the-amazing-7-sutherland-sisters.

Miller, Annie Jenness. *Physical Beauty: How to Obtain and How to Preserve It*. New York: C. L. Webster & Co., 1892.

Mills, Quincy T. *Cutting along the Color Line: Black Barbers and Barber Shops in America*. Philadelphia: University of Pennsylvania Press, 2013.

Mitchell, Dolores. "The 'New Woman' as Prometheus: Women Artists Depict Women Smoking." *Woman's Art Journal* 12, no. 1 (Spring/Summer 1991): 3–9.

"The Modern Juggernaut." *Christian Union* 36, no. 24, December 15, 1887, 667.

"A Modern Masquerade," *Munsey's Magazine*, April–September 1897.

Moler, Arthur Bass. *The Manual on Barbering, Hairdressing, Manicuring, Facial Massage, Electrolysis and Chiropody as Taught in the Moler System of Colleges*. New York: Arthur Bass Moler, 1906.

Morgan, Jennifer L. *Reckoning with Slavery: Gender, Kinship, and Capitalism in the Early Black Atlantic*. Durham, NC: Duke University Press, 2021.

Murphy, Richard J. *Authentic Visitors' Guide to the World's Columbian Exposition and Chicago*. Chicago: Union News Co., 1893.

Musher, Sharon Ann. "The Other Slave Narratives: The Works Progress Administration Interviews." In *The Oxford Handbook of the African American Slave Narrative*, edited by John Ernest, 101–118. Oxford: Oxford University Press, 2014.

Myzelev, Alla, and John Potvin. *Fashion, Interior Design and the Contours of Modern Identity*. Farnham, UK: Ashgate, 2010.

Nabugodi, Mathelinda. "Afro Hair in the Time of Slavery." *Studies in Romanticism* 61, no. 1 (2022): 81–82.

"The New Woman's Newest Idea." *American Hairdresser*, December 1896: 12.

Ofek, Galia. *Representations of Hair in Victorian Literature and Culture*. Farnham, UK: Ashgate, 2009.

O'Hagan, Anne. "Behind the Scenes in the Big Stores." *Munsey's Magazine*, January 1900, 528–537.

O'Leary, Elizabeth L. *At Beck and Call: The Representation of Domestic Servants in Nineteenth-Century American Painting*. Washington, DC: Smithsonian Institution Press, 1996.

Ormond, Richard, and Elaine Kilmurray. *John Singer Sargent: The Later Portraits*. New Haven, CT: Yale University Press, 2003.

"Our Paris Letter." *Harper's Bazar*, June 27, 1896, 542.

Paddon, Anna R., and Sally Turner. "African Americans and the World's Columbian Exposition." *Illinois Historical Journal* 88, no. 1 (1995): 19–36.

Palmer, Mrs. Potter (Bertha Palmer), et al. *Rand, McNally & Co.'s Handbook of the World's Columbian Exposition*. Chicago: Rand, McNally & Co., 1893.

Pastoureau, Michel. *Red: The History of a Color*. Princeton, NJ: Princeton University Press, 2017.

Peiss, Kathy Lee. *Hope in a Jar: The Making of America's Beauty Culture*. New York: Metropolitan Books, 1998.

Penny, Virginia. *The Employments of Women: A Cyclopaedia of Woman's Work*. Boston: Walker, Wise & Co., 1863.

Peyton, Kate Virginia. "My Blonde Wig." *Peterson's Magazine*, November 1876, 318.

"Phalon and Son's Cocoine." *Harper's Weekly*, February 12, 1859, 112.

"Phalon's Cocin" (*sic*). *Harper's Weekly*, December 31, 1859, 842.

"Phalon's Saloon." *Gleason's Pictorial Drawing-Room Companion*, February 12, 1853, 112.

Picquet, Louisa, and Hiram Mattison. *Louisa Picquet, the Octoroon: or, Inside Views of Southern Domestic Life*. New York: Hiram Mattison, 1861.

Pitman, Joanna. *On Blondes*. London: Bloomsbury, 2014.

Plante, Ellen M. *Women at Home in Victorian America: A Social History*. New York: Facts on File, 1997.

Plitt, Jane R. *Martha Matilda Harper and the American Dream: How One Woman Changed the Face of Modern Business*. Writing American Women. Syracuse, NY: Syracuse University Press, 2000.

Pointon, Marcia R. *Hanging the Head: Portraiture and Social Formation in Eighteenth-Century England*. New Haven, CT: Yale University Press, 1993.

Pollock, Griselda. *Vision and Difference: Femininity, Feminism, and Histories of Art*. London: Routledge, 1988.

"Pomades and Oils." *Scientific American*, June 13, 1868, 370.

Potter, Eliza. *A Hairdresser's Experience in High Life*. Cincinnati, OH: Privately printed, 1859.

Potvin, John, ed. *The Places and Spaces of Fashion, 1800–2007*. New York: Routledge, 2009.

Potvin, John. "The Velvet Masquerade: Fashion, Interior Design and the Furnished Body." In *Fashion, Interior Design and the Contours of Modern Identity*, edited by Alla Myzelev and John Potvin. Farnham, UK: Ashgate, 2010.

Powell, Margaret K., and Joseph Roach. "Big Hair." *Eighteenth-Century Studies* 38, no. 1 (Fall 2004): 79–99.

Prettyman, Gib. "The Serial Illustrations of *A Hazard of New Fortunes*." *Resources for American Literary Study* 27, no. 2 (2001): 179–195.

"Professions for Women." *Harper's Bazar*, October 8, 1870, 647.

Rabinovitch-Fox, Einav. *Dressed for Freedom: The Fashionable Politics of American Feminism*. Urbana: University of Illinois Press, 2021.

Raiford, Leigh. "Ida B. Wells and the Shadow Archive." In *Pictures and Progress: Early Photography and the Making of African American Identity*, edited by Maurice O. Wallace and Shawn Michelle Smith. Durham, NC: Duke University Press, 2012.

Rauser, Amelia. "Hair, Authenticity, and the Self-Made Macaroni." *Eighteenth-Century Studies* 38, no. 1 (Fall 2004): 101–117.

Reed, Christopher Robert. *All the World Is Here! The Black Presence at White City*. Bloomington: Indiana University Press, 2002.

Report of the Committee on Awards of the World's Columbian Commission. Washington, DC: Government Printing Office, 1901.

Report of the President to the Board of Directors of the World's Columbian Exposition: Chicago, 1892–1893. Chicago: Rand, McNally & Co., 1898.

Ribeiro, Aileen. *Dress in Eighteenth-Century Europe, 1715–1789*. New Haven, CT: Yale University Press, 2002.

Ribeiro, Aileen. *Facing Beauty: Painted Women and Cosmetic Art*. New Haven, CT: Yale University Press, 2011.

Rifelj, Carol de Dobay. *Coiffures: Hair in Nineteenth-Century French Literature and Culture*. Newark: University of Delaware Press, 2010.

Ripley, Eliza. *Social Life in Old New Orleans, Being Recollections of My Girlhood*. New York: D. Appleton and Co., 1912.

Ritchie, Andrew. "The League of American Wheelmen, Major Taylor and the 'Color Question' in the United States in the 1890s." *Culture, Sport, Society* 6, no. 2/3 (June 1, 2003): 13–43.

Roach, Marion. *The Roots of Desire: The Myth, Meaning, and Sexual Power of Red Hair*. New York: Bloomsbury, 2005.

Robins, Anthony W. "Hotel Albert." http://thehotelalbert.com/photos.html.

Robinson, William H. *From Log Cabin to the Pulpit, or, Fifteen Years in Slavery*. Eau Clair, WI: James H. Tifft, 1913.

Rooks, Noliwe M. "Black Hair, Self-Creation, and the Meaning of Freedom." In *Connecting Afro Futures: Fashion × Hair × Design*, edited by Claudia Banz et al. Bielefeld, Germany: Kerber Verlag, 2019.

Rooks, Noliwe M. *Hair Raising: Beauty, Culture, and African American Women*. New Brunswick, NJ: Rutgers University Press, 1996.

Rowland, Alexander. *The Human Hair, Popularly and Physiologically Considered with Special Reference to Its Preservation, Improvement and Adornment, and the Various Modes of Its Decoration in All Countries*. London: Piper Brothers Co., 1853.

"Saleswomen's Appearance." *Dry Goods Economist*, November 20, 1909, 44.

Santamarina, Xiomara. *Belabored Professions: Narratives of African American Working Womanhood*. Chapel Hill: University of North Carolina Press, 2005.

Schwartz, J. W. "Mrs. L. Shaw." *Printer's Ink*, October 25, 1899: 3–5.

Sherrow, Victoria. *Encyclopedia of Hair: A Cultural History*. Westport, CT: Greenwood Press, 2006.

Sheumaker, Helen. *Love Entwined: The Curious History of Hairwork in America*. Philadelphia: University of Pennsylvania Press, 2007.

Smith, Kim. "From Style to Place: The Emergence of the Ladies' Hair Salon in the Twentieth Century." In *Hair: Styling, Culture and Fashion*, edited by Geraldine Biddle-Perry and Sarah Cheang, 55–65. Oxford: Berg, 2008.

Smith, Willard A., ed. *World's Columbian Exposition, 1893: Official Catalogue, Part VII. Transportation Exhibits Building, Annex, Special Building and the Lagoon*. Chicago: W. B. Conkey Co., 1893.

Snook, Edith. "Beautiful Hair, Health, and Privilege in Early Modern England." *Journal for Early Modern Cultural Studies* 15, no. 4 (Fall 2015): 22–51.

Snyder, C. S. *Decorum: A Practical Treatise on Etiquette and Dress of the Best American Society*. Chicago: J. A. Ruth & Co., 1877.

Spier, K. C. *Universal Exposition Paris, 1889: J. C. Conolly's Illustrated Guide for the Use of English and American Visitors*. Liverpool: J. C. Conolly, 1889.

Square, Jonathan Michael. "Culture, Power, and the Appropriation of Creolized Aesthetics in the Revolutionary French Atlantic." *SX Salon* 36 (February 2021). http://smallaxe.net/sxsalon/discussions/culture-power-and-appropriation-creolized-aesthetics-revolutionary-french.

Square, Jonathan Michael. "Slavery's Warp, Freedom's Weft: A Look at the Work of Eighteenth- and Nineteenth-Century Enslaved Fashion Makers and Their Legacies." In *Black Designers in American Fashion*, edited by Elizabeth Way. London: Bloomsbury Visual Arts, 2021.

Stafford, Jonathan. "Home on the Waves: Domesticity and Discomfort Aboard the Overland Route Steamship, 1842–1862." *Mobilities* 14, no. 5 (September 3, 2019): 578–595.

Sterling, Dorothy, ed. *We Are Your Sisters: Black Women in the Nineteenth Century*. New York: W. W. Norton, 1984.

Stevens, Walter Barlow. *St. Louis, the Fourth City, 1764–1909*. Chicago: S. J. Clarke Publishing Co., 1909.

Stewart, Whitney Nell. "A Protected Place: The Material Culture of Home-Making for Stagville's Enslaved Residents." *Winterthur Portfolio* 54, no. 4 (December 2020): 245–270.

Stitson, J. R. (pseud. for Joseph Scott Stillwell). *The Human Hair, Its Care and Preservation*. New York: Maple Publishing Co., 1900.

Storey, Neil R., and Fiona Kay. *Victorian Fashions for Women*. Havertown, PA: Pen & Sword History, 2022.

Streitenberger, Hiram. *Streitenberger's Manual and Barbers' Hand Book of Formulas*. Chillicothe, OH: Hiram Streitenberger, 1887.

Stroomberg, Harriet. *High Heads: Spotprenten Over Haarmode in De Achttiende Eeuw*. Enschede: Rijksmuseum Twenthe, 1999.

"A Sun Bath after a Shampoo with Packer's Tar Soap." *The Chautauquan* 30, October 1899, 107.

Sutton, Philip. "Maury and the Menu: A Brief History of the Cunard Steamship Company." *New York Public Library Blog*, June 30, 2011. https://www.nypl.org/blog/2011/06/30/maury-menu-brief-history-cunard-steamship-company.

Tarlo, Emma. *Entanglement: The Secret Lives of Hair*. London: Oneworld Publications, 2016.

Thaxter, Celia. *Letters of Celia Thaxter*. Edited by Annie Fields and Rose Lamb. Boston: Houghton Mifflin Co., 1895.

Thompson, Cheryl. "Black Women, Beauty, and Hair as a Matter of Being." *Women's Studies* 38, no. 8 (October 15, 2009): 831–856.

Thompson, Mrs. C., ed. *Mrs. C. Thompson, Importer and Manufacturer of Wigs, Hair Jewelry, Ornamental Hair Work . . .* New York: Mrs. C. Thompson, 1883.

"Thousands Were in Line." *Referee and Cycle Trade Journal* 15, no. 5, May 31, 1895, unpaginated.

Thrift, Nigel. "Space." *Theory, Culture & Society* 23, no. 2/3 (2006): 139–146.

"The Trade in Human Hair." *Scientific American*, March 27, 1869, 198.

"Trade Notes." *American Perfumer*, (February 1922): 537.

Truman, Benjamin Cummings. *History of the World's Fair, Being a Complete and Authentic Description of the Columbian Exposition from Its Inception*. New York: E. B. Treat, 1893.

Truth, Soujourner, Olive Gilbert, and Frances W. Titus. *Narrative of Sojourner Truth . . .* Battle Creek, MI: For the author, 1878.

Tuan, Yi-Fu. *Space and Place: The Perspective of Experience*. Minneapolis: University of Minnesota Press, 1977.

Turkel, Stanley. *Built to Last: 100+ Year-Old Hotels in New York*. Bloomington, IN: AuthorHouse, 2011.

Twyman, Robert W. *History of Marshall Field & Co., 1852–1906*. Philadelphia: University of Pennsylvania Press, 1954.

United States Bureau of the Census. *The Foreign Commerce and Navigation of the United States*. Washington, DC: Government Printing Office, 1866/1867.

United States Bureau of the Census. *The Foreign Commerce and Navigation of the United States*. Washington, DC: Government Printing Office, 1874/1875 (published in 1876).

United States Bureau of the Census. *The Foreign Commerce and Navigation of the United States*. Washington, DC: Government Printing Office, 1891/1892.

United States Department of the Treasury, Bureau of Statistics. *Annual Report and Statements of the Chief of the Bureau of Statistics on the Commerce and Navigation of the United States for the Fiscal Year Ended 1882*. Washington, DC: Government Printing Office, 1882.

Untitled, *American Hairdresser*, January 1896, 20–21.

Usher, Nora C. "Some Things I Learnt in America." *Work and Leisure: A Magazine Devoted to the Interests of Women*, August 1, 1892, 218–220.

Vermeulen, Heather V. "Race and Ethnicity: Mortal Coils and Hair-Raising Revolutions, Styling 'Race' in the Age of Enlightenment." In *A Cultural History of Hair in the Age of Enlightenment*, edited by Margaret K. Powell and Joseph Roach, 135–154. London: Bloomsbury Academic, 2021.

Vieira, Manuel J. *Tonsorial Art Pamphlet*. Indianapolis, IN: Press of the Publishing House, 1877.

Vincent, Susan J. *The Anatomy of Fashion: Dressing the Body from the Renaissance to Today*. Oxford: Berg, 2009.

Vincent, Susan J. *Hair: An Illustrated History*. London: Bloomsbury Visual Arts, 2018.

Wake, Joseph. "The Art of Painting on the Photographic Image." *British Journal of Photography* 24, no. 908 (September 28, 1877): 461.

Walker, Juliet E. K., ed. *Encyclopedia of African American Business History*. Westport, CT: Greenwood Press, 1999.

Walker, Juliet E. K. *The History of Black Business in America: Capitalism, Race, Entrepreneurship*. New York: Macmillan, 1998.

Wanzer, Lyzette. *Trauma, Tresses, and Truth: Untangling Our Hair through Personal Narratives*. Chicago: Chicago Review Press, 2023.

Ward, Maria E. *The Common Sense of Bicycling: Bicycling for Ladies*. New York: Brentano's, 1896.

Wassholm, Johanna, and Anna Sundelin. "Gendered Encounters in Mobile Trade: Human Hair as a Commodity in the Nordics, 1870–1914." *History of Retailing and Consumption* 6, no. 2 (May 3, 2020): 118–136.

Weber, Caroline. *Queen of Fashion*. New York: Henry Holt, 2006.

Welch, Evelyn. "Art on the Edge: Hair and Hands in Renaissance Italy." *Renaissance Studies* 23, no. 3 (2009): 241–268.

Wells, Ida B. *The Reason Why the Colored American Is Not in the World's Columbian Exposition*. Chicago: Ida B. Wells, 1893.

Wells, Ida B. *Southern Horrors: Lynch Law in All Its Phases*. New York: The New York Age Print, 1892.

"What to Do with Oily Hair." *Good Housekeeping*, October 12, 1889, 283.

White, Carolyn L. "The Fall of Big Hair: Hair Curlers as Evidence of Changing Fashions." In *The Importance of British Material Culture to Historical Archaeologies of the Nineteenth Century*, edited by Alasdair Brooks, 162–187. Lincoln: University of Nebraska Press, 2015.

White, Esther C. "The Landscape of Enslavement: His Space, Their Places." In *Lives Bound Together: Slavery at George Washington's Mount Vernon*, edited by Susan Prendergast Schoelwer. Mount Vernon, VA: Mount Vernon Ladies Association, 2016.

White, Shane, and Graham White. "Slave Hair and African American Culture in the Eighteenth and Nineteenth Centuries." *Journal of Southern History* 61, no. 1 (February 1995): 45–76.

White, Shane, and Graham White. *Stylin': African American Expressive Culture from Its Beginnings to the Zoot Suit*. Ithaca, NY: Cornell University Press, 1998.

White, Trumbull, and William Igleheart, *The World's Columbian Exposition, Chicago, 1893*. St. Louis: P. W. Ziegler & Co., 1893.

Whitehead, Karsonya Wise. "Sarah Parker Remond." In *Encyclopedia of African American History*, edited by Leslie M. Alexander and Walter C. Rucker. 3 vols. Santa Barbara, CA: ABC-CLIO, 2010.

Wilkinson, A. B. *Blurring the Lines of Race and Freedom: Mulattoes and Mixed Bloods in English Colonial America*. Chapel Hill: University of North Carolina Press, 2020.

Willard, Frances E. *Glimpses of Fifty Years: The Autobiography of an American Woman*. Chicago: Woman's Temperance Publication Association, 1889.

Willard, Frances E. *A Wheel within a Wheel: How I Learned to Ride the Bicycle, with Some Reflections by the Way*. New York: F. H. Revell Co., 1895.

Willett, Julie A. *Permanent Waves: The Making of the American Beauty Shop*. New York: New York University Press, 2000.

Willis, Deborah, and Carla Williams. *The Black Female Body: A Photographic History*. Philadelphia: Temple University Press, 2002.

Wilson, Harriet E. *Our Nig: or, Sketches from the Life of a Free Black in a Two-Story White House, North*. Boston: G. C. Rand & Avery, 1859.

Wilson's Business Directory of New York City. New York: Trow City Directory Company, 1867.

Winkler, Gail Caskey, and Roger W. Moss. *Victorian Interior Decoration: American Interiors, 1830–1900*. New York: H. Holt, 1986.

"Women Make Good Barbers." *American Hairdresser*, February 1896, 28.

Wood, Jessie M. "The Actress." *Life* 27, March 26, 1896, 233.

Woodbury, William A. *Hair Dressing and Tinting; a Text-Book of the Fundamental Principles Showing the Ready Adaptability of the Ever Changing Mode of Wearing the Hair, for Professional and Private Use*. New York: G. W. Dillingham Co., 1915.

Woods, Naurice Frank, Jr. *Insuperable Obstacles: The Impact of Racism on the Creative and Personal Development of Four Nineteenth-Century African-American Artists*. Cincinnati, OH: Union Institute, 1993.

World's Columbian Exposition 1893: Official Catalogue Exhibition of the German Empire. Berlin: Imperial Commission, 1893.

World's Columbian Exposition Illustrated, April 1893, xiv.

Wrigley, Richard. *The Politics of Appearances: Representations of Dress in Revolutionary France*. London: Berg, 2002.

Yochelson, Bonnie. *Miss Alice Austen and Staten Island's Gilded Age: A Biography in Photographs*. Digital exhibit, 2021. The Gotham Center for New York City History. https://www.gothamcenter.org/exhibits/alice-austen.

Zalc, Claire. "Trading on Origins: Signs and Windows of Foreign Shopkeepers in Interwar Paris." *History Workshop Journal* 70 (Autumn 2010): 133–151.

Zdatny, Steven. "Fashion and Class Struggle: The Case of Coiffure." *Social History* 18, no. 1 (1993): 53–72.

Zdatny, Steven. *Fashion, Work, and Politics in Modern France*. Basingstoke, UK: Palgrave Macmillan, 2015.

Zdatny, Steven M. *Hairstyles and Fashion: A Hairdresser's History of Paris, 1910–1920*. Oxford: Berg, 1999.

INDEX

Note: Page numbers in italics refer to illustrations.